David Hempleman-Adams was born in Swindon, Wiltshire, in 1956. His interest in adventuring was inspired by the Duke of Edinburgh Award Scheme, of which he is a gold medallist. In 1998 he became the first person to complete the explorers' Grand Slam, a challenge that has seen him conquer the North and South Geographical and Magnetic Poles and scale the highest mountain in each of the seven continents, including Everest. A businessman by profession but an adventurer by preference, he lives near Bath with his wife and three daughters.

Robert Uhlig, who wrote *At the Mercy of the Winds* with David Hempleman-Adams, is the Technology Correspondent of the *Daily Telegraph* in London. In 1998 he accompanied David Hempleman-Adams and Rune Gjeldnes to the Canadian High Arctic to document their trek to the North Pole in *Walking on Thin Ice*. He is also the author of *The Daily Telegraph James Dyson's History of Inventions*. He lives in Cornwall with his partner and young son.

D0940397

The *Eagle*, from an engraving made in 1897. *(Popperfoto)*

AT THE MERCY OF THE WINDS

David Hempleman-Adams
With Robert Uhlig

BANTAM BOOKS

LONDON • NEW YORK • TORONTO • SYDNEY • AUCKLAND

AT THE MERCY OF THE WINDS
A BANTAM BOOK : 0 553 81363 3

Originally published in Great Britain by Bantam Press,
a division of Transworld Publishers

PRINTING HISTORY
Bantam Press edition published 2001
Bantam edition published 2002

1 3 5 7 9 10 8 6 4 2

Set in 11/12½pt Sabon by
Falcon Oast Graphic Art Ltd.

Bantam Books are published by Transworld Publishers,
61–63 Uxbridge Road, London W5 5SA,
a division of The Random House Group Ltd,
in Australia by Random House Australia (Pty) Ltd,
20 Alfred Street, Milsons Point, Sydney, NSW 2061, Australia,
in New Zealand by Random House New Zealand Ltd,
18 Poland Road, Glenfield, Auckland 10, New Zealand
and in South Africa by Random House (Pty) Ltd,
Endulini, 5a Jubilee Road, Parktown 2193, South Africa.

Printed and bound in Great Britain by
Clays Ltd, St Ives plc.

For Hilary and Linus,
and my girls

'It is a little strange to be here above the Polar Sea; to be the first to have floated here in a balloon. How soon, I wonder, shall we have successors? Shall we be thought mad or will our example be followed?'

Andrée's diary, 11 July, 1897

CONTENTS

ACKNOWLEDGEMENTS

Many people helped with the flight of *Britannic Challenger* to the North Pole. Unfortunately, it is impossible to acknowledge their invaluable advice and encouragement individually, but I thank each and every one of you for your friendship and assistance.

In particular, I must thank Bill Haynes and David Newman of Britannic Assurance for having the vision to back me, and Claire, Denise, Stuart and Paula for undertaking the donkey work that Bill and David's sponsorship entailed. From my team, I am indebted to Brian Smith, Clive Bailey, Gavin Hailes, Pete Johnson, Tom Shaw, Brian Jones and our meteorological genius, Luc Trullemans, for their consistent help and support. Thanks also to: Rachel Clarke and Sue Earl, who kept me on the straight and narrow at my office; Colin Hill and Peter McPhillips for their assistance; and Patrick O'Hagan for his patience.

Thanks also to HRH the Duke of Edinburgh for his

patronage to *Britannic Challenger*'s flight and to Ian McEwan for writing the introduction.

My wife Claire and my daughters, Alicia, Camilla and Amelia, have tolerated my frequent absences from home and I thank them deeply. I also owe the people of Spitsbergen a particular gratitude for their belief in and support of my dream.

Finally, I would like to thank Robert Uhlig for his perseverance and hard work in the writing of this book. He in turn would like to thank Selina Walker, our editor, for her invaluable advice and enthusiasm, and Robert Kirby, our agent at PFD, for finding a good home for this book.

Finally, Robert would like particularly to thank Hilary and Linus for their love, support and tolerance of the many months this book took him away from them.

—

INTRODUCTION

It is instructive to read here that on his doomed attempt to fly a hydrogen balloon across the North Pole in 1897, the explorer Andrée took along with him a dinner jacket in case he was obliged to feast with the king of some as yet undiscovered Arctic country. That was only three or four generations ago. Go back five or six, and large parts of Africa, Asia, and even the American West were only just being explored by European travellers, or those of European descent. Even in the scale of human time, so tiny against evolutionary, or geological time, the complete exploration of the world is very recent. When Redmond O'Hanlon was setting off to the central Congo eight years ago he was able to show me on his large-scale maps white patches of unchartered mangrove swamps. Now satellite mapping has shrunk the last patches away. We've been everywhere, or rather, others, or their sensing equipment, have been everywhere on our behalf. Good reasons will remain for biologists and geologists and other kinds of scientists to return to remote places, but for the pure explorer, of the kind who simply thrills to be the first to go and come back alive, there isn't much left beyond the deep ocean bed. Everest, 'conquered' as recently as 1953, is now festooned with thousands of tons of litter and abandoned equipment. Six billion of us are crowded on to the planet, and there are more of us on the way. Even if only a tiny percentage are restless enough to undertake hazardous journeys across wilderness to relatively untouched locations, these are going to be pretty well trodden by the end of this century.

The North Pole, however, will not be. It is a purely notional point in a frozen sea whose ice is constantly shifted by powerful currents – as generations of trekkers have found to their frustration, and occasional advantage. The weather conditions can be of an unearthly harshness, and are volatile as well. The 'terrain' is that of ice under great pressure, with ice sheets moving against each other like tectonic plates, throwing up vast fields of rubble, or ice blocks, or leads of open water. Nuclear submarines routinely glide under the polar ice cap, jumbo jets slice through the stratosphere on their everyday business, and occasional summer ice-breaking ships bring tourists by the score, but only those who make the journey on foot from the nearest land can say they've really been to the North Pole.

David Hempelman-Adams and his friend Rune Gjeldnes walked there in 1998, dragging their own sledges in a journey recorded in *Walking on Thin Ice*. No amount of electronics, or the fruits of the latest in fibre and material developments, could replace their reliance on physical fitness, patience, humour, mutual tolerance and goal-obsession. Reasonably enough, David believed he had earned himself a balloon trip next time round.

Perhaps the greatest achievement of this, his latest exploit, was to learn from scratch how to pilot a balloon, and within months set a world record with a trip across the Andes, and then set off for the North Pole. Just as hardy survivalists like to tell you that snake, rat or termite taste 'just like chicken', so balloonists will insist that theirs is, mile for mile, the 'safest form of transport'. I'm not so sure. When I was researching my novel *Enduring Love*, which begins with a ballooning accident, my wife – herself a vertigo sufferer – explored a vast media database with the key words 'balloon' and 'death'. She came up with fifty closely typed pages of disasters, and that was within a two-year limit. Murphy's Law seems to flourish a couple of thousand feet above the ground: what can go wrong goes wrong, and comes down. I've therefore been politely evasive whenever David has invited my teenage sons and me on a genteel excursion above the fields of Wiltshire. I think I'd rather eat a rat.

Nothing in *At the Mercy of the Winds* persuades me to change my mind. The title alone confirms my resolve absolutely. So too does the extraordinary account of the Andrée expedition that is interwoven with the contemporary story. The technology – all polished wood and brass, canvas and gunpowder – reminds one of the science of Wells's *The Time Machine*, and indeed, the Andrée adventure was as ambitious and improbable as a voyage through time. Its sad love story, and the mystery of the three explorers' tragic end, unsolved for more than thirty years, make this a trip to rank with Cherry-Garrard's *The Worst Journey in the World*. By contrast, David returned safely to the family he loves, and had at his disposal an array of the latest in telecommunications, meteorological computer modelling and balloon technology. But ultimately, machines can go wrong, more so when they are complex, and this is a story not of electronics, but of a sleep-deprived man hanging in a basket over a frozen wasteland, surviving by his wits, with no one around for hundreds of miles, and no precise control of his direction. The materials and instrumentation may have been revolutionized, but the human element remains unchanged. I have no doubt that, had he been around at the time, David would have volunteered for the Andrée expedition. Reading of this 2000 ballooning journey to the North Pole, one has a refreshed and enlarged sense of a world still in possession of its ultimate lonely place. And just as it was for all the preceding generations of explorers, only courage, stamina and a peculiar form of bloody-mindedness will get you there on your own.

Ian McEwan

THE DISCOVERY

WHITE ISLAND, NORWEGIAN ARCTIC

5 August, 1930

ONLY THE MURMURING CHUG OF THE PROPELLER TURNING IN the ice-cold water and the steady, low pant of the men's breathing broke the silence. Half a mile or so in the distance, the tiny landmass known to seal and walrus hunters as Inaccessible Island appeared to float like a dazzling white shield on the sea. All around, grounded icebergs dotted the water, their sheer walls of ice reflected in the Arctic Ocean. It was the first time in many years that the pack ice had cracked sufficiently to allow access to White Island, and the hunters were heading for shore.

On board the *Braatvag*, the youngest of the eight sealers and two harpooners crouched against the bitter cold as he scanned the coast for walruses. It was Olav Salen's maiden fishing voyage in the Arctic Sea and the seventeen-year-old was relieved to be freed at last from his cramped quarters in the bow of the ninety-six-ton wooden sloop. He'd been at sea for eleven days; eleven days enveloped in the clammy grip of a polar fog with nothing to do but prepare his hunting equipment, talk to the three scientists on board and reminisce about life in Aalesund, home of the Norwegian polar fishing fleet.

The following morning, as the permanent Arctic summer sun circled in a cloudless sky, Olav emerged from below decks. Ole Myklebust and his second harpooner, Sevrin Skjelten, had already departed in search of walrus, the wake of their boat spreading like a giant arrowhead in the icy sea. With all of White Island visible for the first time, Olav found the sight depressing. It was a foreboding and desolate place; the quiet was broken only by an occasional rumble of thunder from the north as massive wedges of ice slipped loose from the glacier at the centre of the island and plunged into the sea, becoming icebergs that floated south until they melted.

The harpooners soon struck lucky, and by midday Olav and two of his companions were heading for White Island in a whaling boat captained by Skjelten. With its cargo of two harpooned walruses, the boat lay deep in the water until the men hauled the massive seahorses onto the beach, slaughtered them and began to strip off the animals' hides, the dead bodies steaming in the frigid air. It was exhausting work, and after an hour the four men had a raging thirst. As the youngest member of the party, Olav was sent to search for drinking water in the company of his friend, Karl Tusvik.

A short distance along the beach, they stumbled upon a stream of icy water winding between the snowdrifts and granite rocks. Wading across to its far shore, Olav felt his boot kick against something metallic. He looked down. An aluminium lid was nestling on the bank. Amazed to find such an obvious sign of human habitation on an island considered one of the most inaccessible outposts of the Arctic, the men scrabbled across the gravel, slipping on patches of ice and sparse red-brown moss as they scoured the ground, heading inland as they searched for other clues that might explain the metal lid.

In front of them, a short distance up from the beach,

they spotted a dark object poking out of a snowdrift near a rocky hill and ran to it. With their bare hands they frantically scraped the crusted snow from around the tantalizing scrap of material to find, semi-encased in the ice, a wood and canvas boat.

As Olav and Karl began painstakingly to remove as much frost and slush as they could, the boat's contents were revealed: a parcel of books, clothing, hammers, a harpoon, a brass boat hook, two shotguns, a wind gauge, some aluminium boxes and string, and a surveyor's theodolite. The bones of a polar bear appeared to be a more recent addition.

Excited by their discovery and shouting their incredible news, Olav and Karl raced back to where Skjelten and the other sealers were still working on the walruses. All four hurried back to the site, to be joined a short while later by the skipper of the *Braatvag*, Peder Eliassen. As he examined some of the objects in the boat, he noticed their markings: *Andrée's pol. exp, 1896*. Turning to his crew, he was the first to acknowledge the momentous significance of their discovery.

'Gentlemen, you are standing before the remains of the most audacious attempt of all to be first to the North Pole,' he told them.

But the men were to find a far more gruesome sight when they continued their search. About thirty feet from the canvas boat, a mutilated human body was propped up against a rock wall. What few scraps remained of the man's flesh looked like rough yellow leather, the head was missing and most of the torso had been ripped out through the corpse's gaping jacket. Lower down, bones protruded through the tattered clothing. The legs appeared to be in better condition, lying naturally with a pair of Lapp boots still strapped to the feet. A pelvis was later found about two hundred feet east of the body, presumably where polar bears had dropped it.

Shaken by what he had discovered, the skipper returned slowly to the beach, where he approached Dr Gunnar

Horn, the leader of the three-man scientific team on board his ship. Eliassen pulled from his pocket the dripping leather-bound notebook he had picked up in the boat and opened it. On its first page, three words and a year were inscribed – *the sledge journey 1897* – followed by a list of provisions and a week-by-week list of the meals eaten. A second piece of evidence was another diary detailing their death march across the ice, described in a series of intricate astronomical calculations and observations taken along the way.

Without doubt, Eliassen told the geologist, we have found the remains of Andrée and his companions.

At last the ice had given up its dead; the mysterious and macabre fate of three brave Swedes who set off from the frozen archipelago of Spitsbergen more than three decades earlier was about to be revealed. Bound for the North Pole in a hydrogen balloon, they had taken off in 1897 never to be heard of again.

Once the significance of the discovery had sunk in, the scientists grabbed spades, pick axes, tarpaulins and an iron bar and headed for the site, about six hundred feet inland from where seagulls were already picking at the two bloody, skinned walrus carcasses. Carefully they pieced together the evidence for their find. Near the boat several items appeared to have been scattered by scavenging polar bears, including a box of ammunition, some clothing, some instruments and boxes, and a rolled-up Swedish flag. The most compelling discovery lay next to an empty sledge resting on the snow: a handkerchief embroidered with a monogram. The faded red cotton read N.S., the initials of Nils Strindberg, cousin of the famous playwright August and one of Andrée's companions.

Next they examined the grisly remains of the body near the boat. Carefully Dr Horn pulled open the clothing around the mutilated and headless torso. At the back of the jacket a large 'A' had been embroidered into the tattered fabric. Could this stand for Andrée, he wondered? Delving deeper into the corpse's rotten clothing, he found a barely used diary in an inside pocket, a lead pencil and a pedometer. Little had been written on the diary's pages, but it was enough, with the monogram on the jacket, to suggest that the remains were indeed those of Salomon August Andrée.

Nearby, one of the walrus hunters spotted the butt of a gun protruding from the snow and knelt down to scrape the barrel free. It appeared to work – evidence, perhaps, that despite the state of Andrée's body the men had been able to protect themselves from polar bear attack.

On top of a pile of clothing lay a Primus stove, liquid still sloshing around inside. One of the hunters pumped it, and paraffin shot out of the burner in a fine spray – a sign that the explorers had probably not starved to death. Cooking implements, crockery and a china pot of lanolin, used to repair damage inflicted on the adventurers' skin by the cold, were also strewn around the camp.

After a while, Sevrin Skjelten, the second harpooner, wandered away from the main search party. Scanning the ground, he suddenly saw the gaping smile of a human skull, lying bleached on the granite gravel about a hundred feet north of the body presumed to be Andrée's. About four yards from the skull a pair of feet, still encased in Lapp boots, poked out of an Arctic grave, built by wedging the body in a cleft between two large rocks and covering it with stones. Bending down to examine it, Skjelten noticed the corpse's left shoulder protruding from under the stones. A human shoulder blade rested on top of the mound. He wondered whether the body should be left where he had found it, but after discussion with his fellow hunters and the scientists, they decided the grave should be opened and the corpse exhumed so that the explorers could return to Sweden to rest in their native soil.

The skeleton under the rocks was headless too. Maybe this explained his death. The men speculated that bears had ripped off his head and the man's two companions had had to bury the decapitated corpse. Or maybe the skull found by Skjelten nearby belonged to this heap of bones. The exhumation proceeded slowly because the bones had frozen to the permafrost and needed to be hacked free with pick axes and spades.

Once the body was freed, the men attacked the canvas boat. It took only an hour or so to free it from the ice, but a sledge beneath it was completely encased and took much longer. Eventually all the remains were freed and wrapped in a tarpaulin. Finally, the men built a small cairn to mark the resting place of the Andrée expedition, and Dr Horn wrote a short note in Norwegian and English.

In this place, the Norwegian Expedition to Franz Josef Land, on board M/S Braatvag, *Skipper Peder Eliassen, found the relics of the Swedish Andrée Expedition. White Island, 6th August, 1930. Gunnar Horn.*

Stuffing the scrap of paper into a bottle, he placed it inside the cairn. A pole, held in place by three guy-ropes, was wedged into its summit to mark the location.

Then the ten men of the *Braatvag*'s crew laid their oars on the ground, dragged the canvas boat onto them and carried it carefully to the water's edge where, along with the rest of the relics, the boat was loaded onto one of the whaling boats which for the second time that day sank to its gunwales in the icy water.

Once aboard the *Braatvag*, the boat, sledge and human remains were strapped to the decks for the long journey back to Sweden, thirty-three years after Andrée and his fellow adventurers had left in a blaze of reckless ambition.

CHAPTER ONE

THE SPARK

THE CANADIAN HIGH ARCTIC

1 April, 1998

ON APRIL FOOLS' DAY IT OCCURS TO ME THAT THERE MAY BE an easier way. I am four weeks into my third attempt to reach the North Pole on foot. No dogs, no snowmobiles, no daily support from a personal aeroplane. I'm dragging 250lb of equipment and food on a sledge over forty-foot-high frozen ridges of broken ice for more than four hundred miles. Two resupplies to replenish food and replace broken equipment; other than that we're on our own. It's a backbreaking, high-risk endeavour that will see me lose almost a third of my body weight in eight weeks, and I often ask myself why I think this misery is worthwhile.

I am at an all-time low. My back and shoulders are in constant pain from dragging the sledge into heavy winds. I have frostbite injuries on my nose, toes and fingers. The weather has been appalling. At times it has been −55°C, but the wind-chill has made it feel like −85°C.

With Rune Gjeldnes, my polar partner, I've so far

completed a third of the trek from the edge of northern Canada to the Pole. This Norwegian Special Forces marine has become the best of companions – trustworthy, steady and dependable in a crisis; a true friend – and we both know that when we work together we are more than the sum of our two parts. Neither of us would have got anywhere near as far north without the help of the other, and we are as one against our common foes: the debilitating cold, the mental anguish and the sheer physical torture we face every time we venture out of our tiny tent into half a million square miles of the harshest environment on earth.

The worst should, by now, be behind us, but the weather seems to be getting worse and the ice more treacherous with every mile we grind northwards. A few days ago, we struggled for ten hours in a whiteout. It's a frightening, disorientating condition in which the wind blows up the snow at the same time as the clouds above are white. In such circumstances it is impossible to distinguish between the ice beneath our feet and the sky above, or open water – my greatest fear.

To compound our misery, the Arctic has only just begun to haul itself out of its permanent winter darkness and the sun is up for fewer than six hours a day. We are as much in a race against time as in a battle against the elements. From the acutely cold period of twenty-four-hour darkness that ends in early March, to late April, when these high latitudes are bathed in sunshine around the clock, there is a very short window of opportunity when the ice is strong enough to take our weight. Before March it is too cold and dark for the journey; beyond April, the heat of permanent daylight is a comparative luxury but it also breaks up the ice that constitutes our bridge across the Arctic Ocean.

But the Arctic reserves the cruellest of its many challenges for the hours when Rune and I lie asleep in our tent, when the polar currents force the ice on which we pitch camp further southwards in the night than the distance we manage to drag our sledges north during the day.

I lie in my sleeping bag and contemplate the misery that faces us. At times, we drive ourselves to the limit in order to cover six miles in a day, but to our despair we then drift back seven miles in the night. If it goes on like that, in a few weeks' time we'll be back at Ward Hunt Island, our starting point. Of course I know that the currents should eventually change direction, and could even carry us towards the Pole, but it seems a perverse state of affairs, especially as we can only make the journey at this time of the year, when the ice is strong enough to carry the combined weight of two men and their sledges. I am convinced that there has to be another, relatively simple, way for adventurers to get to the North Pole.

The day before, the perils of walking to the North Pole were brought home to me in the worst possible fashion.

I woke up feeling dreadful, and Rune immediately let me know that I looked as bad as I felt. He leaned back in his sleeping bag, pulled on one of the seemingly inexhaustible succession of roll-ups that he smoked, and smiled. 'Why is your right eye that baggy? I cannot remember we have been fighting.'

Rune, as ever, was as bright as a spark and eager to go. I wished only that I could feel the same way.

'It's because I'm getting old. I'm past it for this polar lark, Rune. You'll look like this when you're forty-one and exhausted.'

We did not have a mirror so I could not see if I looked as bad as Rune said. Instead I got Rune to video me for a few seconds, then I looked at the footage in the camera's viewfinder. It was a shock to me. He was right. I looked deadbeat. There were huge rings under my very puffy eyes. I was pale and drawn, and the podgy cheeks that I had four weeks ago had disappeared; in their place, sunken skin hung from the cheekbones I'd forgotten I had.

To add to my depression, I found we had drifted back

overnight by over a mile and the blue skies of the previous day had disappeared. There was relatively little wind but the low cloud left a flat light in which we could not make out the sky from the ground – in other words, another damned whiteout.

We set off after breakfast and within an hour we encountered disaster. The nightmare that had been haunting me for fourteen years and which had stopped recurring only eighteen months earlier came back to torment me, and this time it was real. It was probably the worst single moment I had in two decades of polar exploration.

At the first lead of open water we came to, Rune went ahead with his sledge behind him, and I followed in his tracks. One moment I was crossing what appeared to be a solid section of ice; the next I had fallen, with my skis on, through the ice into the unbelievably cold Arctic Ocean. The less dense 'super-cold' water rises to the surface. It was –4°C. There was no warning that the ice was about to give way, that my recurring nightmare ever since I fell through the ice on the way to the magnetic North Pole in 1984 was about to become a terrifying reality.

Because of the whiteout I had not noticed that the edge of a section of fresh ice was only an inch or so thick. Now I was up to my waist in the Arctic Ocean and panicking. As I fell, I ripped my ice-spikes from around my neck, attempting to dig the two titanium nails into the nearest piece of white ice I could spot, and shouted to Rune, who was about ten or so feet away. He appeared to be oblivious to my state of panic.

I tried to swim, something I find difficult at the best of times, but I could not move my legs with my skis still attached to my feet. I was sinking, aware that I was losing strength and consciousness in the cold water and would slip under the ice if I didn't do something soon.

Rune had already heard me fall in and shout, but in the slow-motion world I was enveloped in he had not yet reacted. I had heard that people's lives often flash in front of them shortly before they die, and at this moment it seemed as if a brief summary of the last few months was being projected inside my eyes. I saw the preparations in Resolute Bay, our departure from Ward Hunt Island and the weeks we had spent together in the tent. Most worryingly, I saw the frostbite on my nose, toes and fingers spreading, and this plunge into the Arctic Ocean ending my bid for the North Pole and the first adventurers' grand slam – climbing the highest mountain on every continent and dragging myself to the four geographic and magnetic poles. This is it, I thought. The expedition is over. I won't recover from this.

But before I knew it, the world around me accelerated and Rune was in front of me, hauling me out of the water's bitter clutches. He dragged me onto an ice floe, where I lay, gasping for breath, my trouser legs already freezing solid like stovepipes.

I wanted Rune to put the tent up double-quick so that I could get out of my sodden clothing and crawl inside my sleeping bag, but he advised against it. 'The best thing you can do is to keep walking,' he said. 'Then your body warmth will dry out your clothes from the inside.' It sounded unlikely to me. I was terrified that my frostbite would now spread across my entire foot and up my leg. I need to get my clothes off, I insisted. 'Trust me, David, it has happened to me many times before. If you stop now, the water will freeze into your clothes and you will never get the ice out of them. You must keep walking.'

So we headed off northwards again, me with my knees shaking for at least the next two hours. Within a very short time we hit ice rubble as bad as any we had on the whole trip. Cataclysmic. Extremely high and no way around it. It took at least three hours to crawl through just half a mile of this nightmarish frozen mess, and it was impossible to spot a clear route in the whiteout.

At the end of the day we came to yet another lead of open water. We decided that we had to cross it before we set up camp, just in case it widened overnight. It took us forty minutes to breach it. By the end of the day I was chin-strapped and I collapsed inside the tent.

We were amazed to discover we had managed to ski seven miles in the last eight hours. Under the circumstances it was brilliant, and I was sure that we would have done ten miles had we had the good visibility and the pans of flat ice that we expected and prayed for. We waited in vain, it seemed.

If only I could find a way to avoid the perils of open water, I think as I lie in my sleeping bag the next day, trying to delay the moment when I'll have to get up and the painful trudge across the ice begins again like some godforsaken Groundhog Day. I think forlornly of the time a couple of weeks ago when we took a day out to recuperate. I had glanced then out of the mouth of our tent to see the vapour trail of a plane crossing thousands of feet above. It seemed such an easy and infinitely more sensible way to travel, and that got me thinking.

Several years earlier, I had heard of Andrée's tragic bid to fly a hydrogen balloon to the North Pole and I'd remembered it ever since because it seemed to make such good sense. The most I can hope to cover in a day on skis is about fifteen miles. Usually it is a lot less, and on occasions we struggle to drag our sledges across even a mile of ice rubble and pressure ridges. By contrast, Andrée expected to fly up to three hundred miles in one day.

But the so-called experts say it was a foolhardy enterprise, and other adventurers argue that it would be mad to try where he had failed so spectacularly and so tragically. It's a challenge no-one has attempted for more than a hundred years, put off by the sheer danger and the tale of the tragic, drawn-out deaths of the only three men to have tried it. They reason that it is obviously impossible because Andrée's single attempt came to naught. Hearing that attitude makes me want to do it even more. And anyway, it is such an extraordinary example of daring and courage that I find it difficult to resist having a go where he failed.

My only misgiving is that ballooning has become tarnished in some people's eyes by all the recent attempts to fly non-stop around the world. There is nothing wrong in the endeavours themselves, but enormous sums of money have been spent by the likes of Richard Branson on numerous flights that use the latest in sophisticated high-tech equipment and still fail. It has left people disillusioned with ballooning. Instead of being something simple and relatively affordable, it is starting to become associated with a rich man's folly, and that is something I want to avoid at all costs.

But the possibility of pursuing these ambitious dreams is all in the future. In the immediate present I have to get to the North Pole, the culmination of my fifteen-year odyssey to become the first person to achieve the adventurers' grand slam. Four weeks later, on 28 April, I finally realize my dream when I stand at the top of the globe, but even then, with a lifetime's ambition finally achieved, my sights are set on a new target. If I succeed in flying a balloon to the North Pole, it will be a genuine world first. No caveats, no weaselly provisos. It is un-explored territory, and therein lies the bait.

The only problem is that I need to learn how to fly a balloon.

Within days of arriving back in Wiltshire, I set about planning my entrance into a new sphere of adventure. My first port of call is Cameron Balloons, the world's leading balloon maker, conveniently located in Bristol, only a few miles from my home. The company constructed the envelopes for several circumnavigation attempts and Don Cameron, who owns the company, is used to people turning up on his doorstep with the kind of dreams that seem unrealistic madness to most people, but which to adventurers are like a junkie's fix.

Even so, my demands are a long way out of the ordinary. I tell Phil Dunnington, Cameron's sales director, fixing him in the eye, 'I'm not interested in champagne balloon flights around the country. I need something different.'

I can tell that Phil regards my request with a degree of scepticism, particularly as I haven't, as yet, set foot in a balloon, but he doesn't dismiss the idea. Maybe my pedigree and experience as a mountaineer and polar adventurer shows through. And maybe Phil's knowledge that I have this tendency to want to establish or break some kind of record makes an impression too, because he then boldly suggests that a flight over a mountain range may be a suitable starting point for such a venture. 'Everest has already been crossed in a hot-air balloon, but I don't think anyone has done the Andes. Our man in Chile is coming over soon. Why don't you come back and meet him?' he says.

It is an engaging proposition. I have already climbed Aconcagua, the highest peak in the Andes, on my way to bagging the seven summits. This would be a return to the scene of a past triumph. And I know that Rune has wanted for some time to attempt an altitude record for a parachute landing on a mountain, so this flight may provide a suitable opportunity.

One week later, I meet Victor Mardones, a short, stocky and unflappable former naval airship pilot who acts as Cameron's agent in Chile. I ask Mardones if my plan to fly a hot-air balloon over the highest point of the Andes is feasible. His answer is equivocal: a gas balloon made the journey in the 1920s, but no hot-air balloon has ever succeeded. Two recent attempts by an American and a Spaniard, he warns, failed because of oxygen problems, and that might queer the pitch with the authorities.

I've always managed so far to find a way around red tape, I reason. The bonus that nobody has done it before is a definite attraction; in fact, it makes it the kind of challenge I find difficult to refuse.

'So I'd be the first, would I?'

'I think you might be. How many flying hours have you got?'

'Er, none actually. I haven't even started.'

There's a pregnant pause while Victor lights up a cigarette, takes a drag, exhales slowly and comes up with a sensible suggestion. 'Why don't you get your licence and we'll talk again then.'

It seems like a fair point. Within a week I am making my first tethered flight with Terry McCoy, an instructor recommended by Phil Dunnington. For my maiden voyage the balloon is tied to a Land Rover in Victoria Park at Bath.

Terry embarks on a curious analogy. 'It's quite simple,' he says. 'Flying a balloon is like making love to a woman.' It sounds spurious to me, but I keep listening. 'If you grab hold of a woman's breast she'll not like it and she'll react violently. It's the same with a balloon: if you're clumsy and whack in the hot air, she'll react unpredictably. But if you're gentle and you caress her, she'll respond beautifully.'

Armed with this straight-talking and unforgettable advice, I begin a high-speed crash-course in the skills needed to gain my licence from the Civil Aviation Authority. The first lessons involve learning how to assemble the canopy – called the 'envelope' by balloonists – and the basket. Then come hours of painstaking practice to master the burner for a smooth take-off and a controlled landing. At first, I have a problem with ground shyness, firing up the burner one time too many as I descend and consequently lifting off just short of touchdown. Then, when I realize my mistake, I thump the balloon down so hard that I put myself in danger of injury.

Nevertheless, after twenty-five hours of instruction, I pass my checkout flight, examined by Brian Jones, who later went on to co-pilot the first successful round-the-world balloon flight. I am now allowed to fly a balloon on my own, and that evening, high on the exhilaration of passing my test, I make my first solo flight, taking off from the centre of Bath. As I watch the golden stone façades of the Georgian crescents mellow below me in the evening sunlight I contemplate my ultimate ambition: to fly a balloon, not quite like this one but very similar, to the North Pole. I land about an hour later, elated at breaking my solo ballooning virginity. Nearby, a pleasure flight has landed, and I wander over. They offer me a sip of their champagne. It tastes great, and I feel as though I have been inducted into a special brotherhood.

Over the next months, Rune and I prepare for our flight over the Andes, seeking expert advice from alpine balloonists and from Brian Jones. There are dozens of questions to be answered, among them whether to use barographs and titanium tanks, the type of propane needed for high altitudes, the need for oxygen breathing apparatus and whether nitrogen is necessary to maintain pressure in the propane tanks.

The most valuable lesson comes at the RAF medical testing centre at Boscombe Down, where a session in a hypobaric chamber plainly illustrates the difficulties of thinking straight in conditions of low oxygen. A female instructor seals us inside a chamber and the air pressure is reduced to the level it would be at a height of 25,000ft. We then remove our oxygen masks and attempt a simple jigsaw puzzle. It seems to me as if I have all the time in the world, but everybody outside the chamber can see that I am fumbling with the pieces. My ability to think is slowing so drastically that I could lose consciousness within three minutes.

The danger we face is made clear to us. If our oxygen fails at any time while we are flying over the Andes, we will initially become dangerously exuberant and then completely unaware of how much our physical reactions are slowing. By the time we realize that our oxygen supply has been cut off, it will be too late to do anything about it. It is a sobering experience.

In mid-November, disaster strikes after I buy a small balloon in which to practise flying and increase my solo hours from the measly three I've clocked up so far. Shortly before I am due to leave for Chile, I take one last solo flight in my new craft, rising in the tiny basket on a crisp autumn morning over Bath. It is a textbook flight until the landing near Marshfield, when I hit the ground with such force that a farmer standing nearby rushes over, thinking I have killed myself. I climb out of the basket gingerly and find I can barely bend over to pack up the balloon. My back is sore, but it is nothing in comparison with the searing pain in my knee. I am due to depart for the Andes in a matter of days and I cannot even walk.

A visit to a surgeon who specializes in treating injuries suffered by Bath's rugby team brings home the bad news. It is a torn cartilage. Fortunately, there is a silver lining to this cloud: the surgeon's experience with sportsmen means I do not need an operation, the usual treatment until five years ago. Instead, a cupful of fluid is drained from the joint and I am prescribed a course of exercises. A week later, a little lamer than I had hoped to be, I hobble off to Chile.

On Tuesday 7 December, a fortnight after arriving in Chile, I find myself standing on a crop duster's airstrip on the outskirts of Los Andes, sixty miles north of Santiago. It is 4 a.m., shortly before sunrise. Rune and I are preparing to launch our bid to fly a hot-air balloon across the Andes.

Since arriving in Chile, I have acquired another half an hour's experience as a balloon pilot, but it was nothing more hazardous than an early-morning test flight of the second-hand 120,000-cubic-foot balloon that Victor Mardones has found for me. Now my experience amounts to a modest four and a half hours, and *Typhoo Challenger*, with its basket stripped to the bare necessities in order to save weight, is by a long margin the largest balloon I have so far flown. Fortunately, it handles beautifully.

It has been a frustrating fortnight waiting for the right wind direction we need to carry us across the spine of South America. Chilean and Argentinian bureaucracy has made the tiresome wait worse. With the two countries still at loggerheads over the precise lie of their common border, negotiating to take off in Chile and to touch down in Argentina is fraught with political wrangling. My intentions were not welcomed by Chilean air traffic control, which initially refused the flight plan, until Victor pulled a few strings and let slip that his father once ran Santiago international airport. As soon as he heard this the airport manager immediately granted us permission, and even phoned a friend in the customs department to ensure that Chilean immigration would approve the flight.

At 22,831ft, Aconcagua is the world's highest mountain outside the Himalayas, but it is familiar territory to me. I failed to climb it in November 1994, but returned and succeeded in reaching the top in February 1995 as part of my assault on the seven summits. Now I'm back to fly across the old foe. I could fly across a lower part of the Andes, but I'm aiming for Aconcagua because it would create an impregnable record: the Andes crossed by hot-air balloon at its highest point.

The only remaining problem is a recurring fault on the ten-litre oxygen tank. It was leaking when it arrived from England and a replacement rubber seal failed to fix it, so Victor found two five-litre aluminium tanks of dry oxygen similar to those used in hospitals.

With the red tape cleared and the equipment prepared, Rune and I run through our pre-flight checks at the airstrip, tense with excitement as our goal looms within tantalizing grasp. The flight will carry us from 40°C to −40°C, so we need to wear layered clothing: shorts under our Arctic thermal underwear, and our cold-weather kit over the lot. Rune has his parachute, but because of the need to conserve weight and bulk, I am without one. Instead, I am wearing climbing boots and a helmet in case we are forced to crash-land on the mountain. I am also carrying a rucksack with rope, crampons, a small tent and a sleeping bag. Nearby, a helicopter with an English television crew is idling, waiting for me to take off.

The clock ticks on. We know that we must take off before the sun rises, while the air is still, and then rise high enough to catch the westerly winds that should propel the balloon across the mountains before the heat of the day sets up the thermals. But nothing seems to be going quite to schedule, and the sense of time running out becomes more acute when one of the launch team causes the balloon to twist on its axis. I decide enough is enough, and take the snap decision to depart. I check that Rune is ready and then fire the burners to lift the eighty-foot-high balloon over the crowd that has assembled. We soar into the early-morning air, climbing over some of Chile's famous vineyards. I check the GPS satellite navigation system and establish radio contact with air traffic control as the balloon begins its steady ascent. It seems to be going well.

According to Victor and the meteorologists, the westerly winds should pick up the balloon at 8,000ft, but there's no sign of any movement when we reach that altitude. In fact, we find we are parked static, still directly above the airstrip. The promised winds have failed to materialize and I know I need to go higher, which requires me to lighten the load immediately if I am to have any hope of crossing the Andes.

There is one easy way out of this predicament, and I don't hesitate in taking it. 'Rune, you're going to have to jump now!' I shout over the roar of the burners.

'What?' Rune replies. It is not the parachute drop he had expected and he is shaken out of his habitual calm by the prospect of a premature exit.

I know that he will do almost anything for me, and that includes sacrificing his own attempt at a record so that I can still have a free run on mine. 'If I get over we'll come back and concentrate on your record,' I bargain, knowing that I have no other choice, but hating myself for having to make the decision.

Without another word Rune is gone. In a single move-ment he leaps over the side of the basket and plummets into the dawn darkness below. It is one of the most traumatic moments of my life, watching the one person I have come to depend on more than any other for my safety and sanity leap straight over the edge. To an inexperienced parachutist such as myself, it seems ridiculously dangerous, and I fear for the man without whom I would not have reached the North Pole and completed my grand slam. Although I am tempted to peer over the side of the basket, I cannot bear to watch him drop in case his chute fails to open. I cannot remember ever feeling as lonely as I do now, in these first few moments after Rune disappears.

But I do not have much time to contemplate Rune's fate. With some two hundred pounds of human ballast ditched, the balloon is now ascending like a rocket and I have to fight to regain control. With my heart in my mouth I repeat the words 'Christ, I hope he's all right' like a mantra until I hear from the ground that he has landed safely. Then I attend to my own predicament, that of a novice pilot rising at a rate of a thousand feet a minute to heights he has never scaled before. I trim the burners, secure my oxygen mask and check my position. Still no wind. I'm going up in a straight line. It's not what I want, and there's little time to spare. I have enough fuel to fly for only five hours and need to head eastwards pronto, so I decide to climb higher in search of the elusive westerly winds. As I rise, I lose sight of the helicopter with the television crew on board. My last remaining human contact has reached its operating ceiling of 21,000ft. Meanwhile, the figures flash by on my altimeter: 22,000ft, 23,000ft, 24,000ft.

At 26,000ft I finally pick up the wind, only to discover that it is carrying the balloon northwards along the Andes. Where in hell's name are the promised winds that will carry me eastwards, across the mountains to Argentina, to success and safety? I drift slowly northwards, looking down on Aconcagua's majestic contours laid out like a map beneath me. I can see the route I followed to the top, past the Condor's Nest and the Berlin Hut where Neil Williams, my climbing partner, and I pitched our final camp before our assault on the summit. Great memories, but this is no time for reminiscing. I've got a job to do, and I tell myself there's only one option: better whack it up some more in search of a westerly wind. The burners roar in the thin air and their flame jets screech in my ears as the balloon surges upwards again. I know that I face certain death if I venture beyond 34,000ft without enriched oxygen, so I level off just short of 32,000ft, the altitude at which passenger jets cruise across the Atlantic.

I feel scared, very exposed and utterly alone. I've never flown higher than a few thousand feet above southern England and here I am close to the jetstream and in utterly unfamiliar territory. Above me, a vapour trail is billowing around the balloon from the burners, and I remember that it was the sight of a jet's vapour trail nearly nine months ago that got me in this tight spot. Unlike a jet aeroplane, I am travelling at the same speed and in the same direction as the wind, so the vapour trail does not streak in a straight line. Instead it snakes around the envelope as I float alone above the magnificent mountain range that lies about ten thousand feet below, wondering what to do.

I tweak the burner to keep the flame alight in the low pressure of the high altitude and then I check my course. Sod it. I am still heading north, but there is little time to consider an alternative plan of attack. The first of my two five-litre tanks of oxygen is almost empty and I need to switch to the second tank within minutes. All I have to do is unscrew the coupling while keeping the mask over my face. It is a simple procedure that I have practised count-less times on the ground, but it is proving more difficult at high altitude. Then I realize: I am used to the −46°C cold at 32,000ft, but the coupling is not. It has frozen solid. It will not budge.

My hands are shaking with nerves. I manage to release the bottle from its binding and I stretch my whole body to its limit in order to hold the coupling up to the propane burner in an attempt to warm it up. But still there is no movement. The mask remains clamped to my face and I glance at the meter to see how much oxygen – and time – I have left. Christ, it's in the red already. In my head I can hear the voice of the instructress at Boscombe Down telling me I have three minutes to live. Where is she now that I really need help?

Faced with the brutal reality that I have only myself to rely upon, I spur my brain on into overdrive, suspecting that my decisions could already be impaired by partial oxygen starvation. I know I cannot keep going without oxygen. Either I will die or I will veer into a part of the Andes where it is impossible to land. The calculation isn't difficult: I can breathe without oxygen at 10,000ft, so I have no option but to drop from three times that height before my tank runs out. There's no alternative; I have to make an emergency descent, one of the most dangerous of all ballooning manoeuvres, and one that I have been told about but never attempted. If I switch off the burners and let the air in the balloon go cold, I will plummet at around two thousand feet per minute. At the very least it will take me eleven minutes to get down to 10,000ft. Many mountains nearby are considerably higher than that and I could crash into them. It's going to be a close call, but I have no choice.

Knowing that to hesitate is to die, I immediately cut the burners and let the balloon drop from the sky. It is intensely frightening hearing the fuel whoosh out as it turns to liquid in the bitter cold, but the most alarming moment comes when the burners' pilot lights flicker and die in the thin air. I know that I may not manage to light them again, and if that happens I will continue to plummet beyond the 10,000ft mark and less than five minutes later I will crash into the ground.

I then tune my radio to the frequency used by the helicopter hovering below and radio a curt Mayday to Mario, its pilot. He sounds worried, and tells me that he has been trying to radio me for some time as he was concerned that he had not had a response to his earlier calls. I have no time to explain why; instead I have urgent news for him: 'I'm almost out of oxygen. I'm making an emergency landing.'

It is the right decision, I keep telling myself as I plunge earthwards at more than thirty feet a second. I am not in a blind panic, and I should be able to land in a reasonably controlled manner, even if the pilot lights do not re-ignite. If it all goes wrong, I know that when the balloon reaches 15,000ft and the air thickens, the balloon should slow gradually of its own accord. Even if I cannot relight the burners, it should land like one of those overloaded circular parachutes used in the Second World War. It may be a colossal crash-landing and I may not be able to walk away from it, but at least I should survive. Or so I was told in my flight training.

But as the dropping balloon gathers speed it starts to spin faster and faster, out of control, towards the rocks below. I know that if I do not arrest the twisting I will not be able to avoid hitting the ground, but I feel unable to do anything about it. I am aware that I am already feeling giddy and light-headed. It is the first signs of oxygen starvation and all I manage to do is to think that I am glad I am over the foothills rather than the barren peaks of the Andes. Then the thermals hit, and they begin to blow me towards the crest of Aconcagua.

Quick thinking is needed. The balloon continues to drop like a stone. Either I light the burners to lift the balloon out of the grasp of the thermals or I will crash into the rocky mountain that is approaching fast. I grapple with the burners, repeatedly willing the pilot lights to ignite, but they refuse. Then I have a brainwave. Luckily, I am alert enough to ask Mario to use the down-draught from his chopper to push me away from the mountains. At my rate of descent, those cliffs are getting too damned close for comfort.

It is something that Mario has never tried before, but he

agrees to give it a go. After what has seemed like an eternity of isolation and fear, it is a great comfort to talk to a fellow aviator. To my immense relief, my novel strategy works. The balloon careers away from the peaks and, as soon as I am out of danger, I manage to light the burners with my welder's sparker. It's a close escape, and I know it. A couple of hundred feet further, maybe fifteen seconds more, and I would have crashed into the side of the mountain. Instead, I hop over a nearby peak and a few minutes later make a relatively controlled landing within a few feet of a monster cactus. I have failed on my first attempt to cross the Andes. Fortunately, I've survived to tell the extraordinary tale.

A minute or so later Mario drops the helicopter down near the balloon and I attempt to lift myself out of the basket. After three hours in the cold air I am incredibly stiff, but any thoughts of taking it easy evaporate when I am surrounded by children who have appeared from all directions on foot and on horseback. I have landed near their playground and they marvel and giggle at the sight of a blue-eyed stranger dropping into their midst from the sky. They help me pick the envelope off the cactus spines and then Mario airlifts my balloon to safety. I am left to share lunch with the schoolchildren of El Sobrante, after which I sit in their classroom and join in an impromptu game of football. Fortunately, the tiny village has a payphone, so I ask a schoolteacher to contact Hermana, Victor Mardones's wife. She passes on my message and four hours later the team turns up, led by Terry McCoy.

'Well, that was a close escape. My boy, what do you think of that?'

I know I am extremely lucky to be alive, but I am undeterred. 'It's all good experience, Terry. Don't think I'm done yet.'

Over the next few days we regroup and reassess our plans. First, the balloon needs to be repaired and recertified as fit for flight. Then I break the uncomfortable news to Rune that he will not be coming along on the next flight. The last flight has made it clear to me that I'll need a third tank of propane to give me time to find the right weather track at the appropriate altitude. The balloon will not carry the extra weight unless Rune gives up his place. It isn't an easy thing to do, but Rune takes it well. I promise him that he can still do his parachute jump if we have enough fuel left after I've made my next attempt to cross the Andes, but it is not a convincing pitch. We both know how quickly time is running out.

The most pressing problem is that of the oxygen supply. I cannot afford to make another mistake. Not only is it costing valuable time, next time it could be fatal. My mistake has been to assume that because the initial plan was to use a single ten-litre tank with one mask, I did not need to fit a second mask when we switched to two five-litre tanks. In the event, my life was saved by the fact that I used up more oxygen than I expected while I searched for the elusive westerly winds. If I'd hit the westerlies straight away, I would have been stranded without oxygen, unable to access the second tank, somewhere over a much less hospitable part of the Andes. It was a serious error of judgement that could have killed me. For the next flight I elect to take three five-litre cylinders and to fit each of them with its own oxygen mask.

The final decision is to switch the launch location from Los Andes to Santiago. It will mean that I won't cross the Andes at its highest point, but the proximity to the Chilean capital will enable us to have an up-to-the-minute weather forecast when I take off. Small changes such as this can make or break an expedition.

Three days after my first abortive attempt, I am once again heading for a launch site in the pre-dawn darkness. As I approach the pristine polo field on the outskirts of Santiago, a jet preparing to land at the international airport relays the information I most want to hear: the winds are from the west and holding steady. The balloon is inflated and Terry gives me his traditional pep talk. As ever, it ends with a reminder that the choice is mine: it is not too late to abandon the flight. But for me there is only ever one option: seize the day and go for it.

I stride purposefully towards the balloon, clamber into the basket, make my final pre-launch checks and then call for the ropes to be released. *Typhoo Challenger* rises slowly and magnificently above a mist that heralds a perfect day. I fire the burners and the climb accelerates, Santiago and the Pacific slipping away behind the balloon along with my worries about oxygen and fuel shortages. When I reach 10,000ft I pick up the wind and move smoothly towards the silhouetted peaks, imperiously beautiful as the rising sun illuminates them from behind. It is still dark at the polo field below, but I am high enough to catch the sun and the balloon is lit up like a light bulb in the sky.

But there is little time to savour the beauty and take in the cool dawn air. I have to concentrate on putting plenty of clear blue sky between the balloon and the fast-approaching 20,000ft mountains. The higher I climb, the faster I travel, as the winds increase in speed. The speedometer has clicked up from ten knots to twenty-five knots by the time I reach my ceiling of 32,000ft. This time there is no panic when the burners cut out. With oxygen to spare, I know the descent towards re-ignition will not be the frightening plunge towards hell that it was a few days ago.

It takes me two magical if lonely hours to clear the peaks. I pass steadily over the 21,555ft volcanic summit of Tupungato, suspended in my wicker basket, at the mercy of the wind and knowing that if I fail, there is no room to land among the summits and I should probably die.

Shortly after 9 a.m., I radio back to base to give Terry and the team my position. I tell them I am east of the Andes and read my longitude and latitude off the GPS location finder. 'Welcome to Argentinian airspace,' comes the reply. I've done it! The Andes crossed solo in a hot-air balloon! All I have to do now is find somewhere to land.

And then I make the mistake of relaxing. When I climbed Everest, I was told that most accidents happen on the way down from the summit, when exuberance and complacency conspire to create overconfidence and carelessness. With the dusty plains of Argentina spread out in front of me, I make a lapse of judgement that almost costs me dearly. Worried about the effect of thermals now that the sun is up, I descend to 20,000ft to look for a place to land. But it is a major error. I lose height too quickly and too close to the mountains, and consequently I stray into a wind pattern that blows me back towards the peaks at a frightening rate. Things would have been fine had I waited until I reached the town that I can see five miles ahead before making the decision to come down. Instead, I panic and, desperate to avoid snatching defeat from the jaws of victory, thump the balloon down on the side of a dirt road. I've made it, but God knows where I am. I'm not even entirely sure that I'm still in Argentina.

I check my GPS location finder. It appears this is Argentinian territory, and the first physical confirmation that I have crossed the border comes when I spot an unmistakably Argentinian gaucho and his daughter approaching across the dusty field. I radio the team back in Chile to tell them of my success. 'Great flight. No problems. Easy landing,' I say to Terry. I give him my position and he tells me I am eight miles west of the village of Pareditas and some forty miles east of the Chilean border. I can hear the team whooping in the background. It feels great. I took off from Chile before breakfast and landed in Argentina in time for lunch.

Nobody will be coming to fetch me for quite some time, so I celebrate my moment of triumph on my own, raising my arms to the heavens that have carried me on my journey and whooping for joy in the empty scrubland. Tears roll down my cheeks as I realize I have set my first ballooning record and lived to tell the tale. Next stop, I think to myself, the Pole.

CHAPTER TWO

THE PLAN

LONDON, ENGLAND

29 July, 1895

THE CAVERNOUS VICTORIAN LECTURE THEATRE WAS PACKED with the cream of the world's Arctic explorers and scientists. In the serried banks of seating, military aeronautic experts were squeezed in beside academics and pillars of the geographic establishment. Along the wood-panelled walls, journalists and writers jostled against a smattering of the plain curious, eager to hear the latest accounts of exploration and adventure as told to the Sixth International Geographical Congress.

Among the audience was General Adolphus Washington Greely, the American explorer of Greenland and Ellesmere Island and founder of the American Geographical Society. In 1883 he led an expedition of twenty-five men through 250 days of Arctic winter. Only seven survived – by eating their own leather clothing. Near Greely sat Rear-Admiral Albert Markham, a legendary figure in polar exploration. In 1875 he sledged closer to the North Pole than any man before. Like the other delegates, they had convened in this stuffy hall on a hot summer's evening because Salomon August Andrée, a Swede who was gaining a reputation across Europe as a pioneering balloonist and an inspired technician, was to give an account of his proposed expedition to the North Pole.

The room buzzed with speculation. Herr Andrée had already spoken in Stockholm, Berlin and Paris of his grandiose plan, and it was rumoured that Alfred Nobel, the inventor of dynamite, a baron called Oscar Dickson and the King of Sweden had put up the funds. To some of the audience, Andrée's proposal was the only remaining way to reach the Pole; to others, it was the latest ridiculous manifestation of balloonacy.

Shortly before the appointed time, Andrée entered the room. He was an unusually large man with a bushy moustache and oiled hair parted just so. Pausing only to chat briefly with an officer of the conference, he approached the lectern.

Andrée knew he faced a high-stakes game. By the end of the nineteenth century, the North and South Poles were the only parts of the planet yet to be discovered. Explorers had circumnavigated the globe by sea and, as far as possible, by land. They had followed the major rivers to their sources and ventured through jungles and across deserts and swamps to investigate the most remote outposts of civilization. After the scramble for Africa, only the inner reaches of the Arctic and Antarctic remained unmapped. For men such as Andrée, the Poles exerted an irresistible pull. He knew that if he succeeded, he would be forever remembered as the man who was the first to reach the North Pole. But if he failed, his audacious plan would be no more than a footnote in polar history.

The buzz in the room subsided into expectant silence. Andrée cleared his throat, then stepped forward to outline his plan in the fluent, accented English he had picked up while working in Philadelphia.

'The history of geographical discovery is one of great

peril and suffering. But of all the areas to be discovered, none has offered such great difficulties to the explorer as the Arctic regions,' he began.

'In hot regions, natives block the way of the explorer, but they can also assist him in his efforts. Lakes and rivers may slow his progress, but they can also carry him long distances, and provide subsistence. Even deserts are not without oases, shelter and food. In the Arctic, however, exploration is quite different.

'The cold only kills. There are no oases in the icy desert, no vegetation, no fuel. The polar ice might carry an explorer across the ocean, but it is a treacherous journey, blocked by gigantic blocks and insurmountable walls of tumbling ice. Ocean currents beneath the ice can speed you towards your destination, but they are just as likely to carry you away or crush your vessel in the movement of the floes. Perpetual summer sunshine lights the way, but it also melts the ice into a thick slush, unable to carry the weight of a man.'

At the time of this address, all attempts to reach the North Pole had used sledges pulled by man, dog, horse or reindeer. And all had failed. Frustrated by the apparent impossibility of reaching the Pole on foot or by sledge, Fridtjof Nansen had set sail from Norway just over two years earlier on the *Fram*. This wooden boat was built in such a shape that when winter came and the ice closed in, it would rise above it instead of being crushed. Nansen's plan was to allow his ship to become frozen on the Arctic ice off eastern Siberia and to be carried by ocean currents over the Pole to Canada. But not a word had been heard from Nansen since the day in 1893 when he sailed from Kristiania.

'The fact remains,' Andrée told the packed room, 'that over the centuries all attempts to cross the polar ice have failed, numerous lives and vessels have been lost and large sums of money wasted.

'It is time to examine whether there is any means of transportation in the Arctic other than the sledge. We need not look very far to discover one that is ideal for the purpose. I refer to the balloon. Not the perfect steerable balloon of our dreams, but one that we can actually make. I am certain that such a balloon is capable of carrying an exploring party to the Pole and home again across the Arctic plains.'

It had been a cold and misty evening in March 1894 when Andrée had first spoken of his plan to balloon to the North Pole. Adolf Nordenskiöld, Sweden's leading Arctic explorer of the day, had approached him at the end of a meeting of the Swedish Anthropological and Geographical Society. Having survived ten polar expeditions, Nordenskiöld knew better than most that the North Pole could not be reached at that time by sledge.

'Walk with me back to my home at the Academy of Sciences,' said the great figure of Swedish exploration.

'It would be an honour, Frihere Nordenskiöld,' Andrée replied.

It was a considerable understatement. For Andrée, a shy and fiercely ambitious man who led a secluded life devoted to his studies and to his position as chief engineer of the Swedish Patent Office, Baron Nordenskiöld embodied all the glamour and influence he craved. Since the day in 1880 when King Oscar created Nordenskiöld a Frihere, a Swedish baron, upon his return to Gothenburg, he had been a national hero in a time of fierce patriotism. His achievements were considerable. He had explored Spitsbergen and led an expedition to western Greenland to study the inland ice. But his greatest feat, which led to the barony, was to have become the first person to sail through the Northeast Passage, from Norway via the Siberian Arctic to the Pacific.

Wrapped in the cold, damp mist, the two men walked slowly up Drottninggatan, or Queen Street, towards Adolf Fredrik Church. The baron's plump cheeks glowed in the cold air and tiny beads of dew condensed from the mist on to his warm, high forehead as he told Andrée of his ambition to investigate Antarctica, at that time the only unexplored continent.

'I have often wondered about using tethered balloons for polar reconnaissance,' Nordenskiöld said. 'I thought they might be useful for making observations, surveying the land for maps and so on.'

The baron outlined his theory that, because of the difficulties of landing on Antarctica, balloons could be used to lift an expedition with all its members and equipment from sea level over the ice walls that surrounded much of the continent and onto the ice shelf.

Hearing the elder statesman of Swedish exploration muse about the virtues of balloon flight was all the encouragement Andrée needed. Seizing the opportunity to interrupt when Nordenskiöld paused to wipe his small, round, wire-framed spectacles, Andrée blurted out his plan.

'I may try to cross the North Pole in a balloon drifting with the wind,' he said suddenly. 'No-one else appears to have realized the magnificent, regular system of winds that is capable of carrying giant balloons with cargo and passengers. I have made many flights with the *Svea*, a balloon I had made a year ago by the best maker in France, and found it an excellent way to travel.'

Nordenskiöld was taken aback by Andrée's sudden enthusiasm. Only a few minutes before, he had been speaking in the highly reserved manner that was expected of a chief engineer of the Patent Office addressing the Swedish Anthropological and Geographical Society. Now he was gabbling like a young teenager smitten with his first love.

'I know how the winds work, how humidity and temperature affect flight and what I can hope to photograph and to hear from any feasible altitude,' Andrée continued. 'I have made many flights, but for me they were not a sport or some pleasurable way of passing the time, but purely scientific experiments to determine how far I could hope to fly and with what accuracy.'

Nordenskiöld found it unusual to hear a man talk with such urgent passion about something as inanimate as a balloon, but for Andrée the *Svea* and ballooning had indeed become an obsession that pushed everything else but his beloved mother out of his life.

'I once flew for two and a half hours, in which time I covered twenty-six miles and rose to a height of thirteen and a half thousand feet,' he told Nordenskiöld. 'Do you know, even up there I could distinctly hear dogs barking.'

Nordenskiöld looked at the large man in front of him with some scepticism. Andrée did not look like a classic adventurer. His hands were soft and his face was slightly puffy, the result of a spoilt childhood, overindulged by his mother, his eccentric demands tolerated by his father. He did not seem driven by a love of the outdoors and a determination to conquer nature. Instead, Andrée appeared to Nordenskiöld to be a bookish type, more at ease with meticulous method than fearless fortitude. It was hard for anyone to imagine Andrée gritting his teeth as he fought against the elements. Maybe that was why he wanted to fly to the Pole, Nordenskiöld thought to himself. That way he would be safely above the desperate existence of life on the ice with which Nordenskiöld was so familiar. Despite these reservations, Andrée's bubbling enthusiasm impressed him.

'This sounds most interesting,' Nordenskiöld told Andrée. 'Any method of shortening the agony of living on the ice for month after month, or even year after year, has to be the way forward. I hope you'll continue to work at your plan.'

'But Frihere, I am almost complete,' Andrée insisted. 'I have designed a balloon to fly to the Pole. All I need is two companions to take photographs and make scientific observations while I fly; an observer and a secretary to join me, the balloon expert.'

Again Nordenskiöld was taken aback. Behind Andrée's scholarly front there appeared to be a man of vision and enormous determination.

'But your plan has a weakness,' Nordenskiöld warned. 'No-one knows if the tradewinds reach the Arctic. What will you do if you get no winds blowing directly north?'

Andrée then divulged his greatest discovery yet, made on his third balloon flight and perfected on his sixth voyage – namely, how to steer the balloon.

'Last October I set out to fly along the coast but I misjudged the wind. When I lifted off, the wind was blowing lightly out to sea, but I still made the journey because I counted on the wind direction changing when I reached a higher altitude.

'The flight was going well. I was above the cloud, making observations of temperature, the clouds, my respiration and thirst at different heights. I then dropped below the cloud and was alarmed to find myself over the water.'

The wind had carried the *Svea* across the Åland Sea, a northern inlet of the Baltic Sea between Sweden and Finland. Andrée had realized there was no chance of returning to the mainland. Spotting a boat that he thought might be able to help, he had tried to reduce the *Svea*'s speed by lowering an anchor down a guide rope that was dangling on the water's surface. This had failed to slow the balloon, so he'd attached two empty ballast sacks to the end of the landing line and lowered them into the water. With their mouths wide open, the sacks had scooped up the water and slowed down the *Svea*.

'I called down to the captain of the vessel and asked him to catch one of the balloon's ropes, but he shouted back that he preferred to lay his boat across my course so that one of the ropes might get caught in the rigging.'

Andrée could see that he had Nordenskiöld's complete attention as he continued.

'I could see the madness of such a dangerous manoeuvre. If my hydrogen-filled balloon came anywhere near the steamer's funnel, the explosion would kill everyone on board the steamer as well as me. I had no choice but to refuse the captain's assistance and endeavour to reach land.'

Unable to hoist the water-filled sacks back up to his gondola, Andrée had cut them free and the *Svea* had increased speed to around eighteen miles an hour. But this was still not fast enough to make landfall before darkness, so Andrée had cut free the guide rope attached to the anchor, leaving several other ropes dangling in the water.

'I noticed that I was rising and sinking, and realized that the partially deflated balloon was acting like a kite in the wind. The guide ropes provided a way of controlling the balloon's altitude without resorting to jettisoning ballast or releasing gas. It meant I could fly further than a free balloon of the same dimensions. With this discovery, I was immediately liberated from flying purely at the whim of the winds.'

Nordenskiöld stopped walking and turned to face Andrée. The street was shadowy, lit only by gas lamps, but Andrée could clearly see Nordenskiöld's piercing gaze through the gloomy mist.

'Does this really mean what I take it to mean?' Nordenskiöld asked.

'Absolutely, Frihere. I scarcely need point out what implications this has for making long balloon journeys for exploration purposes.'

Andrée continued recounting his story, describing how he had ended his 170-mile flight by crash-landing on a lonely islet as darkness fell over the Åland Sea.

'It was an extremely violent landing, but it had one fortunate outcome. All my instruments were severely damaged, including my watch, which stopped dead at seven eighteen p.m., confirming exactly how long I had flown. I then spent an extremely unpleasant night on the island until eleven the next morning, when I was at last spotted and rescued by a boat.'

Andrée had timed his tale well, for the two men had now reached a side entrance at the Academy of Sciences. Nordenskiöld paused before climbing the short flight of steps that led to his apartment.

'This has been a fascinating evening. It has been a

pleasure to meet you and your plans are quite astonishing,' he said, shaking hands with Andrée. 'Please consider me one of your supporters. You must let me know how you progress. You can count on any assistance I can offer. But for now, I must say goodbye.'

The door closed and Andrée turned back towards the street, thrilled by Nordenskiöld's overt support and encouragement. As he walked to his mother's house, he told himself grandly that this was the moment of birth of his polar expedition.

For fear that people would regard him as an idealistic dreamer, Nordenskiöld was only the second person to whom Andrée had revealed the full extent of his ambitions. Even his mother did not know the whole story. He had told her only that he wanted to explore the Arctic and that he thought he might do so by balloon. Gurli Linder alone knew that he dreamed of making his name by flying his balloon all the way to the North Pole.

Andrée knew there was a very simple reason why Gurli would never divulge his plans to anyone else: she was the wife of a close friend, and to divulge the intricate details of his ambitions would be to admit to Stockholm society the extent of her intimacy with Andrée. For Gurli had fallen hopelessly in love with him, a love that Andrée was very much aware of but left unrequited.

The summer and autumn of 1894 were the couple's happiest time together, though Gurli suspected deep inside it was to be their last. They spent many long afternoons walking in the countryside around Stockholm or sailing between the dozens of islands in the Stockholm archipelago, hoping they would not be spotted by someone who knew them. It was a considerable feat to court so obviously, yet go unnoticed. Gurli was a stunning woman, tall, statuesque, with fair hair and a fine figure. It was inevitable that she attracted admiring glances, particularly as Andrée looked rather less imposing beside her. However, it was not Gurli's beauty that had attracted

Andrée, but her intelligence and wit. She was the only person, he felt, who had the sensitivity really to understand him. She alone could comprehend why he always felt he was an outsider, and sympathize with his burning ambition to make a name for himself.

As they walked like any married couple, promenading with the burghers of Stockholm on a Sunday afternoon, Andrée would tell Gurli of the dramatic discoveries he had made with the *Svea*, and how he believed he was on the cusp of a revolution in balloon flight and polar exploration.

Undaunted by his narrow brush with death, Andrée had continued his experiments, proving that he could control the *Svea*'s cruising altitude precisely and in a very straightforward manner. The key was the dragline, which held the *Svea* in a very fine equilibrium. When the balloon rose, the dragline lifted off the ground and its extra weight pulled the balloon back down to the cruising altitude; if the balloon descended below its optimum height, more of the dragline trailed along the ground and consequently the balloon had to support less of its weight. It was as if ballast had been released, and as a result the balloon returned to its ideal cruising altitude.

'Being able to control the cruising altitude is very important,' Andrée told Gurli on one of their many afternoon walks. As usual, she yearned for him to speak about the possibility of a future together rather than ballooning, but Andrée pressed on. 'It means I can prevent the balloon rising to a height at which hydrogen will escape from the envelope, the one action that will limit the distance I can fly. Flying at a constant low altitude will give the *Svea* far greater endurance than any other balloon.'

Gurli listened and looked on with even greater admiration, longing to make Andrée realize the depth of her feelings and wishing she did not have to live such an unusual double life. But she also knew that Andrée had only one love in his life.

'My love is for you alone,' she told Andrée on another

walk in early summer. 'It is constant and everlasting, but it shows no sign of ever being fulfilled.'

Andrée realized the selfishness of his dependency on Gurli, who risked losing her children if her clandestine love was uncovered. He knew too what she wanted to hear, but did not spare her feelings.

'My choice is between you or the expedition,' he told her. 'You must understand that the expedition will always come first.'

Years later, Gurli would write that the pain of that moment still haunted her, but her devotion to Andrée was so absolute that she continued to support him. Recognizing his single-mindedness, she refused to let her unrequited love get in the way of her loyalty and their close friendship.

By mid-July Andrée was using a three-armed dragline and a steering sail that he rigged between the *Svea*'s envelope and its gondola. With its draglines trailing along the ground the *Svea* progressed at a slower pace than the wind, and the sail could be adjusted to catch the wind and change the direction of the balloon.

On one of his last trips, Andrée dropped cards from the balloon. They carried his name, his address and a request that whoever found a card should return it with details of the position at which it was found. From this he was able to plot his route and work out by how much he had managed to steer the balloon.

Again Gurli was the first to hear his good news. Still hoping for a declaration of his love, it was the last thing she wanted to be told on that balmy August evening. As they ate dinner on the terrace of a restaurant overlooking Lake Mälar, just to the west of Stockholm, Andrée told Gurli that he had proved a way of making the *Svea* highly steerable.

Gurli looked radiant that evening. Her golden skin was lit by the moonlight and Andrée could see the flicker of the candles on the table reflected in her eyes. It made them twinkle like the stars he could see above the trees behind her blonde curls. It was not the first time that Andrée had felt a strong physical attraction for Gurli, but again he denied it to himself. He knew that if he succumbed to her attractions, he would gain a lover but lose the motherly support he felt he needed from her more than anything.

'And what does it mean for your plans?' Gurli asked, hoping that Andrée would tell her that his obsession was over now that he had proved he had a way of steering the balloon.

'I managed at times to steer the *Svea* up to thirty degrees off the direction of the wind. I now know that I can make long journeys across land and sea using a balloon equipped with sails and draglines. I am not entirely dependent on the wind, but able to steer the balloon and follow the route I want. It means, I think, that I can fly a balloon to the North Pole.'

'So you are still determined to go ahead with your flight to the Pole? And if you succeed, what will you do then? Will you ever settle down, or will you become one of those people who is always looking for another challenge, unable to find satisfaction in the simple happiness of domesticity?'

'In marriage, one has to compromise one's ambitions,' Andrée replied. 'It is too great a risk to commit oneself to another person who would then be as important to me as I am.'

Gurli's eyes filled with tears.

'As soon as I feel any seeds of love begin to germinate, I am determined to uproot them,' Andrée continued remorselessly. 'I know if I were to let those feelings grow in my heart, they would become deep-rooted. I might be tempted to choose the woman I loved over the expedition, and I have vowed never to let this happen.'

By the time Andrée spoke at the International Geographical Congress in London in July 1895, he had completed nine flights with the *Svea* and worked out what he needed to fly to the Pole.

'Firstly, the polar balloon should have sufficient carrying power for three passengers,' he told the audience in the huge lecture theatre. 'It must also be able to lift all the necessary instruments for making observations, plus provisions for four months and ballast. In all, I estimate the cargo will be about three thousand kilograms. Secondly, the balloon should have an impermeability that will keep it afloat for thirty days. Thirdly, the filling of the balloon with hydrogen must take place in the Arctic regions. And finally, it must be steerable so that it will not be like a vessel drifting at the mercy of the wind, but will to a large extent be under the control of the aeronaut.'

Andrée had finally calculated that he could steer the balloon by up to 27° off the wind. Over a long distance, the effect could be dramatic. Instead of flying in a straight line from Cork in Ireland via Hull to Copenhagen in Denmark, for instance, it would mean the balloon could fly as far south as London and Brussels, or as far north as Edinburgh and Bergen in Norway. Over a six-hundred-mile journey to the Pole, it would mean enough leeway for the balloonists to fly in winds that were not heading directly north.

The basket, Andrée said, should be spacious and comfortable, with berths for three people and an observation platform on its roof. It should have floats and be suspended from a carrying ring, connecting it to the envelope of the balloon in such a way that it could be quickly disconnected from the envelope in an emergency.

Andrée had also calculated that his proposed expedition would cost no more than 129,000 Swedish kronor.* The balloon and basket would cost 36,000 kronor, a canvas balloon shed 15,000 kronor, and the hydrogen apparatus 18,400 kronor. The rest was to be spent on other equipment, technical assistance and on transportation to the north of Spitsbergen.

'We will need a sledge, a canvas boat, a tent, arms and

---

* About £7,120 at the time; equivalent to £440,000 in 2001.

ammunition, and provisions for four months, all in case we need to be rescued if a mishap occurs to the balloon.

'I wish to emphasize, however, that in providing equipment for the expedition, the character of the expedition should not be lost sight of. It is' – and here Andrée paused to stress his point – 'by balloon that the voyage should be made, and it is to the balloon that the travellers must cling. The life-saving apparatus, therefore, will have no further function than life-boats and life-buoys on board a ship.'

Many in the lecture hall were wondering who this man with the remarkable plan was. Some of the geographers present knew him by name and reputation for he had been assistant to the meteorologist Nils Ekholm in the first International Polar Year of 1882–3, when twelve stations were set up around the Arctic Circle to take measurements and pool the results. Andrée had worked at the Swedish station at Kapp Thordsen in Spitsbergen, where other scientists scoffed at his ideas, particularly after he revealed considerable gaps in his academic background. Worst of all, he had to endure the gibes of his colleagues after he had miscalculated the amount of kerosene that would be needed. His arrogance in not double-checking the figure with a colleague meant that the Swedish scientists spent much of the winter under severely rationed lighting.

Andrée's embarrassment among his peers led him to volunteer as guinea pig for an experiment later that winter. For years, scientists had questioned reports that people who lived through the permanent darkness of polar winters emerged into the first sunlight of spring with a yellow-green tinge to their faces. To determine whether facial skin actually changed colour or whether their eyes were simply unused to sunlight, Andrée shut himself in a house for a month. When he emerged from the darkness, his face really was yellow-green.

Even more revealing than his willingness to subject himself to voluntary imprisonment was the entry he made in his diary on embarking on the trial: *Dangerous? Perhaps. But what am I worth?* Such low self-esteem may have been a by-product of Andrée's sober intellectualism. He had an obsessive need for order and a deep-seated belief in the rationality of science. It may also explain why he had a burning desire to prove that he was somebody of note.

From a very young age, Andrée had been exceptionally wilful, always demanding answers from his parents to a barrage of questions. At sixteen, having won most of the academic prizes on offer, he demanded that his parents take him out of his secondary school at Jönköping, not far from the small lakeside town of Gränna where he was born, and allow him to enter the State Technical University. His father died soon afterwards, but Andrée was always more devoted to his mother and for some time seemed unable to have a close relationship with anyone else.

After university he worked as a technical artist and designer before travelling to America, where he first learnt of ballooning from a Mr Wise of Philadelphia, a highly experienced balloonist. But Andrée's frugality and a poor diet resulted in ill health. He returned to Sweden, took up an assistantship at the State Technical University and led a secluded life, immersing himself in books and contemplation, utterly self-absorbed until he joined the International Polar Year experiments and travelled to Spitsbergen. By the time he began to experiment with flying balloons, he was by all accounts a considerable misfit.

With few close friendships and an academic and professional record that he appeared to feel was inadequate, it was perhaps not surprising that Andrée was a dissatisfied man when he made his early balloon flights. Flying above Sweden, however, he was able to let his mind wander. What better way to show the ingenuity of his method of steering a balloon than by undertaking a flight to the one place that still remained out of the reach of man? And if he were to succeed, would it not guarantee him lasting fame, and at last the respect, possibly even the envy, he craved from his fellow academics? And would it not bestow on his fellow Swedes a national pride much needed at this time of wrangling over sovereignty with Norway? If nothing else, he thought, playing up to national prestige might help him secure financial backing. And so he added a few paragraphs of patriotic passion when he delivered his proposal for a polar expedition by balloon to the Royal Swedish Academy of Sciences on 13 February 1895.

'Who is better suited to undertake this endeavour than we Swedes?' he demanded. 'We are a highly civilized people who through the ages have been known for our fearless courage. Living close to the Arctic regions, we are familiar with its climate and trained by nature to over-come it. We should not shy away from the duty that lies ahead. More than any other people, are we not uniquely qualified to accomplish this task? Am I wrong in assuming that, as central and southern Europeans explore Africa, we should explore the white quarter of the world?'

Andrée's address certainly struck a chord among fellow Swedes. Elsewhere his plan was often met with ridicule – one Austrian newspaper wrote that he was a fool and a swindler – but in Sweden he became a national hero even before he had finished raising the funds. In May, Alfred Nobel walked into Andrée's office and asked him if he remembered their meeting eight years previously. When Andrée said he did, Nobel offered to become his first sponsor, and donated almost a fifth of Andrée's budget. He later increased his commitment to the project by stumping up more than half of the expedition's cost. By the time Andrée came to London, fewer than three months later, all the costs of the expedition had been covered, and he had dropped the patriotic appeal to his countrymen from his presentation.

Andrée finished his speech with a final plea to his distinguished audience: 'Is it not more likely that the North Pole will be reached by balloon than by dog and sledge, or by a ship travelling like a boulder encased in the ice? I believe it is possible to venture further into the Arctic in a few days' balloon flight than during a century of exploration on foot.'

A polite smattering of applause ran around the room; some members of the audience were clearly impressed with his proposal, but many were not. Among the sceptics was Rear-Admiral Albert Markham, who rose slowly to his feet. The room hushed instantly.

'I do not wish to discourage efforts, however novel, to reach the North Pole, and I sincerely hope that the proposed enterprise by Herr Andrée may be successful,' he began. 'I cannot, however, encourage it, because of my ignorance of aeronautics. But I may perhaps be allowed to draw attention to the fact that with a balloon we are unable, in thick or cloudy weather, to distinguish anything that we may be passing over.

'I hope that Herr Andrée will be able to return from the North Pole and tell us what he has seen there; but, though he may be travelling only three or four hundred yards above the level of the sea, it will be very difficult for him to know whether he is above land, ice or snow. He will be unable to collect natural history specimens, or take any celestial observations in order to find out his latitude and longitude, without descending to terra firma. His balloon may be blown against a cliff or an iceberg. If it is damaged, how is he to get back?

'These are only a few of the questions I should like to put to Herr Andrée, though I have no doubt that they have already been well weighed and considered.'

And with that, Rear-Admiral Markham sat down, apparently satisfied that the Swedish interloper had been put in his place.

Andrée ought not to have been surprised by these objections. Three years before, the Royal Geographical Society, an inherently conservative body of men who appeared to believe that the Scandinavians should leave Arctic exploration to the British and Americans, had poured scorn on Fridtjof Nansen's plan to cross the Arctic Ocean in the *Fram*. But before Andrée had a chance to reply, another, younger, man stood up.

'I have listened with interest to Herr Andrée's paper.' The geographer Arthur Silva White spoke with a slightly fogeyish air. 'But much as I sympathize with every daring attempt in the cause of science, I cannot regard his project in any other light than that of a bold flight into the unknown. Under the most favourable circumstances, Herr Andrée might possibly reach a higher northern latitude than any previous Arctic explorer, but there are no scientific grounds for supposing that an equally favourable return voyage can be depended upon during the short life of a balloon.'

Uncomfortable at having his cherished ideas challenged so openly, Andrée reddened. It brought back memories of the long winter at Kapp Thordsen, when more experienced men had exposed his ignorance and ridiculed his arrogance. Unable to realize that yet again he risked humiliation for his naked ambition, Andrée jutted out his chin, determined to convince the audience of the plain common sense of his plan. But before Andrée could utter a word, Silva White, stepping sideways from his position at the end of one of the dozen or so benches that were stepped in rows around the lecture theatre, spoke again. He was confident and slightly theatrical, used to speaking publicly, and his self-possession unnerved Andrée even more.

'Nine years ago I carried out a series of experiments in Scotland in order to determine the extent to which an aeronaut can depend upon air currents. It led me to place a considerable amount of reliance upon the chances which an aeronaut may have in reaching a distant spot within a few points of the prevailing wind.

'But these chances depended, and must depend, absolutely on a very precise knowledge of meteorological conditions during an ascent, and upon a very liberal expenditure of gas and ballast – the life-blood of a balloon. Upon neither of these favourable circumstances can Herr Andrée rely. His draglines may enable him to save ballast, but they can have little effect in deflecting the course of his balloon. I therefore regard Herr Andrée's project as foolhardy, and not one to be seriously discussed at a meeting of this character.'

With a flourish, Silva White sat down. The previously silent lecture theatre was now abuzz with chatter. Poor Andrée stood rigid, unblinking, his chin still raised in defiance.

Another man cleared his throat. General Adolphus Greely, at fifty-one one of the oldest living Arctic explorers, was on his feet. 'I have never travelled in a balloon as an amateur,' he began in his slow American drawl. 'But my professional duties have obliged me to give my attention to ballooning in connection with other important questions. In the course of my examination of aeronautics, for example, I have learnt the meaning of the word "permeability".' He paused for effect. 'Let me tell you that a balloon is subject to a minimum loss each day of one per cent of its gas. Hence, if the life of a balloon is to be six weeks, it will at the end of that time have lost about forty per cent or nearly one half of its carrying power. And if Herr Andrée has succeeded in preventing this, then all I can say is that I hope, before starting, he will take us into his confidence.'

The lecture theatre resounded with mocking laughter, and again Andrée's face reddened. He could feel his moustache thicken, which it always seemed to do when his authority was challenged, as it mopped up the beads of sweat breaking out on his upper lip. Out of sight of the audience, behind the lectern, his left knee trembled with nerves as he began to fear that he was losing the battle to convince those he needed to persuade more than anyone else of the validity of his plan.

'I need only say that this practical question has engaged the attention of some of the acutest minds in France and Germany,' General Greely continued. 'Money in great sums has been applied to devise means of durability for the war balloons of those countries. How far they have succeeded is unknown to the general public, but all experts agree that it is a complex and exceedingly difficult problem to resolve. If our ballooning friend has discovered the means, I am sure that Colonel Watson in England will as gladly receive and acknowledge it as I shall do in America.'

Andrée struggled to remain expressionless. He knew he was on weak ground here, as he was relying solely on the advice of Monsieur Gabriel Yon, the Parisian balloon maker who had built the *Svea* and who had assured him that a twenty-three-metre-diameter balloon made of two layers of silk would not lose more than fifty kilograms of gas every thirty days.

'The longest recorded life of a balloon, one which travelled from Paris and landed in Sweden in 1871, was fifteen days. We have also to consider that the balloon must follow the local currents of the air. From the observations made by the Swedish expedition to Spitsbergen in 1883, we know that its typical direction is from the south-west, with an average force of eight or nine miles an hour. Thus, with ordinary luck in his favour, Herr Andrée might accomplish much in six or seven days. But, putting everything in his favour, the question arises: How is he to come back?'

General Greely cast around the room as if looking for an answer to his question. His military training had taught him the quickest ways to ridicule the ambitions of junior officers, and he was using every oratorical skill he possessed.

'He proposes to land on the Arctic coasts of North America. For two years I commanded a geographical polar expedition, and taking observations at Fort Conger, in Smith's Sound, found the prevailing winds to be south-southwest and south-southeast. This is in the east. At Point Barrow, in the extreme west, the direction of the prevailing air current is from the southwest. And so I say it may be possible to reach the Pole, but it appears impossible for a balloon to come back again.'

Andrée could not believe his ears. General Greely, having previously gained the support of his peers and senior officers for his polar ambitions, was now pooh-poohing his own attempt to further scientific understanding of the Arctic. And to add insult to injury, he seemed to be suggesting that the wind blew to the north from all points around the Pole. Where, then, did his massive confluence of wind go? Andrée wondered. Straight up into the atmosphere?

Greely ended his belittlement of Andrée with an appeal to the Congress to dismiss the expedition as ill conceived. 'If Herr Andrée believes in his scheme and is determined to carry it out, and can get the money, I say, let him go, and God be with him. But as geographers, looking at these things from a practical point of view, and having some knowledge of air and currents, this Congress should not give the weight of their influence or their endorsement to this expedition.'

Andrée was incensed, but he knew he must not show it. 'I think that this discussion has wandered from the methods by which I propose to make my polar journey,' he began, a little hesitantly. 'I am quite aware of the problematic task it would be to attempt such an expedition in a free balloon, but I shall not use a free balloon. My polar balloon will have a dragline, always sliding on the ground.

'It has been said that the area I propose to traverse will be covered by fogs, but that is mere supposition. This area is about the size of Europe, and there will be fogs on some places, but not on others. It has also been said that I shall be unable to make out my latitude and longitude. I shall use the sextant.

'Admiral Markham asks how I will return if anything should happen to my balloon. We shall do exactly as others have done – that is, by using sledges and boats. My position will be no better nor worse than that of any previous explorer who lost his vessel. You say that the voyage can only be made in a wind from the south. Well, I shall wait for it in Spitsbergen.

'It has also been claimed that it is impossible to go in any other direction than that of the wind without going up into other currents of air. Yes, if you use a free balloon, but I have not spoken of any such thing. I am going in a balloon with draglines and ballast ropes. Such a balloon can be steered. I have done it before and I think the polar balloon will be much easier to deal with because I can use much bigger sails.

'Finally, the general claimed the balloon would not last as it will lose one per cent a day. My voyage will last twenty to thirty days, and shall consequently lose less than eighteen hundred kilograms as the contents of the balloon amount to six thousand cubic metres. Its carrying power is three thousand kilograms. Consequently, if the loss is at one per cent, it will still have twelve hundred kilograms' buoyancy remaining after thirty days.'

Andrée stood back from the lectern. Raising his head from the notes he had been consulting, he paused. 'I do not ask for money. I have got all that I need, and the attempt will be made.' Looking directly at Admiral Markham and General Greely, he then sat down.

He knew that when he travelled to London, the spiritual home of the geographical establishment, he would face resistance. But, he reasoned, the progress of expeditions to the North Pole had reached a stalemate. Current methods were clearly not working and any advance further north across the ice on foot or on sledge would be accompanied by great risk to human life. This had been acknowledged when he spoke in Stockholm, Paris and Berlin. In Sweden, he had gained the support of Nordenskiöld and Gustaf Dahlender, a leading physicist, and Professor Gustaf Retzius, an anatomist and anthropologist. Professor Gösta Mittag-Leffler had enlisted the French Academy of Sciences to appoint a committee to investigate Andrée's balloon expedition, and Dr Baschin, a balloonist and meteorologist at the Meteorological Institute in Berlin, had passed on his goodwill. Only in London, where his proposal threatened the conservative thinking of the top echelons of the geographical hierarchy, had he faced personal attacks and been so comprehensively ridiculed.

Finally, another military man stood up. 'I am inclined to think that a balloon may be kept in good working condition in the Arctic region.' Colonel C. M. Watson, the former commander of the Balloon Corps of the British Army at Aldershot, did not waste time with a preamble. 'I know of one case of a military balloon which was filled when the snow was on the ground, and it held the gas well for three weeks. A very small balloon will experience considerable difficulty in holding its gas, the holding power diminishing as the dimensions decrease, but the larger the balloon the better its vitality and carrying power.

'Another very important point in this explorer's favour is that he will not be exposed to the great difficulty experienced by aeronauts: variations of temperature. In the Arctic summer there is no night, and it is the variation of temperature that kills a balloon. Herr Andrée has told us that the average variation of temperature at Spitsbergen is six degrees centigrade, and further north it may be even less than that. In my opinion, Herr Andrée has all these influences in his favour – infinitesimal changes of temperature and constant daylight, so that at no time will he be unable to tell where he is and whither he is going.'

In Colonel Watson, it seemed, Andrée had at last found someone who knew what he was talking about, unlike the others, who had based their criticism on their dated personal knowledge of the Arctic and second-hand information they had gleaned on ballooning.

'With the greatest diffidence, I would venture to challenge one other remark made by Admiral Markham, namely that it is impossible to fix the position of a balloon,' Colonel Watson concluded. 'We can tell very well where we are going, and if anyone were to see the results obtained by my officers engaged in balloon reconnaissance, they would realize the excellent nature of the work done, and the accuracy of the maps drawn by them.

'That the attempt will be attended by great risk is a foregone conclusion, and no-one knows this better than Herr Andrée himself. But many expeditions that are attended by risk are worth undertaking. Herr Andrée may never come back, it is true, but nevertheless the attempt should be made, and if it is crowned with success, he will have done more than anyone else before him.

'I cannot but feel this is the most original and remarkable attempt ever made in Arctic exploration.'

Applause filled the lecture hall as the colonel sat down. Although not everybody in the room had been convinced, Andrée could tell that, with Colonel Watson's considerable assistance, he had won over several who were extremely doubtful of his chances before the meeting began.

Now all that remained was for his mission to get underway.

CHAPTER THREE

THE GROUNDWORK

SPITSBERGEN, NORWAY

25 January, 2000

THE PLAN IS IN PLACE. THE WEATHER EXPERT IS ON STANDBY. The balloon is being built and is almost ready to go. The control centre and launch teams are assembled. The sponsor is on board. The television crews and newspaper reporters are waiting for the call. I have completed my survival training and I am ready to depart as soon as the twenty-four-hour darkness of the Arctic winter lifts. Then comes the one piece of news that I do not want to hear.

'No, you just will not do it. It is impossible.' Yngvar Gjessing, Professor of Meteorology at the Polar Research Institute in Spitsbergen, is looking down at a sheet of paper that carries his painstakingly compiled surface wind data. 'The ground winds from March until June are more than twenty-five knots on average,' he says, shaking his head. 'You will not be able to launch your balloon until later in the year when the drainage winds from the glaciers subside.'

I haven't a clue what to do. I need less than five knots

of ground wind to take off. I'm used to the best-laid plans being thrown into disarray at the last possible minute, but this is ridiculous. I have sold the idea to Britannic Assurance; with the money and personnel in place, I plan to take off in just over a month's time. Now, much to my embarrassment, I am standing with Clive Bailey, my project manager, and Stuart Nunn, the events manager for Britannic (he is organizing a competition for Britannic sales staff to win a trip to Spitsbergen), in front of a world-renowned expert who is making it clear to us that my plan to fly a balloon to the North Pole is impossible. A foolish pipedream, no less.

The dilemma is straightforward, its solution less so. I can attempt the flight from Spitsbergen to the Pole from the beginning of April until the end of May. Before then, the Arctic nights are long and the days short. Aside from the discomfort of the cold, the balloon will lose too much height when the sun is not warming the gas inside her envelope. After the end of May, I cannot be rescued from the polar icecap. It will have melted and split apart too much to take the weight of a rescue plane, and the Pole is out of range of most helicopters.

But, as Professor Gjessing is making clear, the ground winds are too strong in April and May for a balloon to take off. By the time the winds become manageable, no rescue organization will agree to pick me up should it all go wrong, for fear that the ice will not take the weight of the rescue plane. Without a rescue strategy in place, no insurance company will cover my flight. And without insurance, I am forbidden to take off. It's a condition of every pilot's licence.

The only consolation is that it is not the first time I have been told that flying a balloon to the North Pole is unachievable. Every time I've spoken to an expert I've been told it is beyond the realms of possibility, which has only made me more determined to find a way to make it work. However slim the chances of success, I've managed to keep my dream alive. I always knew that flying over the

Andes would be a joyride in comparison to flying to the top of the world, but I am determined to make this work, and to stick to Andrée's route. If there is one thing I have learnt it is that the experts are not always right.

The groundwork for my aerial assault on the Pole started as soon as I got back from Chile and phoned Brian Jones, who had passed me on my checkout flight. I let him know of my plans. It was December 1998 and he was extremely busy, working as the project manager for the Breitling round-the-world balloon bid.* He looked at me with what I could tell was a mixture of amazement and disbelief. Compared with him I was the greenest of novices, and he smiled at my audacity, his nose crumpling into his mouth as he told me that flying to the North Pole would be even more difficult than going around the globe. Then he uttered the words that stuck for ever after in my mind: 'David, somebody will fly around the world soon. So many teams have been trying for so long that it will inevitably be done. All that will remain then is the Pole. It's one of the last great aeronautical adventures.'

I seized on that – 'one of the last great aeronautical adventures' – and immediately knew that I had the catchline to attract sponsors, excite the media and fire up a support team. All I needed to do was bring it all together.

Brian put me in touch with Luc Trullemans, a Belgian meteorologist who was forecasting the wind patterns for the Breitling team. His initial response to my enquiry was the same double-edged retort with which I was, by now, becoming familiar. Undaunted, I persuaded Luc to meet me and he flew to Heathrow from Brussels, where he works as a weather forecaster for the Royal Meteorological Institute and for RTL, the satellite television channel.

---

* Later on, in early 1999, Brian replaced Tony Brown as Bertrand Piccard's co-pilot. The pair went into the record books as the first to fly non-stop around the globe in a balloon. It was a fabulous achievement.

I liked Luc immediately. I had been expecting a fusty boffin, but Luc was the exact opposite: dapper, charismatic and utterly approachable. From the moment he came striding up to me at Heathrow I knew that we would get on. He was a man I could work with and trust.

Luc did not underestimate the scale of the task ahead, but he was the first person not to tell me I was mad to attempt the flight. He was excited by the challenge and told me that predicting the weather and wind patterns for a flight to the North Pole was the Holy Grail for meteorologists. 'It is in a different league to the round-the-world challenge,' he said in his heavily accented English. Just hearing his French vowel sounds wrap themselves around the words made the whole enterprise sound so much more romantic. 'There are about twenty occasions every year on which the wind is right to steer a balloon around the world. In the period you want to go, there are, at most, two suitable slots every year. Usually less. You'll be very lucky to get a slot when you want to go.'

I was pleased it wasn't easy. I wanted it to be just as much a challenge for me as it had been for Andrée and his men. I was determined to fly in an open basket, like my Swedish forerunners, and like them to set off from Spitsbergen. I also decided to use the same benchmarks as Andrée. He had believed there might be a mountain at the North Pole. There is, in fact, nothing but the Arctic Ocean, which if you are lucky will be covered by the polar pack ice when you arrive, but, after discussions with the British Balloon and Airship Club, the sport's governing body, and the rest of the team, I decided that I would call the flight a success if I could get within sight of Andrée's mythical mountain. That meant within at least sixty nautical miles, or the last degree of latitude. I asked Luc if it was possible.

'Sixty miles? If you were to get within one hundred miles it would be a fantastic achievement,' he said. Then he dropped the bombshell: 'And if you do get there, getting back will be almost impossible.'

Andrée had been told the same thing, but he had turned his back on the experts and decided to take the risk. I was going to do the same. I had a century's worth of accumulated knowledge of Arctic weather patterns at my disposal, and this, I believed, should ultimately help me reach my goal. And I didn't care if I couldn't get back from the Pole by balloon. I just wanted to get there. If necessary, I would ski back to land or wait for a summer icebreaker to pick me up.

However, the one overriding reason why I was determined to go ahead was that the plan had been hatched in the middle of a successful expedition, and like all my adventures, it was a formula that had always brought me luck. I decided to try the North Pole while en route to the South Pole solo and unsupported. I decided to go for the seven summits when I'd bagged Mount Everest in 1993. The North Pole by balloon had become too enticing a challenge to turn down, and I was not going to give up because the experts said it was difficult or impossible. Andrée never gave in to the sceptics, the detractors or the critics, and I intended to follow suit.

'The winds are extremely unpredictable in the Arctic,' Luc warned. 'Any long-range guidance I can offer you will be less reliable than the instructions I am preparing for the Breitling team. I will be able to predict the wind patterns only a few hours, not days, in advance.' I knew that at the lower latitudes where various balloonists were attempting to circumnavigate the globe the centrifugal force of the world turning made the weather more predictable. There were dozens of weather stations along their routes, all feeding detailed weather data into the massive super-computers that meteorologists use to build up accurate models of weather patterns. 'Where you are planning to fly, David, there are no weather stations,' Luc reminded me, shrugging his shoulders and raising his eyebrows like a textbook Gallic caricature. 'It is an ocean, and the only data I have comes from satellites.'

'All I need to know is whether you think it's possible,' I

told him. I would be flying alone beneath *Britannic Challenger* but Luc would be there in spirit, like a third eye gazing hundreds of miles ahead to see what dangers and opportunities lay before me. If he said it was impossible I would have to rethink the whole enterprise.

'It's not going to be easy, David,' Luc replied, 'and you are making it even harder for yourself if you take off from Spitsbergen. Anywhere else – Canada, Alaska or Siberia – would be easier. Why don't you rethink your launch site?'

I thought of Andrée. He did not know what lay ahead of him when he took off from Spitsbergen. It could have been mountains, it could have been dry land; he even took along a dinner jacket in case he had to dine with the king of some as yet undiscovered country. In the event it was open sea and the polar ice pack. He was a true pioneer. Likewise, I did not know what the weather held in store nor exactly where it would be best to launch, so in the spirit of Andrée I was determined to take off from Spitsbergen, even if the weathermen and other experts told me it would be easier elsewhere.

Luc accepted my decision. 'If that's what you want, then I'll do my best. I like a challenge, but, David, you're making it as hard as can be,' he said.

A few weeks later Luc called me. He had examined all the weather patterns of the last few years and had found only one year that had offered two slots when the winds would have carried a balloon to the Pole. 'You'll be lucky to get one that coincides with a day of calm ground winds,' he added.

That's how I came to find myself standing in front of Professor Gjessing in his Spitsbergen office, being told that I was extremely unlikely to realize my intention to take off in April or May. The problem was that since I had persuaded Britannic to sponsor me, I was committed to taking off from Spitsbergen just then.

I first approached Britannic in June 1999. I knew that any sponsor would regard my proposal as an extraordinarily high-risk endeavour, but I also knew that if they examined it closely they would realize that it was extremely good value for money. It took twenty-two attempts and fifty million pounds for one balloon eventually to succeed in making a round-the-world balloon flight. At least six teams or individuals had taken off in pursuit of that goal, one of them in the 1980s, the rest in the late 1990s, and several other teams had prepared bids that they later abandoned because the weather was not right or because they ran into technical difficulties. I was budgeting on £120,000 for my flight. I was determined that if I did not do it in 2000, I would do it in 2001. And although it was the riskiest adventure I had ever undertaken, I was convinced that it was going to work.

Britannic spent months sifting through my proposal, examining it and re-examining it from every angle. They were very worried. They knew the odds of success were tiny. The round-the-world attempts had been able to learn from previous mistakes. An early Breitling Orbiter flight had come to a very premature end because a tiny fuel clip failed shortly after launch; one of the Virgin Challenger attempts had failed when the balloon broke free of its moorings while it was being inflated. On my limited budget I could not afford such fundamental mistakes, and to complicate matters I was venturing into previously unexplored territory.

Fortunately, one man at Britannic had the vision. Bill Haynes, the marketing director, recognized that if it worked it would be a genuine world first, and that compared with most record attempts it was bargain-basement cheap. In October 1999 he agreed to be my sole sponsor. He told me that he liked the idea because it was unusual and it would be a good exercise for building a team within the company. From that moment on, he and his team were extremely supportive.

I was unused to working so closely with a sponsor – on most of my adventures I have been a one- or two-man band – and in some ways they were too professional for me, with minutes for each meeting, action points and lists of objectives. I did not mind dealing with lots of other people, but the mass of logistics, with contingency plans for emergencies and fallback plans in case the contingency plans did not work and last-resort plans if the fallback and contingency plans failed, did make me hanker after the simplicity of making all the preparations on my own. At times I lay awake at night, unable to sleep for thinking that I had created a huge, unwieldy dinosaur that was beyond my control. But I soon accepted that such a degree of co-operation was inevitable with a high-risk project dependent on many different people not making a single mistake, and I was pleased that Britannic was not some fat-cat sponsor that simply handed over a cheque, sat back and waited for the publicity.

I return from Spitsbergen with two problems that need solving. Strangely, they are both similar to logistical problems that Andrée faced. Like him, we need to find a launch site that is shielded from the ground winds that prevail throughout April and May. And whereas Andrée had to work out a way to transport a hydrogen plant to Spitsbergen, I have discovered that helium is exorbitantly expensive in Norway and need to work out a method of transporting it from Britain to the launch site at a time when the approach to Spitsbergen might still be ice-bound.

Every Monday evening I meet with the project team at the Globe, a pub in Bath, to discuss our plans. The pub is appropriately named as every member of the team but me was involved in some way in the global circumnavigation by balloon. Each member has a vital role, but as project manager and logistics expert, Clive Bailey is the keystone. He is a livewire, always enthusiastic and with a wicked sense of humour. From our first meeting he has called me 'Old Man', so I immediately christened him 'Boy', and the nicknames have stuck.

Gavin Hailes is the launch director and most evenings is

to be found busily stitching the envelope together. Until the moment the balloon leaves the ground, this burly former lance sergeant in the Grenadier Guards will be the one person I depend on more than any other. He is the repository for a wealth of technical information. At work he is quiet and considered, stroking his thick beard while he considers the answer to any question, but he also likes to party and loves pulling practical jokes.

Clive and Gavin recommended Pete Johnson to me as one of the best burner engineers in the world, so I immediately asked him to design and assemble my burners and fuel system. Like so many other experts, he made it clear he thought I was reckless and he actually told me he thought I was mad to attempt to fly to the Pole. But as the archetypical quiet and reflective engineer, sporting glasses like Brains in *Thunderbirds*, his concept of danger is at the other end of the spectrum from mine. I took him to Canada to test the burners and he was fantastic; very thoughtful, very balanced and rock solid once he had made up his mind.

The final member of the team is Kieran Sturrock, who fitted the electrics on the Breitling Orbiter gondola. He offers advice and guidance but does not want to become officially involved as he thinks my plan is too dangerous.

The advice and ideas that are batted around the table every time we meet are invaluable, although my advisers run into some resistance from me when it comes to equipment and support resources. They are all used to the massive budgets of the round-the-world attempts and think nothing of hiring Learjets, but I probably have less to spend than Richard Branson's entertainment budget during his round-the-world attempts.

From a very early stage we decide to aim for a low-tech approach, primarily to keep the adventure true to the spirit of Andrée but also to minimize costs, complexity and the risk of something complicated going wrong. We can keep expenditure down and minimize fuel consumption by flying a relatively small balloon with a wicker basket rather than a large balloon with a heavy sealed capsule. Fuel use will be further curtailed by flying in twenty-four-hour sunshine. We budget for 570 litres of propane, but I reckon I can get by on a lot less.

We also decide on a 90,000-cubic-foot capacity Roziere balloon, less than one tenth of the volume of many of the balloons used for the round-the-world efforts. It means it will cost less than a tenth as much, consume less than a tenth of the fuel and be far easier to manoeuvre.

Somewhat ironically, Andrée has more in common with Branson and the other circumnavigation attempts than he does with me. Andrée's equipment was state-of-the-art in its day, just as the many round-the-world attempts used the most sophisticated technology of their time. I have tried to remain as close to Andrée's approach as possible, even if it means my method is slightly archaic. Andrée had a hydrogen balloon; I am using helium. It's safer, and because it's non-flammable I can adjust my height by heating it instead of relying solely on ditching ballast, but in principle it's a gas balloon, like Andrée's *Eagle*. My Swedish predecessor flew in a wicker basket and so will I, although Andrée's was much larger and more comfortable than the basket I have picked up second-hand for a thousand pounds. In one crucial aspect, however, Andrée's balloon was more elaborate than mine: his was steerable, mine is not. Instead, I will have access to much better weather and wind prediction, which I hope to use to find streams of wind – called 'windtracks' – that will steer me to the Pole. I also have much better communications technology: high-frequency radio and satellite telephones. Andrée had carrier pigeons and corked bottles.

By early February, the balloon and burners are nearing completion and most of the equipment has been gathered. The only remaining problem is whether the container of helium we have recently sent to Spitsbergen on an ice-breaker will arrive in time. It is a nail-biting wait. If it does not make it through the pack ice, the next icebreaker leaves in May – too late for my purposes. Fortunately, the people of Spitsbergen have rallied round, and the most helpful of all is Atle Brakken, the harbour master. His standard response to any request is 'no problem'. It is a refreshing change to many places I have been in the High Arctic, where the locals are adept at spotting your desperation and exploiting it, often demanding exorbitant fees for their assistance.

In late February, about six weeks before I plan to take off, I head down to Plymouth in the hope of making a last-ditch attempt to conquer my fear of water. I have enrolled on an RAF fast-jet survival course, the only programme of its type, and I am hoping it will help me to avoid panicking – and therefore enable me to survive – if I am forced to ditch in the open water of the Arctic Ocean.

Early one morning, I am trussed up in an immersion suit. At forty-three I am by far the oldest occupant of a barge that is hammering across the waves several miles off the Devon coast. My fellow passengers are no older than nineteen, and some of them have yet to start shaving. All of them are considerably fitter and braver than me, as they should be if they want to be jet fighter pilots.

The wind is blowing Force 8, there is six to eight feet of swell and I am convinced the instructors have turned the engine up to full throttle because I am the only civilian. I am strapped into an ejector seat, and then, with little warning, thrown over the side of the barge. It seems extreme to me, but according to the instructors it is the best way to simulate being pulled through the water by a parachute following an emergency ejection from a stricken fighter plane.

Water. Air. Water. Air. My head bobs in and out of the sea, spending more time below the surface than above it. I get a second at most to snatch a breath of air before the rope twists and I plunge under the surface or a wave breaks over me and I swallow another few mouthfuls of the Atlantic.

For Rune, this would be just another day at the office. When we were walking to the Pole he told me of the time he and another Norwegian Special Forces commando were fired from the torpedo shoot of a submarine. They then swam several miles to shore, completed their mission, and swam back out to sea to be scooped out of the water by a low-flying aeroplane. I've seen him treat freezing water with contempt. The day after we reached the North Pole in 1998, I slipped through the ice while we were searching for a flat pan suitable for the pick-up plane to land on. Only my leg got wet, but Rune immediately came to my rescue, jumping into the water with his skis on. To my alarm, he disappeared beneath the surface for a couple of seconds, before emerging from the black water, spitting ice cubes and treading water with his skis still attached to his feet. He seemed absolutely unfazed by the experience, but I was frightened senseless on his behalf.

But for a mere mortal such as me, being dragged at speed behind a powerboat in the cold Atlantic is the scariest thing I have ever done. I am almost paralysed with fear, unable to think straight and help myself. I know what I have to do, but my brain is struggling to cope with the onslaught of water and my body refuses to respond. I know I have to release the buckle that is keeping me in my harness, but I am finding it impossible to move my arms from my sides because of the force of the water. Then I realize that when I twist upwards and my face is above water, I have at most two seconds in which to reach the buckle. On the third attempt I succeed and slip out of the harness to see the boat surging on without me, trailing the sound of the crew shrieking and the ejector seat still bobbing in its wake.

I am petrified. Alone in the water, knowing that some-where in my vicinity a life-raft is waiting, but disorientated and unable to see over the waves to spot it. The barge returns towards me, and as it buzzes past the instructor points in the direction of the life-raft. I swim that way, and more through luck than anything else, I find it. It has not opened, but I manage to release the clips. It bursts apart and self-inflates. I am relieved, but only for a brief moment. I now have to try to climb into the raft in a six- to eight-foot swell while the Force 8 wind whips up a spray that is so thick it is like fog. The sting of the salt water forces me to scrunch up my eyes and I can barely see what I am doing. I try to climb into the life-raft, but flip it over and then have to right it. After several attempts I manage to haul myself into the six-foot-diameter black rubber vessel. Once inside, I find the raft is several inches deep in water and filling fast. I immediately begin to bail it out, making the mistake of telling myself that soon it will all be over. After an hour of frantically scooping water with my sore and chapped hands, I realize that there's no sign of the helicopter that's meant to be rescuing me. With the rise of every wave I think I am about to be tipped back into the sea. I am cold, exhausted, frightened and suffering from seasickness when, after one and a half hours, a helicopter appears and winches me to safety.

It's been the grimmest of experiences, but I am pleased I underwent it. It was extremely helpful, the best course I have ever done. Aside from teaching me that I can survive a nightmare at sea, it taught me that I need an immersion suit and a life-raft when I take off from Spitsbergen. Insights such as that can turn out to be lifesavers on an adventure.

By early March, all the equipment has been gathered. It's a formidable list of over two hundred items ranging from the burners and the basket to plastic spoons, drawing pins and a sewing kit.* Of most importance are the communications and navigation equipment, but still one key component is missing. *Britannic Challenger*'s envelope should have been completed in February; it is now March, and the gasbag is still not ready. In a matter of days I am off to Spitsbergen for a second reconnaissance, and if the weather plays my way I could be

* For a full list of all equipment, see Appendix Two, on page 320.

launching by early April, yet my balloon is not complete. With so many separate elements to this project I sometimes wonder if the logistics are more complicated than I can manage.

Shortly before leaving for Spitsbergen, I head up to Britannic's headquarters near Birmingham to 'launch' the expedition in front of the company's staff. With more than a thousand people watching, I realize for the first time the magnitude of what I have taken on. Because of the scale of the enterprise and Britannic's financial involvement, the outside world is watching, and it dawns on me that I am in the spotlight. It will not be the last time I ask myself what I have let myself in for.

Towards the middle of March, a few days after first light breaks six months of winter darkness in Spitsbergen, Clive Bailey and I once again land at Longyearbyen. For the first time in all our visits to Spitsbergen we can see our remote, desolate surroundings. Ice floes block the harbour and white-iced mountains rise above a fjord. Here and there, where they are not white with snow, the quays are speckled black with coal dust. Mining is the only thing that happens in Spitsbergen, the sole reason a few people live on this Norwegian island far above the Arctic Circle, the most northerly place that belongs to Europe.

I've seen several less welcoming places in the Arctic, but nowhere with mountains the height of those that surround Longyearbyen, from where we hope to launch. We've chosen a launch site halfway up a narrow, steep-sided valley in the hope that it will be relatively sheltered from ground winds. If all goes well, a light wind will sweep *Britannic Challenger* down the valley after take-off. With the fjord ahead of me, I should have enough time and space to gain at least six thousand feet in order to clear the top of the peaks on the other side of the water. Considering that I will be carrying liquid propane and liquid oxygen, the last thing I want to do is crash into the side of a mountain. *Britannic Challenger* could be called a flying bomb, and if I crash I will be lucky not to go up in a colossal bang and a cloud of black smoke. My first reaction on seeing the mountains is that I'll never get across them, and when we visit Professor Gjessing again, he seems to confirm my impression.

'You need some help from a far better person than me,' he says.

With less than a month to go until a first potential take-off, I am, for the first time, plagued by doubt. Maybe I have bitten off more than I can chew. Most of my previous expeditions were incremental increases, a tactic I learnt the hard way after I failed on my first North Pole attempt, in 1983. Then, at the age of twenty-six, I discovered that there is no substitute for experience.

I had attempted to become the first man to reach the geographic North Pole – the top of the world – solo and unsupported, but I had little knowledge of the harshness of the Arctic. It was foolhardy, and from that moment on I knew that the secret of success was to raise the game step by step with each expedition. The next year I headed for the magnetic North Pole, the point towards which all compasses point. It was an easier target, and I became the first person to reach it solo and unsupported. In 1992 I trekked to the geomagnetic North Pole – a theoretical point on the map situated between Canada and Greenland – as leader of a party of five. Then in 1996 I trekked across Antarctica to the geographic South Pole, and a few months later sailed to its magnetic equivalent. It was only with the confidence and experience of those successes under my belt that I attempted the geographic North Pole again in 1997. For the second time I failed, let down this time by equipment failure. Again, I learnt many valuable lessons, and in March 1998 I set out for the North Pole a third time. This time I finally reached the top of the world.

I also built up my mountaineering skills the long, hard and slow way. There's no substitute for it. I started climbing in the Brecon Beacons, then in Snowdonia and Scotland, before heading for the Alps. It was only when I had considerable climbing experience and had slept in a tent at altitude that I attempted Everest and embarked on a quest to climb the highest mountain in each of the seven continents.

But this time I am going in at the deep end. My experience of flying a balloon in the Arctic is limited to two short pleasure flights in 1999, one of which was across the Northwest Passage and one near Resolute in northern Canada. Both were in hot-air balloons. Now I am attempting a flight to the Pole, and not only is it in a helium balloon, of which I have absolutely no experience, but even the experts think it is impossible. Don Cameron, one of the most experienced balloonists in the world, has told me that he has no idea how the balloon will perform in the extreme cold and the constant sunlight of the Arctic. It does not fill me with confidence.

My faith in my prospects aboard *Britannic Challenger* is dented further when Clive and I test the balloon heater on the ground. It fails. It appears that one of the rubber seals has hardened in the cold, and liquid propane sprays everywhere. All I can think is that the consequences do not bear thinking about if the same seal fails when I'm airborne.

After a couple more days in Spitsbergen we get the news that the envelope has been finished and is on its way north by plane. We cross paths with the balloon as we head back to England and I fly on to Brussels for a final briefing by Luc Trullemans on the weather conditions. He shows me the latest tracks – none of them look at all promising – and compares them with some of the best windtracks from previous years.

'I still think you are mad to take off from Spitsbergen,' he says. 'The wind patterns are better from just about anywhere else and there's a high likelihood of strong ground winds throughout April and May.'

The stoical Belgian talks me through my prospects. He emphasizes how small a margin of error I face.

'Luc, my fate is in your hands. If you can find me a

good track north, then I'm going to give it everything I've got.'

'No, David. *You* hold the key to success or failure. I will spot the windtracks on my computer, but you have to find them in the sky. Sometimes only fifty feet in altitude will separate two windtracks heading in completely different directions.'

I know it will be like diving into a river not knowing in which direction the current is flowing, but I am determined to have a go.

'Are you sure you still want to go ahead, and that you can do this?' Luc asks me.

'Luc,' I reply, 'I haven't got a choice.'

CHAPTER FOUR

THE RIVALRY

VIRGOHAMNA, NORWEGIAN HIGH ARCTIC

14 August, 1896

DANE'S ISLAND, A TINY SPECK OF LAND NORTHEAST OF Spitsbergen, basked under the midnight sun of high summer but already the air had a biting chill, a foretaste of the bitter Arctic winter to come. In two months, the sun would set for the last time that year, and the only source of heat and light would drop below the horizon until the following spring.

Long before then, time threatened to run out for Andrée. Only six days remained until the *Virgo*, his expedition's three-hundred-ton steamship, had to return via Tromsö to Gothenburg. Day after day, the balloonists watched the flags flutter from the top of the balloon hangar. Every morning they released small pilot balloons to test the direction of the breeze as they waited for the wind to carry them north. Soon the daylight hours would grow shorter, but for the three polar travellers waiting to depart, for the scientists, technicians and boat crew who supported them, for the tourists and journalists who were watching the spectacle unfold, the days seemed to grow ever longer with the delay. Most newspapers in Europe and America had reported on Andrée's ambitious plan, and the eyes of the world now seemed to be trained on Virgohamna, a natural harbour on the edge of Dane's Island.*

Men worked everywhere; it was like a military operation. An octagonal wooden shed, the balloon hangar, had been built within the protective clasp of a vast black cliff of curving granite. In front of it, the rocky beach was strewn with the equipment, provisions and detritus of a marauding army of carpenters, engineers and boiler makers. By day these men laboured to prepare Andrée's balloon, the *Eagle*, for its flight into the unknown. At night they played accordions and violins, sang, danced and drank under the midnight sun, and speculated on the chances of success for their employer, Salomon August Andrée, visionary technocrat, balloonist and adventurer.

Late in the afternoon of 14 August, as the men were coming to the end of their working day, a lookout came running down from the mountains above the bay.

'The *Fram*!' he shouted. 'The *Fram* is coming into the harbour!'

After months of being the focus of attention, Andrée was instantly relegated to a mere bystander as a weather-beaten ship approached, chugging slowly through the summer mist. He recognized it immediately. As the *Fram* entered the harbour, Andrée could see the unshaven, long-haired crew of the boat that over three years earlier had left Norway under the leadership of Fridtjof Nansen. Dubbed 'the modern Viking' by the London newspapers, the thirty-four-year-old Norwegian was the undisputed pioneer of polar exploration and by far the biggest thorn in Andrée's side.

* Virgohamna, meaning 'Virgo harbour', was actually named after Andrée's expedition boat several years after he used the site to launch his flight to the Pole.

The *Fram* was a masterpiece of shipbuilding. Made predominantly of Italian oak, reinforced fore and aft with steel, and with three tall sailing masts backed up by a steam engine, its hull was much thicker and more rounded than a conventional ship so that it could withstand and rise above the ice when it froze against her sides. Having discovered that the polar ice drifted from Siberia to Spitsbergen, Nansen persuaded the Norwegian government to back an attempt to sail towards the North Pole. With a crew of thirteen he left Oslo in June 1893. Three months later, the *Fram* was frozen into the ice and the long drift began. Now, having broken free from the ice that had held it captive for thirty-five months, the *Fram* was on its slow journey south and was steaming into Virgohamna in search of refuge from the impeding pack ice.

Andrée was consumed with curiosity and ran over to Captain Hugo Zachau of the *Virgo*, demanding to be taken by launch out into the Norwegian Sound to meet the *Fram*. More than anything he wanted to know if Nansen had managed to reach the Pole, which would make his flight largely redundant. Behind Andrée, as he motored out to the *Fram* with several members of his team, the top of the *Eagle* could be seen poking out of the open roof of the seventy-foot-high balloon hangar. If Nansen had failed, Andrée hoped to prove the *Eagle* would carry him further in a week than his great rival had managed in almost three years.

Andrée climbed on board the *Fram* with Captain Zachau and noticed the crew did not appear to have suffered much hardship. Indeed, many appeared to have double chins and bulging stomachs.

'You look very well,' he said to Otto Neumann Sverdrup, a man he recognized as the commander of the *Fram*.

'There is a simple answer: we planned well and took more than enough supplies,' the imposing figure replied.

Sverdrup had a long, inscrutable face, a hard stare, a bald head and a massive, winged beard that stretched out left and right from his chin to form what looked like a hairy carpet. Able to withstand the severest cold with little protection, he used to tease Nansen for being 'thin-blooded' because he wore mittens when the temperature dropped to −30°C.

With his pipe clenched between his teeth, Sverdrup turned to Zachau. 'Have you heard news of our comrades Nansen and Johansen?'

'Surely they are with you?' Zachau responded.

'They left us seventeen months ago. We had reached eighty-four degrees north, so in March last year Nansen and Johansen set out for the Pole on skis. They had twenty-eight dogs and enough food for one hundred days.'

'One hundred days?' Andrée questioned. 'How could they have survived since then?'

'When they exhausted their thirty days' supply of dog food, they planned to keep the animals going for a further eighty days by killing them one by one and feeding them to each other,' Sverdrup replied. 'As for themselves, they hoped to live off fish and polar bear.' The commander looked out to sea. 'That you have not heard news of them is ... depressing. We hoped they would reach home before us and that you would tell us of their safe arrival.'

Andrée's feelings were mixed. The rivalry between him and Nansen was intense. Scandinavian newspapers frequently published articles and cartoons that used their race to the Pole as an analogy for Norway's fight for independence from Sweden. He was pleased the *Fram* had survived her ordeal in the ice unscathed, but he was concerned that his archrival might still return and claim to have reached the Pole by dog sledge.

Eager to hear news and gather information on the state of the pack ice, Andrée shook the hand of each crew member. There were cheers, speeches and champagne. After the formalities, both parties talked among themselves, explored the *Fram* or went ashore to view the *Eagle*. Sigurd Hansen, a lieutenant on the *Fram*, took

Henri Lachambre, the famous Parisian maker of the *Eagle*, below decks to show him the *Fram*'s library. Nansen had insisted it was built and well stocked to maintain his crew's morale through two long, dark winters trapped in the drifting ice.

Pointing to a book on ballooning, Hansen told Lachambre of his longing for home. 'During the coldest days wedged in the ice, when we wanted more than anything to see the sun again and feel its warmth on our skin,' he said, 'we often daydreamed of a balloon like the *Eagle* coming to pluck us from the *Fram* and carry us home.'

The departure of the *Fram* all those months ago had been surpassed only by Andrée's farewell from Gothenburg on 7 June. Sweden had never seen anything like it. A crowd of thousands filled the quayside, their excitement not dampened by torrential rain. As far as the eye could see, tiny black dots bobbed up and down. On the quay it was the top hats and umbrellas of the dignitaries; on the water it was the occupants of an armada of boats. Most of the onlookers were soaked to the skin, but nothing could spoil the carnival atmosphere. Bands played, champagne corks popped and pleasure boats hosted riotous parties. To the burghers of Gothenburg, the exodus of three Swedes into the far unknown, possibly to claim new lands for the nation, was an endeavour of the boldest sort.

Andrée stood by the *Virgo*, a little apart from the crowds. The Swedish nation's expectations weighed heavily on him, and as the brass bands played with militaristic pomp, he asked himself again if he had any right to risk his own life, let alone those of his two young comrades. He thought back to the previous evening, when he had wished his mother farewell, and he thought too of Gurli Linder, the woman whose love he was unable to match, and whom he had told that morning with characteristic insensitivity that his separation from his mother had been the most difficult moment the expedition had brought him.

'Remember, it is you that I long to come back to, Mother,' he had told her as they hugged in the hallway of their home.

'Let me give you one last kiss,' his mother had said, her cheeks wet with tears as she held open the front door. 'This is the first grief you have brought me, August.'

Andrée had leant forward to wipe his mother's cheek dry before kissing her gently and whispering in her ear. 'Don't be uneasy, dear. Your heart is watching over me.'

But Gurli and his mother already seemed far away as Andrée stood on the quayside with his sponsors, friends and assorted dignitaries. It was a time for grand gestures and bold words, so Andrée stepped up to a microphone to address the throng.

'When we succeed, when our feet are on firm ground again, our thoughts will be here with you, where our expedition received its most vital help. But should things not go so well, in the final moment our thoughts will fly back to Gothenburg, and I will always regret that I won't be able to thank you one last time.'

With that, Andrée climbed the gangplank, turned at the top, saluted the crowds and boarded the *Virgo*. To a cacophony of boat whistles, cheers, jubilant shouts and cannon fire, and accompanied by a flotilla of more than one hundred small boats and pleasure steamers, Andrée, his team of eight and the *Virgo*'s crew of twenty-two glided out of the harbour. While families in rowing boats bobbed around the ship, waving their hats in the air to salute the adventurers, Andrée pulled a letter from his pocket. It was from his mother, who had given him strict instructions not to open it until the *Virgo* was underway.

I am so disappointed in myself for having been such a poor, weak creature on that difficult day of leave-taking, she wrote. *But there is one thing I want you to bear in mind, and that is: if, when you return, I am no longer here, you must not depress or blame yourself by thinking that your grand enterprise has had the least influence on my having gone the way of all flesh. And finally, my thanks for everything you have been to me.*

Like many old women, Mina Andrée could often be startlingly direct, but the sentiments in the letter surprised even Andrée. He had not the slightest indication that her health was any worse than usual. For a few minutes he worried that he had left his mother at a time when she needed him most, but those feelings soon evaporated when he thought of all that lay ahead.

Andrée had christened his balloon *Ornän*, the Swedish for *Eagle*, and had picked two men to accompany him in its wicker gondola. Dr Nils Ekholm, senior researcher at the Swedish Meteorological Central Office, knew Arctic weather patterns better than anyone. Andrée had first met him during the International Polar Year fourteen years earlier, when he acted as Ekholm's meteorological assistant at Kapp Thordsen. Throughout 1895, both men had investigated the polar winds in intricate detail. Hampered by a complete lack of data from the surface of the Arctic Ocean, Ekholm had worked out the likely weather patterns using readings from the nearest land-masses and from observation of cloud movements at the edge of the ocean.

'I have calculated that a deep low-pressure area to the west of Spitsbergen should generate a southerly wind strong enough to carry the *Eagle* most of the way to the Pole,' he told Andrée during one of their planning meet-ings. A southerly wind was a wind that came from the south and blew towards the north. 'When the cyclone has passed, the winds created by the next low-pressure area should be sufficient to catapult the *Eagle* to Canada or to Siberia, depending on which side of the cyclone catches the balloon.'

The other man, Nils Strindberg, was an ambitious twenty-three-year-old physicist who had won a com-petition to be the third occupant of the gondola. Impressing Andrée with his scientific knowledge and photographic skills, he had beaten off hundreds of other applicants. Once selected, he constructed a special camera and travelled to Paris, where he learnt to fly balloons.

As the *Virgo* pulled away, Andrée remained taken aback by the huge public interest in his project. Some were fascinated by its technical ambition, but most were bewitched by the morbid magnetism of three young men setting out to risk a slow and lingering death in uncharted territory. Only a month earlier, thirty thousand people had congregated in the Champ de Mars to see the *Eagle* unveiled by Henri Lachambre. The Parisians marvelled at the bravery and courage of the three Swedes and were stunned by the size of their craft.

A technological triumph of the age, the *Eagle* was stitched together from 3,360 pieces of Chinese pongee silk, each meticulously tested before being bonded using a special adhesive that purported to be unaffected by severe changes in temperature or humidity. For months, row upon row of seamstresses worked at Lachambre's factory to assemble the largest balloon ever made. It was held together by nine miles of thread stitched along some fifteen thousand feet of seams, each of which was sealed with an additional layer of single silk. Encompassing nearly 159,000 cubic feet in total, the balloon was spherical in shape with a conical appendage at the bottom, and was varnished several times with galvanized rubber on the inside and outside. When finished and inflated, the *Eagle* stood like a giant rubber ball in its hangar, with the men who built it looking like ants beside it.

A net of Italian hemp was soaked in acid-free petroleum jelly and tallow to prevent it absorbing moisture. Strung over the rubber ball of the balloon, the net's forty-eight loose ends were used to attach the envelope to a carrying-ring, which bore the wicker-basket gondola where Andrée, Ekholm and Strindberg would spend the flight. To prevent snow, rain or fog from freezing to the envelope, a silk rain canopy was stretched over the upper half of the net. Should they fly too high, the pilots could pull ropes to release gas from two valves in the envelope.

In the event of an emergency or crash-landing, a hefty tug on a special rope would tear a five-square-yard 'rending flap' out of the side of the envelope to release its entire contents in a matter of seconds.

The gondola was a cylindrical basket woven from wicker and Spanish cane, with a slightly sloped base so that it would tip and not rotate if it hit the ground. Inside it were three berths. Most of the expedition's equipment and provisions were stuffed in pockets around the outside or attached to a hundred buckled cords that hung along the inner wall in place of shelves. The roof of the car formed the base of an observation platform and was reached by rope ladder; an instrument ring, at about chest height above the roof, carried attachments for cameras and meteorological and other instruments.

The list of equipment was as amazing as it was long. Enough food for six weeks on board the *Eagle* and two months on the ice was packed in aluminium and copper crates. Weighing nearly three-quarters of a ton, their contents included compressed bread, condensed milk, wines, spirits, fresh water, butter, Belgian chocolates, sardines, liver paste and whortleberry jam. To enable them to cook while flying, Ernst Göransson, an engineer friend of Andrée, had devised a paraffin cooker of which Heath Robinson would have been proud. To keep the naked flame of the stove away from the highly explosive hydrogen gas in the envelope, the cooker dangled on a rope some twenty-six feet below the gondola. Food was stirred by remote control and inspected by a mirror on a stick. When ready, the men puffed down a long tube to extinguish the flame and the meal was hauled back into the balloon.

The *Aftonbladet*, a Stockholm evening newspaper, presented the expedition with thirty-six carrier pigeons, together with twelve buoys made of cork and copper wiring. These were painted in the blue and yellow of the Swedish flag. The plan was to release the pigeons and buoys at regular intervals to inform the world of their progress. One buoy, larger than the rest to carry a full report of the voyage and maybe a memento or artefact from the Pole, was reserved for despatch from the most northerly point reached by the expedition. It contained a trigger that on impact with the ice would drive a spike into the frozen surface and raise a little union flag of Sweden, in the hope that, before long, it would float on the ocean currents back to civilization.

Of most interest to the few balloonists in the Paris crowd was the novel arrangement of draglines and sails. The three draglines weighed nearly a ton, stretched for almost a mile and were different lengths to prevent them becoming entangled. The top section of each dragline was made of hemp, attached to its lower coconut-fibre section by a screwing device. Should the three aeronauts suddenly need to release a dragline that had become caught in an obstruction, they could unscrew the device from the wicker gondola. Each dragline had also been weakened at a point about 150ft from its end, so that it would break automatically if it became caught. A second set of eight lines, each about 240ft long, were intended as standard ballast lines and were designed to hang freely when the balloon was at its cruising altitude. If the *Eagle* dipped suddenly, the weight of these ropes would rest on the ground, causing the balloon to return to its intended flying height. Three sails, 818 square feet in area, could be hung from a bamboo pole suspended between the carrying-ring and the envelope. With these, Andrée was confident he could steer the *Eagle* towards the Pole.

However, one man was alarmed by what was on show. Gabriel Yon, the French balloonist who had built Andrée's first balloon, the *Svea*, was convinced that the millions of pinpricks formed by the miles of stitching would allow too much gas to escape for the *Eagle* to stay aloft longer than a few weeks. The supplementary silk strips, intended to seal the seams, were not sufficient, he told anyone who would listen. Those who needed to hear it most did not heed his warnings, however. By the following day, the *Eagle* was bound for Sweden.

On 22 June, a fortnight after leaving Gothenburg, the *Virgo* arrived at Dane's Island. Andrée and Ekholm had spent several hours inspecting various sites on three islands, eventually settling on Dane's Island because it had a north-facing beach with several hollows that would protect the *Eagle* from ground winds. It also had a small wooden hut built by Arnold Pike, a British explorer, where Andrée had permission to set up his expedition headquarters.

The landscape was as unwelcoming as it was dramatic. Black granite mountains topped with snow backed the rocky beach; plates of ice floated in the bay and the temperature hovered just above freezing. Only to the north was the vista unimpeded – six hundred miles of clear sky, freezing ocean and solid pack ice lying between the island and the Pole.

The launch team disembarked and immediately began its preparations for the flight. Every day, every hour was precious for they did not know when the wind would swing round to the south, nor for how long any such wind would continue to blow north. Nobody wanted to miss what might be the one chance they would have to launch the *Eagle* towards its goal.

The site for the balloon shed was cleared of snow, and a round, level platform built over the rocks. A violent storm delayed its construction and provided a frightening portent of what lay ahead, but by the last day of June everything had been unloaded from the *Virgo*. *The hydrogen apparatus is ashore, so the most difficult part of unloading is over*, Andrée wrote in his diary that evening. *With luck, in three or four weeks, the only job left is to get to the Pole. That may present difficulties. It is amusing to engage in hypnotism on such a large scale.*

The assembly of the balloon hangar now went ahead. First constructed in Gothenburg, each component of the hangar had been meticulously labelled before being dismantled and packed away. Octagonal and wooden, with four storeys held together by steel bolts and a balcony running around the top storey, it had an adjustable top wall that could be swung around the building to shade the envelope from the wind until the last moments before the *Eagle* took off. Andrée oversaw the work, his fastidious attention to detail irritating the carpenters and builders. Whenever anyone proposed an alteration or a potential improvement, he told them he had already considered every eventuality and had made changes where necessary.

At last he could see the embodiment of his dream beginning to take shape. *The start will take place in July as soon as the weather is favourable, at a moment when the air is sufficiently clear and when there is a fresh southerly or almost southerly wind blowing*, he wrote in his diary.

On 11 July, after finishing his watch at 2 a.m., Andrée stole ashore, leaving the rest of his team and the crew asleep on the *Virgo*. Unable to contain his excitement any longer, he tucked under his arm a copy of *Journey of the Vega*, his hero Adolf Nordenskiöld's account of his discovery of the Northeast Passage, and scrambled up the shore to where the wicker gondola of the *Eagle* was covered with a tarpaulin. Pulling back the heavy covering, and whispering a quiet prayer of dedication in the cold night, he climbed inside. With a sleeping bag as a cushion and a blanket over his head to block out the midnight sun, he fell asleep dreaming of the day when he would return to Sweden a hero, the first man to reach the North Pole.

The next morning he hurried back to his cabin. *There was a fresh wind blowing, and the car was arranged in such a position that it swayed with the wind*, he noted. *I had with me the first part of the* Journey of the Vega *and read a few pages, placing it on the bookshelf that had been newly set up. In this way I christened the new vessel as best I could.*

Work on the *Eagle* continued apace. The draglines and

ballast lines were soaked in petroleum jelly and tallow, and repeatedly tested by dragging them across the ground and through water. The envelope was unpacked and valves attached, and the hydrogen plant was assembled. But bad weather again held back their progress, a heavy snowfall drenching much of the equipment, and it was not until 23 July that the lengthy and hazardous process of filling the envelope with hydrogen could begin.

Producing the gas was an exercise on an industrial scale, using three tons of iron filings, forty-one tons of concentrated sulphuric acid and seventy-six tons of salt water. A large lead-lined and airtight vessel was filled with the acid, water and iron filings. The iron reacted with the acid to produce iron sulphate and hydrogen, which fizzed off. The gas was then bubbled through a coke chamber to remove impurities and passed over quicklime to remove any water condensation, which could freeze within it. As the balloon inflated in the shed, those who had not seen its full size before stood back and watched in silence. It was like a vessel from another civilization.

Four days later, the top of the envelope could at last be seen poking out of the top of the balloon shed, prompting Andrée to write proudly: *At four o'clock inflation of the balloon was completed. This so-called impossible undertaking is now accomplished*. But another week was to pass before all the provisions had been packed on board and the gondola attached to the envelope. By the first days of August, much to the relief of an extremely impatient Andrée, the *Eagle* was ready to fly.

Dear Papa, Nils Strindberg now wrote to his father, *the balloon is now inflated. The wind is unsuitable, but we can wait a day or two; a few details are to be adjusted*. But Captain Hugo Zachau put an end to his hopes of relaying more good news. Irritated by the delays and frustrated by what he regarded as lack of discipline and poor organization among the scientists, Zachau informed Andrée that he had to return to Sweden. 'I must sail by the twentieth of August. The owners of the *Virgo* will not allow it to stay beyond then,' he announced. The boat had a re-inforced steel hull to protect it against light ice, but its insurance policy would not cover it beyond the end of the month.

Typically, Andrée had been oblivious to the pressures facing the other members of his party. 'But everything has turned out so well and to plan,' he protested. 'If nature will only perform its role now, we will soon be ready to launch.'

And so the men sat and waited for a wind to carry them north. A trial balloon was released, but it climbed too fast into the sky, disappearing into the cloud before Ekholm or Andrée had a chance to judge the wind direction. Still the wind blew stubbornly from the north, occasionally veer-ing slightly to the east or west as if to tease the men waiting at the edge of the bay. Andrée gazed beseechingly at the flags fluttering on top of the balloon hangar.

A mood of unease began to settle on the camp as people began to ask themselves the questions they dared not ask Andrée. Would the wind to the north ever come? Would all their work be in vain?

Unlike other balloon flights, which were generally launched in calm weather conditions, Andrée planned to launch the *Eagle* into the brunt of a southerly gale. Aware that he was breaking the first rule of ballooning, he was nonetheless convinced that it was worth it. 'The strong wind should enable the balloon to penetrate as quickly as possible far into unknown regions, and in the direction of the Pole,' he told his team members.

But Andrée and Ekholm had made a crucial mistake in their weather predictions. They had assumed the weather was the same every June, July and August, but they were wrong. Increasingly depressed that there was still no sign of the winds to the north that he and Ekholm had fore-cast, Andrée began to fear the worst. *Last night I was obliged to face the possibility that we may not be able to launch this year*, he wrote in his diary on 4 August. *Zachau cannot wait beyond August 20th. Any longer and his vessel will not be insured. Consequently, we must begin to pack our things on board the* Virgo *on the 14th. Ekholm thinks, too, that we cannot make an ascent any later than this.*

And Ekholm had other worries on his mind. From his meteorological studies he knew the wind was more favourable in July than August, but he had also been examining Strindberg's tests of the permeability of the envelope, and was convinced the *Eagle* was leaking gas faster than Andrée would admit. 'By my calculation, with every day that passes, the *Eagle* can carry one hundred and eleven kilograms less. That's how much gas it is losing because of leakage through the silk envelope. It will only get worse after the *Eagle* is launched as the wind pressure on the envelope will increase the daily loss,' he told Andrée.

Andrée called over Henri Lachambre, who had travelled from Paris to assist with the launch. Lachambre insisted that Ekholm was wrong, and that the *Eagle* would lose only fifty to sixty kilograms of carrying capacity a day.

'If I'm correct, the *Eagle* will fly for one to two weeks only. It is not enough. It would be mad to take off,' Ekholm insisted.

As the wind continued to blow stubbornly from the north, everyone on Dane's Island began to realize that the launch of the *Eagle* was no longer possible. *Today we have ground the scissors with which the balloon is to be cut open,* Andrée wrote despondently on 16 August. *Tomorrow, eight carrier pigeons are to be released, each carrying the same communiqué that the attempt, for this year at least, has been abandoned.*

The next day, with the wind pushing ripples across the bay towards the shore and clouds still heading south, Andrée issued the order for the balloon to be emptied of gas. Once again, Strindberg wrote to his father. *Dear Papa, we return with mixed feelings. What will be said of our failure? We have done all we could. If Andrée raises money next year, we may have more chance of success.*

Their heroic dreams seemed to be at an end.

A week later, Andrée arrived in Tromsö to find Nansen celebrating the fact that he had reached 86°14′ North, the furthest point north any man had ever gone, although he was still 226 nautical miles short of the Pole. Congratulating his Norwegian rival, who had spent the winter on Franz Josef Land where he had managed to gain around twenty pounds in weight, Andrée headed for Sweden, his pride severely dented.

Andrée returned to his job at the Swedish Patent Office, Strindberg to his family, and Ekholm to the Swedish Meteorological Central Office where he publicized his concerns about the viability of the balloon and his belief that its permeability did not live up to Andrée's claims. He soon resigned from the expedition over the matter, and was quickly replaced by Knut Frænkel, an athletic engineer who was sent to Paris to be taught balloon navigation by Lachambre.

A few months after his return, Andrée wrote to Alfred Nobel, requesting further funding and explaining Ekholm's resignation. Shortly before he died in December, Nobel met with Andrée and offered him a larger and improved balloon to replace the *Eagle*. Andrée refused. Dejected and humiliated, he turned to Gurli for comfort, who realized there was less likelihood then than at any other time that their romance would blossom.

'Why did you not take Nobel's offer, August?' Gurli asked him one night.

'To do so would have been to concede to that traitor Ekholm's criticism. I had no choice but to refuse,' he answered.

'You have told everybody that there are no hard feelings, but in your heart you will never forgive Ekholm, will you?' Gurli asked.

'No,' came the answer.

Andrée retreated further into his shell, immersing himself in his work at the patent office with even more gusto than before. That winter was long and uncomfortable for him, made more so by the Norwegian press crowing about Nansen having won the first round of the polar race in the context, yet again, of Norway's struggle for national independence. Despite their rivalry, however, the two men continued to write to each other, Nansen unable to hide his glee in a postscript to one of his letters. *I believe Macbeth's golden words should be placed on your banner. 'I dare do all that may become a man; who dares do more is none.' It is in drawing this boundary that true spiritual strength reveals itself.* Andrée was stung by the implied criticism. *Since I have proven that I am capable of returning, I am greatly tempted to do just the opposite*, he replied.

Although in public Nansen pretended to be supportive of Andrée's expedition, in private, to Andrée's face and behind his back, he dismissed the endeavour as ridiculous. In April 1897, Andrée was called upon to make a speech in Nansen and Johansen's honour at a banquet in Stockholm, where the two men were awarded a medal from the Swedish-Norwegian Union government. In his reply, Nansen complimented Andrée on his bravery and ingenuity in seeking a new way to reach the Pole. Although he flattered Andrée, it was obvious to those in the know that Nansen did not believe a word he was saying.

'Calm down,' he told the people at his table when he sat down. 'Banquets are banquets. In any case, why shouldn't one encourage idiots?'

CHAPTER FIVE

THE ENGAGEMENT

STOCKHOLM, SWEDEN

October 1896

FOR NILS STRINDBERG, IT ALL BEGAN WITH A PAIR OF TINY galoshes.

By late September, the youngest member of the Andrée expedition had returned to Sweden. As the carriage he had taken from the central station drew up outside his family home in one of the best districts of Stockholm, he was surprised to see that despite the inglorious ending to his travels, it was decked with bunting and a banner. Exhausted and dejected, Nils was in no mood for celebration; he was looking forward to seeing his brothers, sitting down to a large plate of his mother's good cooking and then retiring for a long sleep in his old bedroom.

The cheers began before he even opened the door. When he pushed it open he found the hallway packed with relatives, close friends and some business associates of his father, Johan Oscar, a wholesale merchant of considerable standing in Stockholm.

'Nisse, my darling Nisse.' Rosalie Strindberg threw her arms around her son's neck. 'Come inside. Welcome home. We're so pleased to have you back.'

Streamers rained down on Nils as he warily entered the hall. It was not what he had expected, but he knew his family, which was good old Stockholm stock, believed in welcoming its younger members back into the fold, and it was not every day that a son returned from an expedition to the Arctic.

Before Nils had even taken off his coat or put down his bags on the mat, his mother called her husband over by his nickname. 'Occa! Come over here, and bring some wine for your son.'

Nils smiled weakly. For a man who had just turned twenty-four the fuss was all quite overwhelming, but he was pleased to see his beaming father approach, his plump face rather red from the port wine he had been drinking.

'Well, well, my adventurer son. Let me take a look at you,' Occa said. 'Back from the wilds. I've been reading all about it in the *Aftonbladet*.' He winked at his son as he threw a thick arm around his shoulder. 'But I'm sure you have some tales to tell that weren't in the newspapers.'

Johan Oscar stepped back and looked his son up and down. He didn't appear any different from the day he left; maybe he looked a bit more tired, and he had certainly picked up a ruddy tan from the midnight sun, but otherwise he was the same old Nils. Open-faced and somewhat shorter and darker than most Scandinavians, his parents often said he could easily pass for a Frenchman or an Italian. As ever, Nils was impeccably dressed in a three-piece suit, a wing-collared shirt and a loose-knotted bowtie. A thin strand twisted upwards at either end of his neatly waxed black moustache; his hair needed a trim to return it to its usual tidiness, but otherwise there was no change for the worse. In fact, his father mused, it looked as if Nils had lost some weight.

'That Arctic air seems to have done you good,' Occa

said. 'Your waist is not as thick as it was when you left home and your collar is not as tight as when we last saw you. But I'm sure all that will change when you get some of your mother's cooking inside you and you're back behind your desk at the university. Maybe now that you're famous they'll promote you from Assistant in Physics to something better.'

Nils smiled again. 'All in good time, Father. Now let me get inside the door and put these heavy bags down.'

Nearby stood Tore, Nils's younger brother, who was training to be a sculptor. The Strindberg family broadly fell into two categories. There was the artistic side, like Tore and his cousin August, the famous playwright and novelist whose *Miss Julie* was still the talk of Stockholm society, and there was the technical side, like Nils and his elder brother Sven, who had travelled from Helsinki, where he worked as an engineer.

'Sven, how are you?' Nils called out to his brother. 'You've come a long way on my account.'

Sven smiled. 'Never mind me. Come into the salon and tell me about your adventures.'

Nils shrugged off his overcoat and the two brothers walked into the formal parlour with its dark sideboards, heavy furniture and large table decked with a lace tablecloth. They talked for a while about Nils's journey home and his experiences at Dane's Island. Slowly, Nils relaxed and turned to the matters on his mind.

'I'm pleased to be back here rather than stranded on some distant polar ice plain, but I had hoped I would be returning home in different circumstances,' he said. 'I cannot deny I am disappointed, particularly – and do not repeat this to anyone – in Andrée.' Nils glanced around the room before taking his brother into his confidence, then spoke quietly. 'He is a fine man, but there were times when I wished he would have acted more spontaneously. We did not get the wind we wanted, but still I cannot help thinking that maybe Andrée was too cautious. Even in failure his response was measured.'

Sven was surprised. 'You should be thankful you have returned fit and healthy. For that alone you owe Andrée something,' he said, prodding Nils's chest with his finger. 'Nisse, you must remember that Andrée is nearly twice your age. And as the leader of your expedition, he is bound to be more cautious. It would be wrong if he were not.'

'I know, I know. But I am worried. On the voyage home, there was talk of returning to Dane's Island next year. But we are not a happy team; Dr Ekholm is highly critical of Andrée and his methods, and I have some concerns that Ekholm's fears about the safety of the *Eagle* might be justified. I will have to consider carefully whether to join Andrée again.'

Drinking several glasses of wine apiece, the two brothers talked intimately for some time. Eventually the subject turned to more familiar matters.

'Enough of my travels,' Nils said. 'What I really need to know is: have you heard of – or, even better, seen anything of – Anna Charlier? You know, I thought of little else while at Dane's Island.'

Nils had first set eyes on Anna Charlier in the mild summer of 1894. He had not been long out of university and was making a modest living tutoring the children of wealthy Stockholm families who had come to holiday in the beach resorts of Scania, a province in southern Sweden. His path crossed several times with Anna's during that flower-filled summer; Nils taught natural sciences and the violin, while Anna taught literature and languages.

The Scanian peninsula was Anna's home – her father was the postmaster in the nearby town of Klippan – and Nils often turned to her for directions and advice. Very soon he found he was seeking her assistance even when he knew the answers to his questions. There was something about Anna's gentle manner and the soft, lazy way she smiled that made him want to see more of her.

For weeks, Nils struggled to think of ways of asking Anna for a date. Knowing that the families for whom they both worked would not approve of a romance between tutors, he had to resort to subterfuge. Shortly before he was due to return to Stockholm, he came up with an idea. 'I am preparing some photographs for an exhibition in Stockholm. Maybe you would let me take your portrait?' he asked Anna as he handed over the Skjöldebrandt girls into her charge. 'I've already photographed these two young ladies, but I've yet to capture a masterpiece.'

The following Sunday, Nils borrowed a pony and trap from one of his employers and drove Anna inland from the beaches and summer resorts of the flat coastal region. They headed for the beech and pine forests in the southern part of Scania, with a basket containing a picnic of meatballs, herring salad and bitter lemonade beside Nils's self-built camera in the back of the trap. As the pony trotted along the country lanes, Nils stole glances at Anna sitting bolt upright beside him. The sun shone off her curly light brown hair. Despite her attempts to pin it tightly to her head beneath a straw hat, wisps of it trailed around her ears in the wind. Nils found it enchanting. A pale summer dress, with a bow around its high neck, was drawn in tightly at her narrow waist; Nils thought it emphasized her figure perfectly, although he was slightly alarmed to notice that she was fractionally taller than him when they sat side by side.

After riding for an hour or so, they parked the trap on a small bridge and climbed down to the river bank, where Nils took some photographs of Anna lying under a tree with the picnic spread out beside her on a checked blanket. They chatted easily about the children they taught and the foibles of their employers, agreeing that the Dahlanders were the most demanding of all the families.

As Anna talked, Nils watched her large, sensuous lips move, waiting for her mouth to break into one of its languid smiles. It was the kind of smile that other women would spend years perfecting in front of a mirror, but to

Anna it came naturally – provided the circumstances were right. Nils soon discovered it was difficult to prompt Anna to smile in the way he found so attractive. When he told jokes, Anna would respond with a thin smile, pulling her lips taut, but when she was telling a story or listening to Nils, the leisurely, apple-cheeked smile readily softened her face. How I wish I could make her smile so magically every time I come near, he thought to himself. And how I wish to kiss her on those full lips.

All too soon for Nils they had to return home. The pony and trap had to be returned so that its owners could take it to church that evening, and for most of the journey back Anna and Nils sat in comfortable silence, enjoying the warm breeze and the rhythm of the pony's hooves.

'I shall soon be leaving for Gothenburg,' Anna said, shortly before the journey ended. 'The end of summer is approaching and I need to find winter employment.'

Nils also had to leave the seaside, but he was returning to Stockholm in the hope of a teaching post at the university. 'Well, I shall write to you and send you the photographs,' he said. 'And if you like them, maybe we can meet again?'

Anna agreed, and they exchanged addresses, but Nils's hopes of seeing Anna again were not to be fulfilled. He was offered a job surveying in Norrland, a region of mountains, forests and sawmills in the north of Sweden, and he left home for his new position immediately after arriving back in Stockholm.

More than a year later, in the winter of 1895 and shortly after being appointed Assistant in Physics at the University of Stockholm, Nils entered an exhibition of amateur photographs at the Industrial Palace in Stockholm. His pictures of Anna were among his entry. They won him first prize, but he put his memories of Anna to the back of his mind. He had more pressing things than romance to consider, for he had recently been selected as the third member of Andrée's proposed expedition to the North Pole. While in Paris, learning to fly balloons, in the spring of 1896, Nils often thought of Anna and the afternoon they spent together two years earlier, but he abandoned all hope of seeing her again. After all, a woman with such a winning smile would long since have married, he told himself.

Sven had no news of Anna. 'What should I know about some girl in Stockholm or Gothenburg when I spend all my time in Helsinki?' he asked dismissively. But a few weeks later, Nils was delighted to discover that Anna Charlier was tutoring the children of some family friends, the Petersons. For Nils, it meant one thing: that she was likely still to be single. Immediately, he began to plot another meeting. He also wrote to Sven, who had returned to Helsinki.

Why did you not tell me that Anna Charlier was tutoring Doreotea Peterson's children? I must say it was the most exciting news I have had in a long time. Only you know how I really feel and how much I want Anna to know that memories of her made my life worth living at a time when there seemed to be little to look forward to.

You have not met her, but you have seen the portrait I took when we were both tutors in Scania. Even from one of my photographs you ought to be able to see why I find her so enchanting, but in case you are blind to it, I will remind you why she is so sweet and nice. From the moment I met her I knew there was something special between us. She has a warm, gentle manner and I find talking to her so easy. Need I bore you again with details of the effect her smile has on me? Maybe the moment we first met was the right time in my life for something wonderful to happen, but I prefer to think that it was simply that she was always meant to be the one for me.

After dinner the next evening, Occa Strindberg brought up the subject of who to invite to a Sunday dinner in honour of their friends the Dahlanders, who had just returned from America. Naturally, Nils wanted to invite Anna Charlier, but he dared not say so immediately, and instead played along with his parents' and brother's conversation, waiting for an opportunity. During a lull in their discussion, he took a sip of his port.

'Maybe we should invite Lindsröm, Father. He was such a good friend to me when I was in Paris learning to fly balloons. And Lindsröm will get some music going; it's been a long time since I played my violin. And perhaps we should invite the Peterson children's tutor to make up the numbers. Her name is Anna Charlier, I think, and I hear she is a very fine pianist.'

'Now that is a good idea! Some fresh blood in this stale salon – I like the sound of that. And when did we last have some music in this house, Rosalie? Nils seldom plays his violin these days, and you know how much I like to hear a song.'

Nils's mother smiled benevolently at Occa. He had been in such good form since Nils returned from the Arctic, and she loved to hear her husband and Nils talk of his exploits at Dane's Island.

'And why not invite Andrée, Nils?' she added. 'I have not seen him since you returned from Dane's Island. He works too hard at that patent office and I've always thought he does not look after himself. He could do with a good home-cooked meal.'

'Stop her, Nils, before she invites that traitor Ekholm,' Occa interjected. 'Andrée, fine. But Dr Ekholm is not coming to this house.'

Once again, Nils embarked on a detailed explanation of why Ekholm's well-publicized criticisms of the *Eagle* were not without foundation, but despite this he had been angered by recent suggestions in the newspapers exhorting him to follow Ekholm's example by resigning. He was now determined not to quit. 'I will not be persuaded that I ought to desert Andrée,' he argued. 'I gave my word last year, and I will keep to it now, even if the quality of the *Eagle* is not quite satisfactory.'

Nils's aunt, who was silently embroidering a cushion, spoke for the first time. 'Do you really think it is a good idea to invite so many younger people? They always eat so much. Perhaps we should just invite the Dahlanders, Brita and maybe Bertil? It will be a more civilized evening without the noise of the piano and Nils's violin.'

How typical of my aunt, Nils thought. Always the same crowd, always the same faces. He opened his mouth to object, but his father beat him to it.

'No, no! Let Nils invite his friend. After all, he has been leading a very solitary life, stuck in the Arctic for so long. And I'm sure Miss Charlier would welcome some company from people her own age after being cooped up with the Peterson children.' He then lifted his hand and gestured towards his son. 'Nils, go and make the arrangements now, before someone else tries to change my mind. Lindsröm, Andrée and Miss Charlier it is to be.'

It was shortly before a quarter to seven that evening, and Nils was due at the Society of Physics for a lecture. Anxious that Anna would refuse his invitation, or, worse still, not remember him, he pulled on a coat and ran straight to the Petersons' house. A few minutes later he was back at home and poking his head round the door of the salon.

'It is all arranged. The children are sick and the Petersons have given Miss Charlier permission to come on Sunday. She will not come for dinner, but she will join us afterwards.'

Explaining that he would be late unless he left immediately, he hurried away, full of excitement, humming a popular Swedish tune – 'It's a dream, just a haze' – as he headed into the centre of Stockholm. It was a cold night; winter was approaching, bringing back memories of the cold summer on Dane's Island. As he ran across the bridges linking the central islands in the old town of Stockholm, he could feel the characteristic shiver in the air that heralded the first snow. Before long, the Royal Palace, Houses of Parliament and churches in old

Stockholm would be decked in white, and if it was a particularly cold snap, the bay would freeze over and children would be skating where the ferries were now carrying passengers between the many islands of the archipelago. Somehow, Nils mused, the thought of a frozen Stockholm was more inviting than that of Dane's Island – picture-postcard prettiness versus the harsh reality of the empty Arctic wilderness.

For the rest of the week, Nils found it difficult to concentrate, so full of Anna was his mind. He had been relieved of his usual duties as Assistant in Physics in order to lecture to students on the technical aspects of the abandoned North Pole expedition. He explained that Andrée had chosen him from hundreds of candidates for his photographic skills and scientific expertise. Before the departure from Gothenburg, he told the students, he had investigated the friction of the draglines and the permeability of the balloon cloth. He admitted that he had failed to consider the seams and had subsequently re-evaluated the airworthiness of the *Eagle*, but as he spoke, it was as if his mind was switched to automatic. The tutorials and lectures passed in a daze while he counted down the minutes to his meeting with Anna. His anticipation surpassed even the excitement he had felt when he learnt that Andrée had selected him for the expedition. Then, the prospect of several months of preparation had dented the thrill somewhat; this time, with only days to go until he saw Anna again, he could feel his heart trembling with expectancy.

On Sunday morning, he rode on his velocipede, a boneshaker bicycle made of iron and wood, with his friend Gustav Lang, and after lunch he visited the Peters and the Wallings. At last evening came, and it was time to change into a formal suit and dress shirt with a stiff winged collar. After washing, he greased his hair close to his head with a razor-sharp parting and went downstairs to greet the guests. The only person he did not know was Jöns Johansson, a lecturer at the Karolinska Institute, but he was soon telling him about his exploits with Andrée, who was already at the table.

The dinner party seemed to be a success – most of the talk was of ballooning – but Nils fretted throughout. What time had he told Anna to arrive? he asked himself. What would happen if she came too early? Now that the time of Anna's arrival was almost upon him, Nils wanted to delay the moment, fearing that perhaps she might not be quite as magnificent as he remembered.

The doorbell rang and, wiping his hands, which were damp with nerves, on his napkin, he rushed to the front door. His throat tightened, and he worried that his voice would quiver when he greeted Anna. But a young student, requesting some information from his tutor, was waiting on the doorstep. Nils invited the student inside, but as he was explaining what the student needed to know, the doorbell rang again and, to his alarm, Anna slipped past him into the dining room where the guests were finishing their pudding. Bustling the student out into the night with a promise that he would see him in his office the next day, he returned to the dining room, only to find that Anna – or Miss Charlier, as he had to call her – had already been introduced to his father.

As host, Nils moved politely around the table, speaking to each of the guests in turn. Making small talk to anybody else but Anna was agonizing, and he could hardly bear it when he saw her talking to other men in the room. He willed the evening to speed by so that he could offer to escort her home.

To make matters worse, Andrée was talking to Nils's mother, speaking lovingly of his mother Mina, but gradually the conversation turned to cultural matters and, to Nils's embarrassment, Andrée was beginning to show his ignorance of anything beyond patents and ballooning. His academic career had been fairly distinguished, but he had immersed himself in all subjects except for literature and art, areas in which he had such little interest that it would later be regarded as a character defect.

'We never manage to invite you to the opera or to an exhibition, Herr Andrée,' Rosalie said.

'The artificiality of the opera is not quite my thing. It would be wasted on me; I prefer the dependable real world,' he replied. He also told Rosalie that he could see no point in attending a concert or an art gallery.

'Well, maybe you would come to the banquet next week in honour of Selma Lagerlöf? She has won a literary prize for her *Gösta Berling's Saga*. I trust you have read it?'

'No, I can't say that I have, but I have read *Münchhausen*, and I suppose that is about the same thing.'

Rosalie Strindberg smiled curtly and, turning to her sister, whispered an aside. 'I suppose if you are single-minded enough to organize and fund a trip to the North Pole by balloon, then your interests might be quite narrow. You simply have neither time nor inclination to take notice of much outside your own little world, but I had not expected him to be so self-centred.'

At last, Anna offered to play the piano, and the atmosphere became more solemn. It came as a relief to Nils after the bright and rather artificial chatter around the dinner table, and he found himself beaming with proprietorial pride when the other guests praised Anna's playing.

The party broke up half an hour before midnight, and Nils offered to accompany Anna home. To his joy, she accepted immediately, but his feeling of triumph was short-lived. Several men, Andrée included, went with them, and yet again Nils found it impossible to snatch a moment alone with her. All too soon they arrived at the Petersons.

'Perhaps we could meet tomorrow?' Nils suggested as he and Anna stood on the threshold of the Petersons' house.

'You played so well,' Andrée interrupted. 'I hope to hear you play again soon.'

'Thank you. I enjoyed it too. I do not often get the chance to leave the house, and even less to play the piano.'

Anna put her key in the door. Hands were shaken,

farewells bid, a good night's sleep wished. Then, much to Nils's frustration, she quickly vanished inside.

Hiding his disappointment at the way the evening had gone, Nils walked back with Andrée. As usual, it was impossible to speak of anything but the expedition with Andrée, who was incensed by what he perceived to be Ekholm's treachery.

'Had the winds played our way in Virgohamna, we would not be having this conversation and we would be standing here triumphant after reaching the North Pole,' Andrée said. 'But Ekholm could not see that; instead he carped and sniped about deficiencies in the *Eagle*, forgetting the work I had done to build the best balloon the world has seen.' Andrée kicked at patches of frost at the side of the icy pavement as they walked. 'I have much higher hopes for Knut Frænkel. He is a civil engineer and an outstanding gymnast, and he came to visit me recently at my office.'

He then stopped and pulled a piece of paper out of an inner pocket of his jacket. 'Here, have a look at this. It's Frænkel's application.' Nils took it and read:

To Chief Engineer Salomon August Andrée,

I refer to our conversation of the 19th. I herewith apply for the position vacated by Dr Ekholm as the third man on the polar expedition proposed by the Chief Engineer for next year. I am 26 and a half years of age and have a healthy and strong physique. I have passed my matriculation and graduated from the Royal Technical High School's Department of Highways and Hydro-engineering.

Your obedient servant, Knut Hjalmar Ferdinand Frænkel, civil engineer.

'I hope to confirm his replacement of Ekholm very soon,' Andrée said.

'And what is he like, this Frænkel?' Nils asked.

'I think he is a reliable sort, but his best qualities are his courage and his physical strength.' Andrée was already admitting to himself the likelihood that if the *Eagle* ever took off, the return journey from the Pole would probably be made on foot. 'He does not have Dr Ekholm's meteorological expertise, but I have no doubt he could soon acquire it. And at twenty-six, he is almost half the age of Ekholm and twice as strong.'

Nils stayed silent. It was a moot point. At forty-eight, Ekholm was only six years older than Andrée, but considerably fitter and stronger than him. In physical terms, Andrée would always be the weakest link.

'Come and meet Frænkel at my offices next week. Then you can judge for yourself how good a candidate he is,' Andrée told Nils, and they walked on in silence.

By the time Nils returned home it was the early hours of the morning, and he had abandoned any hope of seeing Anna again. She was obviously not interested in him, he told himself, and it would not have impressed her that he had hardly spoken to her all evening. Tired and despondent, bemoaning his cowardice at not making the most of his chances when she was so near him, Nils went to bed, determined not to think of her again.

But when he came downstairs several hours later to look for his notebook, which he eventually found in his overcoat pocket, he discovered a pair of tiny galoshes bearing the initials A.C., tucked into a corner of the cloakroom.

'They must be Miss Charlier's,' his brother Tore pointed out. 'I will take them back to her. Don't you worry about it.'

Once again Nils could feel his chances of speaking to Anna slipping through his fingers. This time, however, he resolved to seize his opportunity while he could.

'You should take them back, of course. After all, I walked all the way to Miss Charlier's house last night. But it's too much to ask of you. She was my guest, so I will return them myself.' Bristling at his elder brother's condescension, Tore tried to insist that he should go, but Nils was adamant. 'I'm going into town anyway. I will take them on my way to the university.'

There was no time for breakfast. Grabbing Anna's galoshes, Nils rushed outside and was soon bounding up the steps to the Petersons' house and knocking on the door.

'Do you not know what time it is, Strindberg?' The gruff sound of Herr Peterson's voice came through the heavy door. 'What the hell do you want?'

'I am very sorry to disturb you, Herr Peterson. I need to speak to Anna,' Nils shouted back.

'What on earth for? It's much too early.'

'She left her galoshes at my parents' house last night. I have brought them back for her.'

'Could it not wait, Strindberg?' Nils heard a noisy sigh. 'If you wait, I will fetch her.'

The faint sound of footsteps receded down the hallway. A short while later, Anna was at the door. The sound of her voice made Nils's heart race. The thought of her standing, alone and so close, on the other side of the door brought back memories of the afternoon they had squeezed in side by side on the trap's small bench. Nils wondered if Anna's lazy smile was on her lips, or whether she was scowling at being hauled out of bed at such an early hour.

'Herr Strindberg! Why are you here so early? I cannot open the door to you at this hour. Can you please leave my galoshes outside and I'll collect them later.'

Nils thought quickly. This was not what he had hoped for, and unless he could come up with a good response, he would miss his chance of seeing Anna again. 'I will leave them,' he said. 'But would you do me the honour of meeting me later today?'

There was a long silence. 'I can meet you in Drottninggatan at one o'clock,' Anna said at last. 'I have to look after the children until then. Now I must go. Thank you again for returning my galoshes.'

*　*　*

At the allotted time, Nils was in Drottninggatan, Stockholm's main street, which led from the Riksdag, the Swedish parliament on Helgeandsholmen Island, surrounded on three sides by water, to the main shopping area in the oldest part of Stockholm. He was chatting to a friend he had bumped into when he spotted Anna, wrapped in a dark coat trimmed with fur and wearing a matching hat, approaching on the other side of the street. Waving in Anna's direction, Nils crossed Drottninggatan and walked briskly towards her.

Anna was clearly pleased to see him; she beamed her wide smile long before Nils had stopped in front of her. The smile was better even than Nils had remembered it. He had not appreciated at dinner the previous evening quite how much Anna had blossomed over the last two years, and she radiated now with all the beauty of a young woman in her prime.

'You are more beguiling than I remember you,' Nils said, wishing straight away that he had not let his thoughts slip out quite so obviously. Anna's face, already pink from the cold, reddened further, and Nils noticed how she pulled her lips taut in the same tight smile he had tried to avoid two years earlier in Scania. Maybe it is not disapproval when she smiles like that, he thought. Maybe it's embarrassment. How charming.

Anna's eyes watered in the cold and her warm breath clouded the chilled air between them. It made Nils want to throw his arms around her, but he knew he must not. He had decided on his intentions as he lay in bed last night, and consequently had important business to attend to.

'Why don't we walk down towards the shops?' he said, offering his arm to Anna.

She took it readily, and they walked seven or eight blocks towards the centre of town, past Ahlens, the department store, where Anna stopped to gaze at the party dresses in the window and Nils yearned to buy her one, until they came to the front of Oscar Berg's coffee house.

Nils seized the opportunity. 'Let me buy you some hot chocolate and pastries. They're very good here.'

They took a table in the corner, where Nils hoped they would not be interrupted. But it was not to be. It seemed as though every woman who passed their table knew Anna. Most stopped to greet her, and several stayed for a long chat; in all the time they spent in the coffee house, Nils barely opened his mouth. Then Anna asked him the time.

'It's two o'clock,' he told her. 'Why do you ask?'

'I have to join the Petersons at their country house at Johannisdal and need to catch a boat at a quarter past three. Before then I have some shopping to do.'

'In that case, we should leave immediately,' Nils replied.

Paying the bill quickly, he helped Anna into her coat, and they left the restaurant. They stopped at Lajas, a toyshop, to buy a birthday present for one of the Peterson girls, and then they turned towards Skeppsholmen, the island at the heart of Stockholm. Nils led Anna past the Grand Hotel on the waterfront and across a small bridge until they were on Skeppsholmen, directly opposite the Royal Palace.

At last they were alone. Dropping on to one knee, Nils took Anna's left hand between his and asked her to marry him.

'I think I know the answer,' Anna answered, 'but why the question after all this time? I have not heard from you in more than two years.'

Now it was Nils's turn to blush. He looked at Anna; there was no sign of the lazy smile. Instead, she fixed him firmly with her green eyes.

'I have thought of you every day since we said goodbye in Scania,' he said. 'Since then I have not had the opportunity to see you again, but as soon as I did I knew that I wanted to spend all my time with you.'

Anna's face lit up. This time her smile did not come

lazily but rushed across her face. 'I, too, have waited for you all this time. After that afternoon in Scania, no other man caught my eye again. While I was in Gothenburg I thought constantly of you, hoping you would write, but I heard nothing. I was on the point of giving up hope when you appeared at the Petersons'. I must admit I was taken aback when you hardly spoke to me in front of your parents last night, but as soon as I saw you I knew that you were the man I wanted. So yes, of course I will marry you.'

Nils was overwhelmed. He simply could not believe this beautiful woman had so readily agreed to marry him, or that she, too, had waited so long for him. They kissed, and then they kissed again, until Anna reminded him that it was almost a quarter to three. In half an hour, her boat would leave for Johannisdal and Nils wanted to tell his father about their engagement before Anna left.

They hurried to Vasagatan, the parallel street to Drottninggatan, where Anna picked up the provisions she had been asked to collect by the Petersons, and then they ran to Occa Strindberg's office. They arrived just in time; Nils's father was on the street with his briefcase under his arm, about to leave.

'Father, let me introduce you to my fiancée,' Nils said.

Herr Strindberg looked at the couple in disbelief. Rocking back on his heels, he raised his eyebrows and opened and closed his mouth several times. 'I need to have a word with you, Nils,' he said. 'In private.'

Nils and Occa apologized to Anna and stepped aside.

'What do you mean by proposing to this young lady when you intend to return to Dane's Island?' Occa demanded. 'It is hardly the most responsible thing to do.'

'Father, I have thought it all through. I would not be standing here introducing you to my fiancée if I did not believe I would spend a long and happy life with her.' Nils paused. 'I spoke at length with Andrée last night. He is taking steps to ensure the *Eagle* will be airtight when we return to Dane's Island, and he is having it enlarged to ensure it will fly for as long as he originally planned. I am convinced that next time we will be successful and that we will all return unharmed. If I didn't feel this way, I would not have proposed to Miss Charlier.'

Occa pursed his lips, gripped his briefcase tighter and narrowed his eyes. 'If your engagement is a sign of the confidence you have in Andrée, in your abilities and in the state of the *Eagle*, then I can hardly disapprove. I am very pleased for you.' Turning to Anna, his face softened from surprise to happiness, and then delight. 'This is the most marvellous news. Congratulations to you both! And Anna – I may call you Anna now? – let me kiss you.' He leant forward and kissed Anna gently on her cheek. 'Well, well, well. Does your mother know about this, Nils? I wonder what she will say.'

'We have had no time to tell her, sir. We are catching the boat to Johannisdal at a quarter past three, where Anna must join the Petersons.'

'A quarter past three?' said Occa, glancing at his pocket watch. 'You must leave immediately. I'll come with you and we can talk along the way.'

The trio arrived at the quayside breathless, but with five minutes to spare. Wishing them bon voyage, Occa waved as Nils and Anna ran down the gangplank to the *Sjöfröken*, a single-decked passenger ferry painted white, with a black roof and gunwale. Nils helped Anna on board through the iron balustrade at the bow of the small boat, then stepped back onto its short foredeck and waved to his father from beneath the red and gold flag of the ferry company.

For the first time that day, Nils and Anna had time to relax, to enjoy each other's company, the tranquillity of the crossing and the fresh air. Chatting and staring out into the bay, where the autumn sun was dipping towards the horizon, they sat on their own on the open rear deck. The setting sun turned the white of the pretty steam ferry orange and gave a soft glow to their faces. Above them, a row of maritime flags fluttered in the breeze.

'I am immeasurably happy,' Nils told Anna. 'I thought I would never see you again.'

'I feel that way too,' Anna replied. 'I have never been so content and excited at the same time.'

An hour later they arrived at Johannisdal, a popular site for summerhouses in the southern part of the Stockholm archipelago. No-one had come to meet them, so they walked to the Petersons' house undisturbed, relishing the privacy of every step along the way.

It was dark by the time they reached the house. The warm glow of gas lamps in the sitting room, where they could see the girls drinking coffee, spilled in shafts into the garden. Nils squeezed Anna's hand as they made their way up the path, but before they had time to knock, the girls spotted them and leapt to the windows. Seconds later, all the Petersons burst through the front door, shouting with joy and laughter at the news of Nils and Anna's engagement.

After dinner, the Petersons left Anna and Nils alone. They listened to the girls playing music in the next room before walking slowly through the town, Anna listening intently to Nils talking of Andrée's single-mindedness in his pursuit of a polar first.

'Did you know your name, Charlier, is almost the same as the French name for a hydrogen balloon?' Nils added at one point. 'They were named "Charlière", after Jacques-Alexandre-César Charles, the French physician who invented and first flew in a hydrogen balloon.'

Anna smiled at her fiancé and warmed to his infectious enthusiasm. 'Well, I hope it is a good omen.' She did not dare speak of the dark thoughts that had crossed her mind: it is bad enough to be a widow, but to lose your love before you have married is possibly worse. Instead, Anna began to talk of her dreams of having children and of creating a home with a dependable man.

It was an enchanting evening, and as its end neared, Nils could not bear to think of real life crashing in on such a magical time.

*   *   *

Nils and Anna's love deepened through the winter and blossomed early in the spring, when they attended a ball in Stockholm. Like many social occasions in early 1897, it was dominated by balloon fever. Nils and Anna, the guests of honour, were asked to lead the balloon dance.

To Nils and to many of the men at the ball, Anna looked captivating in her white, high-necked ball gown, her puffed sleeves revealing her pale arms. A comb holding a white rose looked beautiful against her brown hair.

At the end of the dance, it was Anna's duty to spin a pointer on a card placed at the centre of the dance floor. At one end of the pointer was a balloon, at the other an arrow; whoever the arrow pointed to had to dance with the woman who spun it. By the end of the evening, Anna had played the game so many times that she'd become adept at making the arrow tip point every time at Nils. The lovers danced together all night, walking home at the first light of the winter sun, stopping only to kiss in doorways.

As the cold receded, they spent lazy spring days in the country, on one occasion travelling back to Scania to revisit the scene of their courtship. Again, Nils took photographs of Anna, and told her of the photographic equipment he had designed especially for the expedition. Almost inevitably, it seemed, the subject of their conversation came round to Andrée, Anna asking Nils what he thought of his mentor.

'He embodies in every respect the ancient saying "to speak once and stand by one's word is better than to speak a hundred times",' Nils said, 'and that impresses me. But although he is self-possessed and discerning, it has always concerned me that Andrée does not act spontaneously. There is wanting in him the spirit of fresh, impulsive action.'

Despite their intimacy, Anna still found it hard to broach the one topic that was on her mind: the looming deadline that would see them parted. Nils, too, never mentioned it. In a matter of weeks, they both knew, he would depart as part of Andrée's team for a second attempt at the North Pole. How could he discuss it with Anna without worrying her, without the danger that she might change his mind? At times there was nothing he wanted more than to settle down with Anna and their children in a country home, but he was a young man who knew that he had been given a unique opportunity. Much as he feared that his domestic dream might never come true, he also knew that if he resigned from the expedition he would regret the decision for the rest of his life. After all, he told himself, he had captured Anna's heart by having the courage to seize the day, and potentially greater things that lay ahead should not now daunt him.

Alone at home, as he prepared to leave for Dane's Island, Nils looked at the photographs of Anna he had glued into his diary. There was one picture of her with seven members of his family, sitting formally around a table. Beside it he had written: *My old love for Anna is revived. Engagement party, exchange of rings. Strangely, the more I talk to her, the more I like her.*

A few pages further on was a photograph of Anna on one of their days in the country, dressed in a loose blouse with a flowery pattern, a frilly neck and a bow at the back. Her skirt had two stripes running around the hem, and she was wearing an elegant hat with a large bow and a stiff brim perched at a jaunty angle. Behind Anna was a windbreak made of roughly hewn branches, and in her hands she clutched a bunch of flowers. But the most noticeable details, as ever, were Anna's warm smile and her clear eyes fixing on the camera. Beside it, Nils had scrawled: *It was difficult to resist her then.*

On the next page was another photograph, this time of Anna lying in a field, with her hands behind her head and her sleeves billowing. Once again she was smiling beguilingly. Beneath it, Nils had written his most personal thoughts: *A wonderful moment. We sat and talked and kissed. I told her I loved her and we longed to embrace*

one another. Each time we meet it is more heart-rending.
What is the right thing to do? Hold back or let go? I must
hold back. It is certainly the correct behaviour.

The night before his departure, Nils and Anna attended
a large art exhibition in Stockholm. *Anna and I were out*
the last day together and enjoyed ourselves very much,
although we wished that we had had more time for each
other, Nils wrote in his diary, tucking the tickets from the
exhibition into the box of mementoes he intended to take
to Dane's Island.

The next morning, Nils made his final arrangements,
checking and rechecking that he had everything he needed
to take to Dane's Island. He shook his father's hand, and
kissed his mother and brother. Then came the moment he
was dreading. As he turned to Anna, tears welled up in his
eyes. He kissed and hugged her tightly and, out of earshot
of the Strindberg family, whispered some words that only
she could hear: 'You *shall* be my wife.' Anna's lips
trembled, and she gripped Nils's hand tightly as he stood
beside her, making his final farewells to his parents. Anna
and Nils then excused themselves so that they could say
goodbye in private. Outside on the porch, Nils hugged his
beloved fiancée again and looked deeply into her green
eyes.

'Don't be sad, my love. I shall soon be home again.
Now, give me one of your magical smiles that look as if
you could swallow the world, so that I leave with a
pleasant picture to remember you by.'

Anna smiled weakly, unable to muster her usual
winning grin. 'Take care of yourself, Nisse. And write to
me every day.'

Nils bent to pick up his bags. He kissed Anna one last
time, then, without turning back, walked down the steps
to where a carriage waited to take him to his train bound
for Gothenburg.

CHAPTER SIX

THE COUNTDOWN

SPITSBERGEN, NORWAY

May 2000

THE CALL COMES AT MIDDAY. I AM WORKING AT MY DESK, about to break for lunch, when an email comes through from Luc Trullemans, my Belgian weather god. After weeks of waiting for the right weather pattern, I am on the point of giving up hope. I had planned to take off in April. Now it is early May, and there are only about three weeks left until I shall have to cancel the attempt. I am becoming extremely despondent; I'm worried that in attempting to follow in the footsteps of Andrée, I too will wait in vain for the wind to carry me north.

I now regret not heading back to Spitsbergen on 25 March, when Luc first called to say that according to his forecasts he could see a wind stream directly from Spitsbergen to the Pole. It was a perfect track, but it was too early. My equipment was not quite ready to go, and neither was I. However, it was a useful early warning, an indicator that we needed to be able to respond quickly to changes in the weather. Since then I've been ready to leave home at twenty-four hours' notice, but there has not been a whisper of a southerly wind. The team is also on standby. A pack of ten rolling air tickets waits at the airport, with reservations on every Spitsbergen flight from now until the end of the month. To crown the misery, the entire team is under strict instructions not to drink a drop of alcohol, in case we get the call.

I feel I now know how Andrée must have felt, the tension of the countdown clock ticking in unison with a growing sense of despair as the promised wind fails to show. I am getting under my wife's feet at home – usually I am away on an expedition at this time of year – and I have even tidied my office – very strange behaviour.

Every day, shortly before lunch, I open an email from Luc. Since 25 March, its contents have always been the same. Like Andrée staring up at the flags fluttering in the breeze, praying for them to point north, I plead that the email will contain news of an approaching weather pattern that promises a fair wind. It has been a long time since the wind last blew to the north, when, on 8 May, I click on Luc's latest email.

From: Luc Trullemans
To: David Hempleman-Adams, Clive Bailey, Brian Jones
Sent: 08 May 2000 12:11
Subject: Weather for Spitsbergen

Dear all,
I think that we are missing a slot forecasted for tomorrow, Tuesday, around 6Z.* The wind will be not too strong at surface and I have a trajectory around 14,000ft going to the Pole area in 72 hours (at this time further than 88°N) but becoming undefined later on.
For the next four days (Wednesday until Saturday), the forecast becomes worse with too much wind on the ground and the wrong direction at high levels.

* The Z in the time refers to Zulu time, or GMT. Thus, 6Z is 0600 GMT.

Luc's English always needs some interpretation, but the message is clear. A track to the north will hit Spitsbergen tomorrow morning, but that's sooner than we can get there. I call him to ask if there's any chance it may linger. He tells me that he'll call me in the morning to let me know if I should pack my bags.

It's an outside chance, but it's enough for me. I can feel my heart pounding in my chest as the adrenalin kicks in. All thoughts of lunch are immediately cancelled. Instead, I phone round the team to let them know Luc's news. Then, I try to get through the day without thinking about Luc's next email.

By the time I get home I am a bag of nerves, restless and unable to eat. I sleep very little that night, getting up six times to go to the bathroom. I spend most of the night staring out of the window at the clear moon in the sky, wondering what the weather is like in Spitsbergen and hoping we have not missed the last trajectory before the polar ice melts too much to take the weight of a rescue plane.

At breakfast the next morning I am irritable; the chatter of my three daughters fails to distract me from my hope that Luc will have good news for me today. By midday, I am feverish with excitement. I keep clicking on the email software with my mouse, willing Luc's next forecast to arrive. Then it appears.

From: Luc Trullemans
To: David Hempleman-Adams, Clive Bailey, Brian Jones
Sent: 09 May 2000 12:01
Subject: It was the good one!

So I am very disappointed because the track of this morning was a good one between 12,000ft and 16,000ft. This explain the difficulty I have to make a precise forecast for more than 72 hours in the area. In this case I found only the first sign of a good trajectory Sunday afternoon (−40h) with a confirmation yesterday morning (at −24h). We have to think over all this.

Weather outlook for Thursday until Saturday 13/5/2000.
For the next days, I have too much wind at surface and
still bad trajectories at higher levels. The wind would only
decrease next Sunday . . .
Next news tomorrow at 14Z.

Luc has voiced the concern that has been building at the
back of my mind. The weather over the Pole is so unpredictable that he cannot forecast it more than three days
in advance, and I am too far away from Spitsbergen to be
able to react sufficiently swiftly to such a rapid change in
wind direction. With tension building at home and people
constantly phoning to find out if I have left yet, I decide I
have to go and wait in Spitsbergen. It takes some
persuading to get Cameron Balloons to let Gavin Hailes,
the launch director, go, but eventually they do. By 15
May, the entire team is encamped at a guesthouse in
Longyearbyen.

Moving to Spitsbergen turns out to be one of the best
decisions I have made. The wind direction is still no use –
the current track would carry the balloon directly to
Warsaw – but at last I am actually doing something
positive rather than stagnating behind a desk in England.
Outside it is bitterly cold, –15°C, but nothing compared
to what I have experienced in other parts of the Arctic.
Spitsbergen is near the Norway Current, a branch of the
North Atlantic Drift, itself an extension of the Gulf
Stream that brings warm water up from the Gulf of
Mexico to the North Atlantic. The current keeps the
islands much warmer than they ought to be at this
latitude, but the ground and buildings are still covered by
snow. The fjord is iced over, it is stormy, and the main
form of transportation is the snowmobile, but I'm pleased
to be here. Now that we are in Spitsbergen we have a
chance to get everything ready to launch at short notice,
and I can stock up on sleep.

Having recently returned from sleep-deprivation

training at the Centre for Human Sciences, part of the Defence Evaluation and Research Agency at Farnborough, I now know the value of a good night's kip. DERA told me I need to sleep for at least six and a half hours in every twenty-four hours, but I know that will be made very difficult by the featureless environment around the balloon, the round-the-clock sunlight and the cold. Consistent sleep deprivation will cause a total deterioration in my ability to perform even simple tasks, and I'll fail to react quickly and correctly to emergencies. A night without sleep, the sleep scientists told me, is equivalent to being over the drink-and-drive limit, with the same kind of symptoms: slurred speech, loss of memory and an inability to respond to stimuli. I am more worried about not being able to sleep in the balloon than about the cold or the loss of oxygen. It's the biggest challenge I face should the flight ever get going.

Atle Brakken, the harbour master, offers us the fire station as our headquarters soon after we arrive in Spitsbergen. He moves the fire engines out so that we have somewhere warm to work, although that is a relative term; the toilet is frozen over and the inside of the windows iced up.

And so Groundhog Day begins: get up; go through the checklist; shower; breakfast; check emails. Then, the rest of the morning to kill: modify the balloon equipment; practise filming; go through more checklists. For lunch, a bowl of soup at the café, followed by more preparations and checking in the afternoon: stow equipment; pack up the dinghy; check the sparkers on the gas burners; test the HF radio, the batteries, the Argos, the immersion suit and the bolt cutters; read and reread the ditching drills for water, mountains and ice. At the end of the day, supper, and then off to bed in the basket so that I can get used to sleeping cramped between the equipment.

This monotony continues for the rest of the week, and I begin really to appreciate the agonized waiting that Andrée went through on Dane's Island. The only thing that changes is the landscape as the Arctic winter gives way to the midnight sun and the launch site, which was solid ice, melts into a lake of water surrounded by brown mud that sticks to your boots like dog food. We move the launch site from beside the fjord, which would have provided a straightforward climb out of the valley, to a higher position on the school football field. It is a more complicated place from which to launch, but we have no other choice.

At least twice a day I poke my head out of the fire station window to look across at the power station nearby. Like Andrée, I am searching for a sign that the wind is blowing to the north. But every day the smoke from the power station chimney doggedly trails south. It makes me realize just how difficult it must have been for Andrée to take off with no more information than that offered by some flags flapping in the wind. At least we have one of the best meteorologists in the world working for us.

By the beginning of the second week, most of our visitors have flown back to England, leaving just a core of five in Spitsbergen. I, too, want to go home. As ever, I am torn between the hunger for adventure and solitude, and the pull of my family. I have been clambering up mountains or trekking across polar wastes every springtime since my eldest daughter Alicia was born. I love the challenge, but I desperately miss my wife and children, ironically more on the easy days than on the days when the going is particularly hard. When it's −50°C and the wind is blowing in my face, I am usually too exhausted to think much of home. All my attention is focused on survival. But when the sun is high in a cloudless sky and I am all alone in a stunning landscape, I wish Claire, Alicia, Camilla and Amelia were beside me to share the experience. And when I think of my daughters causing havoc at home, I wish I was there, doing what comes naturally for a dad.

Before he departs, David Newman, a marketing

manager with Britannic, suggests that we go for a walk. Britannic has been very supportive so far, but I fear they may be on the point of wondering when they will get a return for their money. We leave the guesthouse and head for the fire station, a half-hour walk down the bare, rocky valley. We are already in the last days of May and I had always said I would not fly after 1 June, when the ice at the Pole becomes extremely slushy and no rescue plane will countenance a pick-up. The Arctic pilots are especially jumpy at the moment because a Polish An-2 biplane sank through the ice at the Pole about ten days ago, leaving four Americans and a Norwegian stranded on top of the world.

David comes straight to the point. 'I know you're itching to go, but don't feel under any pressure from us. Don't take unnecessary risks because you're worried that we will not stand by you. If you say the weather is not right and there's no slot this year, then we will understand and continue to support you.'

It is just what I need to hear, and it comes at exactly the right time. I'm hugely relieved. Nevertheless, I don't want to give up yet. I have a hunch we will get a good slot soon.

'We've got everyone here and we've got all the kit ready,' I say. 'Let's take it up to June the tenth. It's way past a safe pick-up time, but as far as I'm concerned we've already passed the point of no return, so let's keep going.'

If things go wrong, I will have to trek back to 85° North latitude – some three hundred nautical miles from the Pole. Only then will I be within reach of a helicopter, if it can winch me off the ice. Even then, it will be touch and go. The helicopter will need to make several trips just to get to me from Spitsbergen – it would have to fly out and deposit two fuel caches before even attempting a rescue mission – and I'll have to abandon all my equipment on the ice. If the helicopter cannot make it, I tell David Newman, I'll wait for a passing icebreaker.

That afternoon, David flies back to England, leaving Gavin and me from the core project team in Spitsbergen.

Groundhog Day continues its monotonous grind, but at least the time allows me to familiarize myself totally with the kit and to get more sleep.

The next day we head up to Longyearbyen airport control tower to speak to Anton, the local meteorologist. He shows us a satellite map of the weather over the Pole. Gavin spots it first, pointing at a swirling band of cloud on the map. 'If that high pressure slipped down a little bit further, and then moved slightly to the east, we might be on,' he says. It's a long shot, but it could come right. However, Luc pays it no attention in his next meteorological briefing.

The following day we drive up to the control tower for another look at the satellite map. The high pressure has moved southeast, as we had hoped. And again Gavin is optimistic. 'It just needs to slip a little bit more. Keep your fingers crossed and it may do it.' But Luc's weather report email that evening again makes no mention of the anticyclone.

By Thursday, we have been following the anticyclone's movement for three days and I am a bundle of nerves. The satellite map at the control tower again shows it is moving southeast, towards Spitsbergen. I can bear the suspense no longer, so I call up Luc to ask him if there is a chance. He replies: 'Maybe Saturday.'

On Friday, the high starts to come round. Luc sends an email saying that it looks good. It sets my pulse racing.

From: Luc Trullemans
To: David Hempleman-Adams, Hempleman/Spitsbergen, Clive Bailey, Brian Jones
Sent: 26 May 2000 15:10
Subject: Best combination in tracks

This is one of the best combinations in tracks.
I worked it out with AVN06Z at first and continuing with

MRF00Z later on.

Everything happens around 2,000–3,000m with a start tomorrow around 17Z.

I will try the same job this evening with AVN12Z and will send you the results at 08Z00.

Be ready! We never knows that this will be confirmed!

Luc

We're on, it seems. Luc has identified a combination of two tracks – using meteorological computer models called AVN06Z and MRF00Z – that should carry me north. However, I cannot help thinking that we have been at this stage before, only to see the high-pressure zone collapse. I am not going to get my hopes up.

That evening, Luc's next set of calculations arrives by email.

From: Luc Trullemans
To: David Hempleman-Adams, Hempleman/Spitsbergen, Clive Bailey, Brian Jones
Sent: 26 May 2000 20:52
Subject: Its looking good

I worked a lot for you, my friends, and this are the results:
The weather on the ground will deteriorate Sunday night and early Monday with increasing winds and snowfall.

Before then, the windspeed will stay between 3 and 10 knots!

The best tracks I calculated were tomorrow afternoon between 12Z and 18Z.

The next trajectories are only examples and those heights can change a little bit during the next runs.

Some scenarios are possible, for example:
12Z NR17111 (between 1,700 and 1,900m) followed by NR17126 for 1,700m and going between 2,300 and 2,500m, followed by NR17123 for 1,900m and going between 1,300 and 1,700m.

15Z NR17141 (between 2,200 and 2,400m) followed by NR17145 for 2,200m and going between 2,200 and 2,400m, followed by NR17143 for 2,300m and going between 1,600 and 1,700m, followed by NR17147 for 2,400m and going between 1,600 and 1,800m.

18Z NR17115 (between 2,500 and 2,800m) followed by NR17131 for 2,700m and going between 1,900 and 2,100m, by NR17134 for 2,500m and going between 2,700 and 3,000m, by NR17137 for 2,800m and going between 1,500 and 1,700m.

It's nice but really sharp to do . . . I think it's workable.

Next update will happen tomorrow morning with AVN00Z at 9Z and tomorrow noon with the new MRF00Z around 12Z.

Continue your prayers, David!

Luc

This jumble of numbers and letters spells good news. The first number in each batch, as before, is the time; 12Z is midday GMT, 15Z is 3 p.m. GMT, and so on. Each code, such as NR17111, is a wind stream that Luc has calculated should carry *Britannic Challenger* north; these are called windtracks (NR simply stands for 'number'). The altitudes following each track, such as 1,700 and 1,900m, indicate the height range at which I should find that particular track; sometimes the altitude is exact, more often it is a rough guide or there is an alternative height at which I might find the track. And the sequence of tracks is the procession of wind streams I will need to catch to maintain a northern direction. At the end of the message, Luc has written that he will send a forecast prepared using the Aviation computer model for midnight GMT – that's AVN00Z – at nine o'clock tomorrow morning. The medium-range forecast from midnight GMT, or MRF00Z, will follow at midday tomorrow.

In short, Luc's message means that I should be able to take off tomorrow between midday and 6 p.m., although the ground winds will be tricky. The later I take off, the higher I will need to fly to catch a track to the north. I phone Luc.

'It's going to be difficult, David,' comes the response in his suave French accent. 'Do you think you can fly with the accuracy needed to catch the tracks?'

I am not confident, but I don't let Luc know it; I've already decided to go for the Pole come what may. The chances of everything coming right – zero ground winds, the right track to within sixty miles of the North Pole and then a suitable track to take me to Canada – are tiny, but nothing ventured, nothing gained.

'I won't know until I try,' I reply. 'It's in your hands. If you think the track's good, I'm going.'

Luc continues to work through the night, feeding satellite data into various forecasting models. Spotting a clean windtrack spinning out among all the movements of an anticyclone shooting around the globe is a phenomenally complex operation. The best track, he tells me, could carry the balloon to within about twenty-four nautical miles of the Pole. I've been this close to take-off before, only to see something scupper the launch, so again, I'm not getting my hopes up.

On Saturday morning, Luc sends his next email.

From: Luc Trullemans
To: David Hempleman-Adams, Hempleman/Spitsbergen, Clive Bailey, Brian Jones
Sent: 27 May 2000 11:28
Subject: Still looking good!

It's now or never!
The strato-cumulus clouds observed over the region have base around 300m and top around 500m.
The windspeed of 6 to 8 knots this noon will increase slowly this evening and exceed 10 knots next night.
Visibility will stay higher than 10km.
The temperature will stay around freezing level.

In attachment you will find the vertical sounding forecast for 12Z and 18Z over Longyearbyen.

After this general forecast I will write now about your potential flight to the north, based on AVN00Z!

Starting at 12Z the obliged level will be between 1,600 and 1,700m (take care of the hills in the north!).

At 14Z the level increases a little bit, around 1,900m.

At 16Z the level would be between 2,100 and 2,200m.

At 18Z it's between 2,300 and 2,400m.

Afterwards I think the windspeed will be too strong to inflate the balloon.

Those tracks are nice but very sharp in levels. If you take this slot, you must fly with the highest concentration and with constant look on the GPS and altimeter but I will bring you in 3 to 4 days up there.

For outlook in tracks, I need the MRF00Z this noon (around 10Z30).

Many thanks!
Luc

Like Luc, I really think this is going to be the one. It really is now or never, but before I have time to contemplate what lies ahead, the team is invited out for dinner for the first time since we've been in Spitsbergen. None of us wants to turn down the invitation to dinner with Anna Ekeblad and Jill Dalviken, both of whom work for the Spitsbergen tourist office. But we need to work through the night if we want to catch tomorrow's track. There is so much to do. Luc, who sends another email that evening, finally makes up our minds for us.

From: Luc Trullemans
To: David Hempleman-Adams, Hempleman/Spitsbergen, Clive Bailey, Brian Jones
Sent: 27 May 2000 18:12
Subject: Go for it!

Everything seems still OK.
This is looking good.
Start preparing.

Luc

The nerves in my stomach twist tighter. I just want to get the balloon off the ground and think about what to do next once it's in the air. However, before then, I've got a dinner party to attend.

While the other members of the team go off to buy chocolates and flowers, I head down to the church. I've been a couple of times before and, although I'm not at all religious, I feel compelled to make a visit. Something tells me we need some help. Inside the chapel, I take off my shoes and sit at the back while a girl practises the piano at the front, near the altar. It is a beautiful piece of music and it reminds me of home. As the melody swells around the church, I am filled with a certainty that I will take off and that the flight will go well. Everything comes together at that moment and I just know we will launch the balloon tomorrow. I don't know why or how I know it. It's probably just instinct, but it is an uncanny feeling of inevitability.

The girl finishes the piece and turns around. She looks startled, shocked that I am sitting at the back of the chapel, and she hesitates when I ask her to play it again. At first she refuses, saying she is too shy, but then she concedes. Again, it is beautiful. And again, I just know that tomorrow will be the day. All the pieces have fallen into place. I would lay money on it.

The dinner party with Anna and Jill is very subdued; the atmosphere is nervous and tense. There are seven people in the room, and we are all going through tomorrow in our heads. Hardly anybody drinks wine, as we know we'll need clear heads for the next twenty-four hours. I am on orange juice. While Anna and Jill serve a delicious meal of venison stew and vegetables, I am running off pre-flight checklists in my head and trying to gauge the earliest time I could leave without seeming impolite. I just want to go and get on with it, and I try to think of an excuse. Eventually, I abandon all attempts at politeness. 'I must go, I'm afraid. I need to prepare myself for tomorrow. It's not every day you get the chance to fly to the North Pole, and Luc says we may have a favourable weather slot.' Feeling a little guilty, I slope off to the fire station to get an early night. I'm in bed by nine o'clock with a promise from Gavin that he will wake me at six.

While I sleep, Gavin rounds up as many people as he can find to help him move the balloon envelope, lying packed up like a giant sausage outside the fire station. With the help of a dozen villagers, he carries it up the valley to the launch site, where he has already parked two containers that hold the launch kit.

At six in the morning on Sunday 28 May, Gavin wakes me. As usual, he is direct. 'Get your arse in gear, David. I'm off to prepare the oxygen equipment.'

The morning of reckoning has come; after waiting for so long, I am suddenly filled with apprehension. This is the riskiest challenge I have ever undertaken and it's not too late to abandon it. But before I dive into deeper intro-spection, there's more banging at my door.

'David! Up!' It's Gavin again. I pull myself out of my sleeping bag. Gavin looks exhausted, and I realize that it's too late to turn back. I owe it to him, if to nobody else, to launch today.

I dress quickly, taking care to make sure I have put my Z stone on beneath my protective Arctic clothing. I have worn the Z stone on every expedition since Mount Everest in 1993, when at Nanche Bazaar, the capital of the Khumbu region in Nepal, I ran into a former Sherpa climber who was running a tea shop and stall in the local market. He was selling Z stones, said to be lucky mascots for climbers, at two hundred dollars each, but I blanched at the price, not least because it was half the Nepalese average wage. I wanted to buy one of the stones, so I made a deal with the Sherpa. I would pay him fifty dollars

138

up front, and if I made it to the summit of Everest and the stone lived up to its claim of guaranteeing a safe return, I would pay him the rest. If I didn't make it to the top, the price would remain at fifty dollars. Neither of us spoke about the third option – if I did not make it back to Nanche Bazaar at all. He accepted the offer, I made it to the top and, quite delighted, I paid him the rest of the money. I also have a string of worry beads in my pocket given to me by Rajiv Wahi, the managing director of Typhoo. I carried them to the North Pole in 1998, so maybe they will help me get there again.

I stumble out of the fire station to find a group of Norwegians helping Gavin to transport *Britannic Challenger*'s basket to the launch site. It seems everybody in Longyearbyen wants to lend a hand. One of the locals even insists that he provides his heavy-lifting equipment for free. While breakfasting on my own, nerves rise up from my stomach and I struggle to finish my toast. I'm anxious and feeling intimidated by the danger. But more than anything, it is the scale of the endeavour that frightens me. I stop several times while eating to ask myself if I have taken on more than I can manage.

Then the wait for the next vital forecast begins. I have had my hopes dashed at the last minute twice before; two good forecasts, and then the third is a stand-down. At last, Luc's email comes through.

From: Luc Trullemans
To: David Hempleman-Adams, Hempleman/Spitsbergen, Clive Bailey, Brian Jones
Sent: 28 May 2000 09:26
Subject: Go

This is definitely the one.
The tracks are good but the wind will drop and if you do not get off by six o'clock you will have missed it.

Luc

I want to go immediately. I am desperate to take off and I don't want anything to get in the way. The whole village has started to rumble and attention is now fully focused on us. Up at the launch site, Gavin has inflated four small helium balloons and positioned one at each corner of the football field. 'To get this balloon off, they all have to be straight,' he tells me.

When I look at the balloons, there are only two. The wind has already ripped two of them out of the ground. It doesn't bode well. I remember the words of Yngvar Gjessing at the Polar Research Institute. Maybe he was right when he said, 'No, you just will not do it. It is impossible.' According to his records the ground winds average around twenty-five knots from March to June.

At the back of my mind is the concern that I will have only one shot at this. There will be no going back once we start pumping the helium into the balloon. No second chance. I just hope it does not end up like one of Richard Branson's attempts to fly around the world. That would be disastrous.

The launch site is bedlam. Gavin has come into his own, issuing orders and getting all the equipment together in the right place at the right time. He is the only person who knows the precise sequence in which things have to be done. The police cordon off the football field with tape and stand guard. It seems the entire population, a thousand souls, has turned out to watch. Meanwhile, I am without transport, running up and down the valley, wearing myself out and feeling aggrieved that we only have a few hired cars.

At midday, Gavin and I head up to the airport for a briefing on the ground winds. The tower meteorologist tells us that we have only until about six o'clock. Any later and the ground winds will be too strong to take off. I'm very worried that we will miss the last chance this year to get a good track to the Pole, particularly as Gavin looks concerned as we drive back to the launch site.

'I don't know if I can get the balloon inflated by six o'clock,' he says. 'There's not enough time.'

It is not what I want to hear. I look him in the eye. 'You can't let me down now. You've got to do it.'

Gavin, as ever, is direct. 'Then you have got to make a decision now. I can start pumping the helium in straight away, but once I start inflating the balloon, that's it. No going back. You take off, whatever the last-minute forecast says. Do you want me to start or not?'

I think of Andrée and how he prevaricated in the last moments, wondering if he was embarking on a suicide mission. But I know that if Andrée was in my position, he would go, and I feel the same. I've waited two years for this moment, and I'm not going to give up now.

'We've *got* to go,' I say, 'whatever the conditions. I have no choice.'

Gavin grins at me, a twinkle in his eye. I can tell he is as excited as I am. 'Right,' he says. 'Let's do it.'

Within minutes the valley is filled with a screeching sound, like a banshee. It is the helium entering the valve at high pressure to inflate the balloon. The envelope rises slowly, gradually taking shape on its side until it lifts off the ground and half the population of Spitsbergen is holding onto ropes to prevent it taking off.

I'm relieved that everything around me is a hive of activity. I cannot bear to think about what lies ahead, and thankfully I don't have the time to focus on anything else but the rapidly approaching moment of take-off. But before then, there's a lot to be done.

Colin Hill, a friend who has flown out to Spitsbergen to see me depart, wants me to talk to Manx Radio, his local radio station. I manage to bark a few words into a mobile phone, hoping that the interviewer at the other end of the line understands that I am very stressed. Colin then hands me a flower, thinking it appropriate for an Englishman to wear a rose on a flight. I remember that Andrée, Frænkel and Strindberg wore roses, and take it from Colin, hoping it will prove a good talisman.

The governor turns up for a chat just at the moment of greatest pre-flight panic, when I am trying to rattle through my pre-pre-flight checklists, my pre-flight checklist and my pre-take-off checklist. I speak briefly to him, knowing that he has it in his power to deny me permission to take off. Thankfully, he gives *Britannic Challenger* full clearance. I then tie a replica of Andrée's flag, given to me by the Andrée Museum, to the balloon. It is a combination of the Swedish union flag and the Norwegian flag. Below it, I string a Canadian flag, a Russian flag, the Stars and Stripes and a British union flag. They are the flags of all the nations where I may have to land, plus my national flag. I'll need all the goodwill I can muster.

The closer the clock ticks to six o'clock, the deeper the pit at the bottom of my stomach. Several times I think I am going to throw up; my nerves are getting the better of me. Gavin comes over and assures me the nausea will subside once I am in the air. It is nerves of anticipation more than anything else, but I am suddenly gripped by a fear that, like Andrée, I may be embarking on this dangerous journey only because the world's spotlight is now focused on me. Do I have to go? Have I reached the point of no return? Is this foolhardy? These questions race around my mind. After all, nobody has managed to fly a balloon to the North Pole before. Surely there must be a reason.

I am a novice balloonist, and I know that sometimes a little knowledge is a dangerous thing. Does this mean I am looking at this flight too simplistically? Is it unrealistic to hope to do this in a basket? I am daunted by what lies ahead and plagued by very strong doubts about my own capabilities. Do I have the right knowledge of what I need to do? I ask myself. After all, I've never flown a Roziere balloon before. All I have is the licence, but the test was entirely theoretical. This could be the most stupid thing I've ever attempted, I tell myself, and immediately I scuttle into the empty container that held the helium tanks to reread in private Don Cameron's notes on how to fly the balloon.

The notes remind me that a Roziere balloon, which has a helium cell inside a hot-air envelope, is not as responsive as a hot-air balloon. The gas cell can break if you go up too fast and the main difficulty is levelling off at the right height. Gavin has meticulously weighed everything to get me to a ceiling of 8,000ft, where Luc says I should find the track north – provided I don't crash into the side of one of the very steep mountains that encircle the launch area.

At six o'clock *Britannic Challenger* is fully inflated and around a hundred people are holding ropes to prevent the gusts of wind coming down the mountains from blowing the balloon down the valley. I change into my expedition kit: three layers of thermals below my immersion suit, an orange neoprene one-piece ensemble with a chunky zip, integral gloves and shoes, and tight seals to keep the water out. Over the top of the suit, I pull on a jacket stitched with my sponsor's logo badges.

After a quick chat with the governor, I do some television and radio interviews. Gradually, it occurs to me that this massive gathering – the villagers, the officials, the television and radio crews, and the journalists – is here because they know there is as much chance of this going horribly wrong as there is of it succeeding. It's a chilling thought, and I quickly banish it to the back of my mind. Then I bid farewell to my team and to Atle, Anna and Jill, who have come to watch the launch.

The hardest moment comes when Gavin steps forward to say bon voyage. We have worked long and hard on this project and he has devoted all his time and loyalty to it. I know that he wants more than anything to join me in the basket, arguing that two people would be better so that one person can sleep while the other navigates, but he bites his lip and just tells me to give it my best shot.

'How do you feel, David?' Gavin asks me.

'Sick. I feel like I'm about to throw up. Sometimes I think we're attempting the impossible.'

'If it was easy, David, it would have been done,' he says, and turns away.

It's what I need to hear. He's right. It brings me to my senses and whets my appetite for the challenge. 'He's right!' I tell myself quietly in the basket. 'Many have tried, but nobody has succeeded. This is my chance to claim this challenge as a first. I'm going to do it.'

The countdown starts and passes in a blur. Before I have time to think about what lies ahead, Gavin cuts the rope and *Britannic Challenger* takes off, at 6.05 p.m. local time (1605 GMT), rising very slowly into the sky. As the spectators become smaller beneath me, I try to think of Andrée, and Claire and the children at home, but I am seized with dread. I stand in the basket, watching the ground recede. I am frozen in position, unable to do anything but gaze out at the spectacle, marvelling at the snow-covered mountains and the fjord below me. After a few minutes, the ground disappears as I enter the clouds, and I am brought to my senses by the cold, clammy fog all around me.

I pull out the satellite phone to contact Brian Jones and Clive Bailey at the control centre, but before I can get to work I emerge through the top of the cloud and spot a 6,000ft-high mountain less than a mile away. I need to gain height quickly, so I reach down to release some ballast. But when I look over the side, it all comes rushing up at me. For the first time in my life, I am suffering from vertigo. I've climbed mountains over 20,000ft high and never had a problem. Now, when I am on my own for a week or more, at heights of up to 30,000ft, I feel giddy whenever I look towards the ground. Sprinkling some ballast sand over the side, I grit my teeth and close my eyes. My immediate concern is to get clear of the mountains; I'll deal with the causes of the vertigo later. As *Britannic Challenger* climbs higher into the blue sky and the peaks spread out around me, I realize that I am able to cope with my nausea as long as I stare ahead at the horizon. But if I look down, I feel queasy, as if a wind is whooshing up from the emptiness beneath the basket.

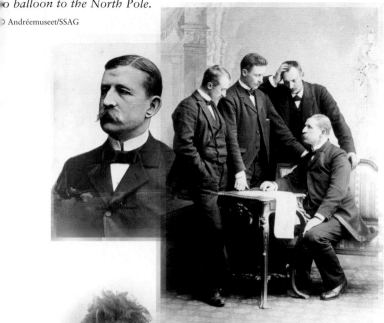

Salomon August Andrée in 1897, shortly before embarking on his second attempt to balloon to the North Pole.

© Andréemuseet/SSAG

ABOVE: *The 1897 expedition team. From left: Nils Strindberg, Knut Frænkel, Vilhelm Svedenborg and (seated) Salomon Andrée.*

© Andréemuseet/SSAG

The two women in Andrée's life: his mother, Wilhelmina, and Gurli Linder, whose love for him was unrequited.

Andréemuseet/SSAG; © Tekniska Museet, Stockholm/photo Andréemuseet/SSAG

The engaged couple: Anna Charlier and Nils Strindberg.

© Andréemuseet/SSAG

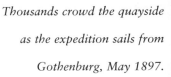

Thousands crowd the quayside as the expedition sails from Gothenburg, May 1897.

© Andréemuseet/SSAG

A crew member of the Svensksund (left) and Alexis Machuron prepare for a hunt before the launch on Dane's Island, June 1897.

© Roger-Viollet, Paris

ABOVE: Kapa Allt! *Andrée, Frænkel and Strindberg in the hangar shortly before the launch on 11 July, 1897.*

© Andréemuseet/SSAG

LEFT: *The top of the* Eagle *pokes out of its hangar on Dane's Island, July 1897.*

© Roger-Viollet, Paris

The Eagle *rises ponderously into the air and, watched*

anxiously by the men on shore, moves out across the bay.

The ropes trailing in its wake are the ballast lines.

The Eagle *disappears over the horizon and out of sight for ever. The wood in the foreground is the remains of the hangar, which had to be dismantled on take-off.*

© Roger-Viollet, Paris

Andrée and Frænkel in front of the beached Eagle *on the polar ice, 14 July, 1897. Strindberg is behind the camera.*

© Roger-Viollet, Paris

Andrée and Frænkel haul the canvas boat across the ice on the way towards Cape Flora, July 1897.

© Andréemuseet/SSAG

Camp: a canvas tent with a single sleeping bag and a boat strapped to a sledge were the only protection the three men had against the bitterly cold wind. © Andréemuseet/SSAG

Big-game hunters: Frænkel and Strindberg stand over a polar bear, 30 August, 1897. © Andréemuseet/SSAG

ABOVE: *Stockholm, September 1930. A day of national mourning at the state funeral of Andrée, Strindberg and Frænkel.* © Andréemuseet/SSAG

LEFT: *A page from Strindberg's notebook with navigational calculations and a description of the halo effect of the sun, 22 August, 1897.*

© Andréemuseet/SSAG

BELOW LEFT: *Details of the dinner to celebrate the King's birthday on the ice in Strindberg's Almanac 18 September, 1897.* © Andréemuseet/SSAG

BELOW RIGHT: *The gold locket Anna gave Strindberg on his twenty-fifth birthday. Inside was her picture and a lock of her hair.* © Andréemuseet/SSAG

After about half an hour, the wind catches the balloon and I start to track, although I do not know in which direction I am headed. I test the burners – they work – and unfold the microwave link to the television crew that should be chasing me in a helicopter. I unreel about a hundred feet of aerial for the high-frequency radio and try to contact Stuart Nunn and Gavin on the ground below, using the VHF radio. There is no response, so I switch to HF and try to contact the control centre. Silence. Then I attempt to speak to the tower at Longyearbyen airport, but again the airwaves are silent. I switch to the satellite phone. It also doesn't work. This is odd. I work out that I am tracking west and approaching the airport, so I try the tower again. They cannot hear me even when I am flying directly overhead. This is bad news. I switch on my GPS satellite navigator, but it also does not work. Likewise the Magellan, which is meant to send emails, and the Orbicom, which should transmit my latitude, longitude and altitude back to the control centre. I've been in the air for less than an hour and already the flight is in jeopardy. All I know is that I am tracking in a vaguely westward direction, but neither I nor anyone else knows where I am headed. I have no navigation equipment and no communications. I am worse off than Andrée – at least he had some pigeons.

Unable to take instruction from the control centre on which course to take to avoid crashing into the mountains, I rely on instinct. It's easier said than done the first time you fly out of a fjord surrounded on all sides by 6,000ft peaks. I don't know in which direction I am flying, so I decide to play it safe. I climb to 10,500ft, and then continue up to 11,000ft to be sure of crossing any mountains ahead. For the next half an hour, I keep trying the communications equipment, vowing to ditch the balloon if the comms do not work by the time the coast of Spitsbergen is in sight. It's all very well having all this technology, but it's not much good if it is faulty, and I don't want to venture beyond the shores of Spitsbergen out of contact. The futility of flying without communications or navigation equipment is brought home when the helicopter turns up to film. I cannot get my VHF radio to work, so I cannot speak to the pilot, nor can I send any television pictures via the microwave link.

After about ninety minutes, I decide there is nothing I can do about my lack of communications, and that it would be better simply to relax. I sit down on my coolbox to take some photographs while the balloon tracks gracefully through the mountains. It is astoundingly beautiful. The clouds clear, and I can see the ground. I pull out my GPS again in the hope that it may start working, and to my relief the readout shows that I have covered about ten miles. There's more good news. The track is heading north, and I manage to locate my position on a map, which I confirm with visual sightings of the mountains around me.

But I still have no communications, and without my briefings from Luc Trullemans I am flying blind. I check the seals, hood and whistle on my immersion suit. I might need it to save my life. Without it, I'll last no more than about three minutes if I have to ditch in the water. With my thermals on underneath the suit, I should be able to survive for about an hour in the freezing water. I also check that my life-raft is ready and fitted with its foam insulator mat and thermorest mattress. I stuff some flares into the raft and make sure the emergency location transmitter is working. I'm taking no chances.

At 8 p.m., I manage at last to get the HF radio to work. It's a massive relief when I hear the voice of Stockholm Radio come through the speaker. I give them my position.

'Seventy-eight degrees and thirty-six minutes north; fifteen degrees and fifteen minutes east. I'm at ten thousand two hundred feet on a heading of three-five-one degrees, flying at twelve and a half knots. Please inform *Britannic Challenger* control centre.'

Ninety minutes later, I hear the chirpy voice of Clive Bailey, patched through from Birmingham by Stockholm

Radio. I give him my new position – nineteen nautical miles further north than the position I gave Stockholm Radio earlier – and tell him that most of my communications equipment is down.

'So what are you going to do, Old Man?' he asks.

'I was going to ask you that question, Boy,' I reply.

'It's your call while you're still over Spitsbergen and can see where you might land. I'm not entirely sure where you're heading.'

I tell Clive to rely on the Argos transmitter for my position, but he tells me that the control centre is having trouble receiving data from it. The Argos is meant to pinpoint my position to within one hundred yards and send the reading via satellite to Washington DC, and then on, via email, to Birmingham. We decide to switch the Argos to its emergency setting to see if that will prompt the system to work. After more than three hours in the air, I am still worried that my comms could fail again at any time, but for the moment, the panic is nearly over.

My next task is to get the autopilot working, but I am having trouble with the burners. The slightest touch on the controls and *Britannic Challenger* shoots up five hundred feet or more. This sensitivity makes it impossible to set the autopilot to a particular altitude because a single blast of the burners takes the balloon off the track it is supposed to be following.

I make several attempts to set the autopilot, including approaching the altitude I want from below, in the hope that by the time *Britannic Challenger* stops rising it will be on the correct track and will lock on to it. None of my various attempts works. At 11 p.m., I speak to the control centre and tell them I do not trust the autopilot. Clive tells me to keep playing with it, as I will not be able to sleep until I've got it mastered.

'You know what to do, Old Man. I told you months ago. RTFM – you know what that means, don't you?' he says.

'Yes, Boy. Read the effing manual.' And with Clive's reprimand ringing in my ears, I pull out the laminated instruction booklet, but it is of little help. Clive promises he will call the autopilot manufacturer in America for guidance.

Shortly after midnight, he radios me with directions on how to set the autopilot and strict instructions to get some sleep. I'm still buzzing on the adrenalin rush of the launch and not feeling at all tired, but Clive warns that it will soon catch up with me.

The autopilot manufacturer suggests switching off one burner completely and turning off the fuel line to the other burner. This should enable the autopilot to set itself. If it tries to blast the burners, nothing will happen, I'm told, and it should be able to lock on to an altitude without the balloon shooting up. I try it, and it works. Great. It fixes on my chosen altitude of 9,800ft. I turn one of the burners on, but only by a third so that any adjustment made by the autopilot will be subtle. At last I can relax a little and take in the view.

My reverie is brief. At 1 a.m., Clive radios to say that Luc has sent an urgent message instructing me to descend to 6,000ft in one hour's time in order to maintain the track north. At 3 a.m., Clive radios with another set of tracks. Luc has calculated tracks of 12° east of north at 8,200ft, 7° east of north at 7,700ft, 19° east of north at 6,000ft and 355° at 4,000ft. Clive advises me to stay at 4,000ft if possible. I'm tired, becoming confused in the featureless landscape, and I'm over open water, so a low altitude is probably safest as I will not need to use supplementary oxygen.

I keep going through the night, feeling tired but unable to sleep under the Arctic sun and fraught with unease that the autopilot is still not working all that well. I have little appetite and cannot face my Arctic rations. Instead, I eat the sandwiches and mushroom soup that I packed in Spitsbergen and keep my fingers crossed until shortly after seven o'clock in the morning of Monday 29 May, when I beat the British solo endurance record of thirteen hours.

It is a wonderful moment, but I have little time to savour it. So much lies ahead.

CHAPTER SEVEN

THE DEPARTURE

VIRGOHAMNA, NORWEGIAN HIGH ARCTIC

21 June, 1897

A NORTHEAST WIND WHISTLED AROUND THE RICKETY balloon hangar as Nils Strindberg sat alone in the semi-darkness, thinking of Anna and writing to his brother. It was nine o'clock in the evening and the only light came from the midnight sun outside, squeezing through the cracks between the wooden planks of the hangar. But Strindberg dared not light a candle or a paraffin lamp during his watch; a few feet away the hydrogen apparatus was pumping its highly flammable gas into the massive envelope that cowered nearby, half-inflated like a lump of spongy dough.

I can't help thinking how lovely it will be to come home. I know my little Anna is sad now, but how happy we will be when we're together again, he wrote, before telling Tore about the expedition's struggle to get to Virgohamna and of their many difficulties while preparing for the launch.

* * *

On 18 May, he, Andrée and their new third man, Knut Frænkel, had left Gothenburg aboard the *Svensksund*, a Swedish gunboat. Like the year before, they had departed in front of a crowd of tens of thousands, but in place of their former naïve optimism, Strindberg and his two companions were gripped by a grim determination to get it right this time. All on board the *Svensksund* – including Lieutenant Wilhelm Svedenborg, the mission's back-up man should any of the three adventurers drop out, and Alexis Machuron, the balloon specialist who had replaced his uncle, Henri Lachambre – knew it was judgement time: they had to come back with the Pole conquered or not return at all.

Watching Gothenburg disappear in the haze of the horizon, Strindberg thought back to his last moments with Anna in Stockholm. As the *Svensksund* wound its way northwards along the long Swedish and Norwegian coast to Tromsö, he fingered the art exhibition tickets he'd put in his waistcoat pocket. They were a memento of their last evening when they had chatted excitedly, both aware that they had little time left together. Back then, Strindberg had thought it impossible to imagine not being with or seeing Anna every day; now, those months since the engagement spent almost constantly in each other's company felt like another lifetime. Already Anna seemed a million miles away, particularly as the only way to keep in touch was by letter. Strindberg regretted not looking from his coach at Anna standing on the steps of his parents' house on the morning he left for the station. He might never see her again, and he wished he could turn the clock back so that he could see whether her last glimpse of him was through a veil of tears or with a beguiling smile on her lips.

Once he had arrived at Gothenburg, Strindberg had watched as the balloon, its net, the gondola, the draglines and the hydrogen apparatus were stowed in the *Svensksund*'s hold. A steam engine and all the expedition's provisions were on board the *Virgo*, destined to meet with the *Svensksund* at Tromsö on 27 May. All their equipment had been reassessed and, although Andrée was reluctant to admit it publicly, Strindberg knew that he had smarted at Ekholm's criticisms of their previous attempt and had incorporated changes that should improve the *Eagle*'s chances of success. The balloon now sported two additional chambers around its equator; this buoyancy-boosting belt increased its volume from 159,000 to 170,000 cubic feet. It was enough, Andrée insisted, to ensure a thirty-day flight despite Ekholm's continuing claims to the contrary.

There was another change: Knut Frænkel. The third man of the expedition was an unknown quantity, but Strindberg had met him several times since Andrée had awarded him his place and had come to like him. If nothing else, Strindberg was relieved that at twenty-six, Frænkel was closer to his age than Ekholm and Andrée. An extremely athletic engineer, Frænkel had spent much of the last six months in Paris; when he was not making the requisite nine balloon flights to master the necessary piloting skills, Frænkel had spent much of his time dealing with the attentions of the press, which was still intensely interested in everything to do with their polar attempt. Strindberg and Frænkel in particular were amazed that polished copies of themselves and Andrée were on display at Madame Tussaud's waxworks in London.

On 30 May, three days after slipping their moorings at Tromsö, the *Svensksund* and *Virgo* arrived at Dane's Island. The voyage had been mercifully free of ice but, as they approached Virgohamna, they encountered pack ice of the densest kind, wedged into the natural harbour by the sea currents and the northerly wind. Strindberg had spent much of the voyage photographing the two ships, and his first view of the familiar black granite mountains of Dane's Island was through his large camera. Lifting his head from the viewfinder, he turned to Frænkel.

'So you see it now for the first time, Knut. What do you think?'

Frænkel looked up at the black granite mountains and down towards the shingle-covered beach. 'If I could start a balloon journey anywhere, this would be the last place I would choose. But that's the thrill of the challenge, isn't it?'

Strindberg looked out at the familiar curve of the bay. It was an unwelcoming place, all hard black rock and white ice edges around the mountain bowl. 'Returning to Dane's Island brings back the uncomfortable memory of failure from last year, but this time I feel it will be different,' he replied. 'We know what we have to do to be ready, and we are here earlier. There should be plenty of time to catch a wind to the north.'

But to Andrée, the sight of Dane's Island was one that filled him with dread. 'It's impassable! We will have to wait for weeks until the ice melts,' he shouted to Count Ehrensvärd, the skipper of the *Svensksund*.

Ehrensvärd simply smiled beatifically at Andrée and issued an order for the stern tanks to be filled with water. With her bow raised high, the *Svensksund*'s propeller sank beneath the ice. Strindberg watched in astonishment as the gunship pushed ahead. The pack ice creaked, groaned and squealed as it was forced apart by the boat's metal hull. Even so, it took the best part of a day for the *Svensksund*, with the *Virgo* following in her wake, to force her way to within sight of the shore.

Andrée paced the deck, Frænkel fidgeted and Strindberg's stomach churned as they waited for the first sight of the balloon hangar. Would it have survived the ravages of an Arctic winter? Strindberg wondered. He knew that winds of forty to fifty knots had blown for months on end, whipping up shards of ice that became wood-piercing projectiles. 'There is every chance the balloon hangar will need rebuilding from the ground up,' he told Frænkel.

At last they spotted two flagstaffs. If the posts still stood, Andrée told Strindberg and Frænkel, their balloon hangar should have survived. At 7 p.m. the *Svensksund* and *Virgo* weighed anchor near Arnold Pike's shelter and the three men set off to examine the damage to the hangar. Strindberg joined the crews as they clambered from the ships onto the ice floating in the bay, leaping from floe to floe until they reached the solid plate of ice bedecking the beach, whooping with triumph when they eventually set foot on the rocky upper shore.

Andrée, however, considered himself too grand to scramble across the tumbling ridges and insisted on being ferried in one of the *Svensksund*'s boats. Photographing the procession, Strindberg looked upon his companion's reticence bemusedly; he knew that Andrée would consider climbing over ice an unnecessarily risky action, but he also knew many of the other onlookers would regard his insistence on being conveyed by boat as ridiculous. The six sailors charged with rowing the boat struggled to dip the paddles of their oars in the water. Eventually, they gave up, instead using their oars to push against the ice, slowly inching the boat towards the frozen beach. In the boat, Andrée, Frænkel, Svedenborg, Machuron and two other passengers sat out the short journey, which dissolved into utter farce when the *Svensksund* fired a salvo of six cannon shots as Andrée stepped ashore.

Ignoring the pomp, Andrée hiked up to the balloon hangar, where he found much of its wooden structure encased in six feet of snow and ice. Much to everyone's relief, the parts of the structure that could be seen seemed to have escaped relatively unscathed.

But there was still a lot of work to be done. Over the next fortnight, the carpenters worked on the balloon hangar while the other members of the expedition hauled the equipment and supplies onto land. It was gruelling work, but Strindberg welcomed it as a distraction from thoughts of Anna. For Frænkel, the preparations could not be completed fast enough. He wrote to his brother of his frustration: *Brother Haakan, Life is humdrum. We rise at 8.30, except Andrée and the crew, who start at 6.30. Breakfast is awful. Rotten eggs for those who want them, tea without cream unless you take condensed milk – disgusting. Then we work on the balloon hangar or the hydrogen apparatus and take observations and so forth until our twelve o'clock lunch. After this I go back to work or perhaps go hunting with one of the officers until 6 p.m. Sometimes during these outings we find the remains of old Dutch fishermen who tried their luck in the northern wastes; a gruesome sight.*

Under Andrée's orders, the ice in the bay was dynamited to make the passage between the ships and the shore more accessible, but moving the eighty tons of sulphuric acid and twenty-three tons of iron filings needed to produce the hydrogen appeared back-breaking to Strindberg as he photographed the men laboriously carrying them up to the boat house.

Two days later, when the open water between the boats and shore had refrozen into an even more chaotic jumble of blocks than before, Strindberg photographed the expedition's ten strongest members attempting to haul the *Eagle*'s envelope ashore. Under Machuron's direction, the men hacked a channel through the ice and then tried to drag the envelope, wrapped in sacking like a two-ton sausage, through it. It took them more than a day, an ordeal made worse by two pressure ridges, which they blew apart by ramming dynamite deep into their cracks. Eventually, with the help of Frænkel and another ten men hauling on ropes, they managed to drag the balloon up planks smeared with animal fat to the balloon hangar. At last, on 15 June, the envelope was spread out on the wooden floor of the hangar and inflation could begin.

'Before it is filled with hydrogen, the envelope must be tested to ensure it has no leaks,' Andrée insisted.

As well as having the envelope enlarged in Paris, he had addressed Ekholm's concern that gas was leaking through the millions of needle holes along the balloon's seams. Extra strips of silk had been fixed to the seams like sticky bandages. Under Machuron's guidance, the colossal envelope was pumped full of air and nine of the

Svensksund's crew crawled inside the globe to cauterize the strips with a rubber varnish. Strindberg checked on the work several times, marvelling at the stamina of the men who would work for ten or twelve hours without a break and emerge gasping for fresh air, intoxicated by the fumes of the varnish.

With the seams sealed, the hydrogen apparatus was fired up. On 21 June, Strindberg took his turn watching the hydrogen being pumped into the gasbag. Slowly the lighter hydrogen expelled the heavier air from the *Eagle*'s envelope as Strindberg continued his letter to his brother Tore: *It is strange sitting here, this year again, thinking that I am betrothed to the best girl in the world, my beloved Anna. I may weep at the happiness lost which I may never see again, but my tears do not matter as long as Anna is happy. She loves me and I am proud that she might be moved by my death. But let me be optimistic. The balloon is varnished and more airtight than last year. The summer stretches out before us with good winds and sunlight. Why should we not succeed? I believe wholeheartedly we will.*

A few days later, the balloon stood fully inflated, straining at its mooring ropes in the hangar. Strindberg took more photographs as the sailors clambered up and over it, holding strips of cotton soaked in lead acetate along its seams to detect any trace of a leak. As a scientist, he knew that sulphur impurities in the gas would turn the lead acetate black and indicate where the *Eagle* had a leak. To his relief there were few escapes, and as the day drew on the crew and sailors gathered to celebrate with champagne. The groundwork had gone relatively well, and for the first time since he arrived at Dane's Island, Strindberg felt his spirits lift at the thought of getting underway at last. With Andrée and Frænkel, he had spent the last few days massaging Vaseline into the guide ropes, a task that left all three of them with swollen hands covered in a mass of blisters, bruises and cuts.

At last the gondola was attached to the balloon, filled with its equipment and provisions, and the final stage of pre-flight preparation began. Everyone worked on, stopping only at midsummer's night. The two ships' crews, the engineers, carpenters and labourers, the balloon experts and gas technicians, and, of course, Strindberg, Andrée and Frænkel commemorated the occasion by drinking 530 pints of beer donated by a Gothenburg brewery. Trestle tables were set up on the rocky beach. Some of the men sang or played guitars, accordions or violins, and with the Arctic midnight sun circling overhead, they toasted the three balloonists, wishing them good fortune on the journey ahead. Strindberg took photographs of it all.

On 25 and 27 June, the *Express* and the *Lofoten*, two tourist steamers, called in at Virgohamna. The *Virgo* had already departed, taking many of the sailors with it, and Andrée in particular resented the intrusion of sightseers, but Strindberg bounded over to them.

'Have you got any mail for Nils Strindberg?' he demanded of the captain of the *Lofoten*. 'I am expecting letters from Stockholm.'

The captain pulled out a sheath of letters, and within them Strindberg found several from Anna.

'Can I persuade you to take some letters back to Sweden?' Strindberg asked. 'I have two or three that are most urgent and which cannot wait until the expedition returns to Tromsö.'

'I'll come to a deal with you. The *Lofoten* will carry your post to Sweden under the proviso that some of her passengers can wait in the bay on the *Express* until your balloon has launched. They have come all this way; they would not like to leave before the main event.'

'I shall speak to Chief Engineer Andrée. It is his decision as to who sees the launch. If he says yes, he will expect something in return,' Strindberg said, before setting out to find Andrée.

Strindberg returned to the *Lofoten* a short while later.

'Chief Engineer Andrée agrees, provided the *Express* carries Svedenborg, our fourth man, to the Seven Islands after the *Eagle* launches, so that he can set up an emergency depot of provisions as far north as possible.'

The two captains consented. The *Lofoten* left a few days later, but the *Express* remained anchored in the bay, watching, until at last, on 1 July, the *Eagle* was ready to fly. It was considerably later than Andrée, Strindberg and Frænkel had hoped, but Strindberg consoled himself with the fact that at least they were ready earlier than the year before. All the seams had been thoroughly tested, all their equipment was stowed and Andrée declared the mission ready to depart whenever a southerly wind arrived to carry them north. Once again, they waited for the wind to turn.

On 6 July, the shout came.

'A southerly wind! The wind is from the south!' the lookout yelled. The wind, which for weeks had been blowing from the northwest or northeast, had veered round so that it was blowing directly to the north. The launch crew were put on immediate standby, the balloon topped up with hydrogen and the technicians given notice that they should be ready to remove the north wall of the balloon hangar.

Andrée spent the day running between the balloon hangar, his meteorological instruments and Arnold Pike's shelter, which he had again commandeered as the mission headquarters. Everything appeared to be ideal for a launch: the wind was in the right direction, and the barometer was falling.

'These are perfect conditions, aren't they? We should launch,' Strindberg said as Andrée tapped the barometer yet again with his pen. He was surprised that Andrée had not already sent them running to the balloon hangar. 'Are these not the conditions you said we needed for the *Eagle* to launch?' he persisted. 'You said we needed a southerly wind and falling atmospheric pressure. We've got both.'

'Call the crew,' Andrée answered. 'I have an announcement to make.'

The entire contingent of expedition members and onlookers assembled outside the makeshift headquarters in Pike's hut, waiting for Andrée to step out and speak to them. After a short wait, he appeared.

'The wind has come too quickly and the barometer is falling too fast. I think it best if we postpone our launch,' he declared.

A murmur of disappointment spread through the ranks, but it soon became clear that Andrée had made the right decision. Within hours the wind increased to gale force, whining through the steel cables securing the wooden balloon hangar to the narrow strip of land in front of the black granite cliff. As the balloon hangar behind them shook through the night, the technicians on watch outside it struggled to stand upright at their posts.

In the early hours of the following morning, when the wind was at its fiercest, Strindberg joined a group of men trying to keep the *Eagle* from slipping its moorings inside the hangar. It was a terrifying sight.

'Hydrogen is clearly escaping!' Strindberg shouted to the men. 'The smallest spark will send everything up in a cataclysmic blast!'

'Tighten the cables! Tighten the cables or we will lose the balloon!' Andrée shouted, but his words were lost in the howling gale.

Even with five tons of sand ballast, the *Eagle* continued to rise and fall by more than six feet in the hangar. Several times it threatened to break free of its moorings. Beneath the dark shadow of the *Eagle*, Strindberg, Andrée and a team of more than a dozen men struggled to fasten the carrying-ring of the envelope to the floor of the hangar. For hours they fought to control the giant wavering orb. Eventually, exhausted and drenched by driving rain, they anchored the *Eagle* with ropes and nets so that it could move neither up and down nor sideways. By 4 a.m., their battle was over. The storm had died down to be replaced, with depressing predictability, by a breeze from the north.

Routine returned to Dane's Island over the next days. Only the engineer Stake still worked, refilling the balloon with the hydrogen that had been battered out of it by the storm. Strindberg took photographs and wrote to Anna, and Frænkel explored the mountains. Andrée brooded, collected moss and wrote his diary. *I have proposed to my companions that up until the 15th of July we choose only the most favourable wind for our launch, but thereafter we must make do, if it is sufficient to enable our departure. After such delay, we are entitled, nay, we are bound to attempt an ascent. My companions are unreservedly with me in this. And it is in accordance with this principle that we shall act.*

When he was not writing to Anna, Strindberg checked and double-checked their equipment, which was lying in heaps on the floor. The guide ropes were coiled in a pile – he assumed they were ready for the flight, but no-one appeared to have examined them or tested that they were in working condition. The collapsible boat and the survival equipment had been stowed in the *Eagle*'s gondola, again without so much as a cursory glance. Strindberg shrugged his shoulders. Surely it was safe to assume that they were up to scratch, especially after all the preparations the year before.

The days ticked slowly by. Once again Strindberg became aware that the world's attention was focused on this frozen beach at the northernmost tip of the Spitsbergen archipelago, where the winds continued to blow the low, drifting clouds in all directions but north. The rain and the low whistle of the wind hitting the mountains as it came in off the bay served only to wind up the tension and expectation. As usual, Andrée withdrew into the certainty of scientific method, examining his calculations and increasingly barking stern orders to the ground crew. For Strindberg, the launch could not come soon enough. He struck up a friendship with Machuron, finding the Frenchman a kindred spirit who understood how he missed Anna's loving smile and warm words.

'My feeling for Anna is so tender,' Strindberg told Machuron, explaining that he was torn between the excitement of the adventure that lay ahead and the possibility that once the *Eagle* lifted into the sky it might be a very long time before he saw Anna again. 'Will the wind ever turn?' he despaired. 'The sooner the *Eagle* launches, the sooner I will be back with my love.'

It seemed to Strindberg that every pair of eyes was watching him and his two companions, willing them to take off, if only to see what would happen if Andrée's grand plan ended in disaster.

Early on the morning of 11 July, Frænkel and Svedenborg were woken again in their bunks on the *Svensksund* by the shouts and heavy footsteps of one of the crew running down the gangway to their cabin.

'The wind is from the south to the north, and building!' the sailor shouted.

From the porthole next to his bunk, Frænkel could glimpse between the ice floes patches of water rippled by gusts from the south-southwest. Two Norwegian whalers had anchored in the harbour, taking shelter in case the wind built to a storm. There was no sign of Andrée or Strindberg.

At 8 a.m., Andrée appeared on the *Svensksund's* deck and headed for shore. An hour or so later, he returned. 'The time may have come, but give me an hour to decide,' he said. To Strindberg, he appeared nervous. 'In the meantime, Frænkel and Strindberg, write your last letters, pack your bags and be ready to board the balloon at a moment's notice. This may be our only chance.'

Frænkel returned to his cabin to dash off a last note to his family. *Dear Mother, time for only a few lines now as we may cast off today. The wind is not the best in direction or strength, but we have waited so long now that we must take this chance. If you hear no more this year we may be wintering in the Arctic. A winter camp on*

Franz Josef Land presents no difficulties. I must finish here! Love to father, sisters, brothers, Haakan and friends, from Knut.

For Andrée, the choice was clear. He could either risk his life and those of his companions, or return to Sweden, probably to be reviled, certainly to be ridiculed, definitely to serve the rest of his working life assessing others' attempts to exploit technology to conquer nature. Ahead lay either a safe future at the patent office or a last-chance gamble in which he staked everything on glory, fame and the respect of his nation.

Over that next hour the clouds increased their speed across the sky, indicating that while the windspeed was relatively constant at ground level, it was becoming much faster at altitude.

Then Andrée reappeared on deck to lead his launch crew of Frænkel, Strindberg, Svedenborg and Machuron ashore. Climbing to the top of the balloon hangar, they inspected the balloon.

'What do you think?' Andrée asked Machuron.

'The wind is gusty, and that might be a problem during take-off,' Machuron replied. 'Provided you clear the balloon hangar without mishap, the wind should not pose any danger once the *Eagle* is in the air.'

'And Svedenborg? What are your thoughts?' Andrée asked.

'Yes, the squally wind could impale the balloon on the hangar, but you have to take a chance with the wind. I think you should attempt it.'

Next Andrée turned to Frænkel, who was avoiding his gaze. 'What do you think, Frænkel? Shall we try or not?'

'It is not just for me to say. We should not go unless we all decide it. For my part, all I can say is, I will if you will.'

Finally, Andrée looked at Strindberg, the only other member of the launch party who had experienced the disappointment and humiliation of returning to Sweden with a dream in tatters. Strindberg understood Andrée better than the other men. He knew that for Andrée the flight of the *Eagle* had lost some of its spark since the death of Mina, his mother. He also knew that high among the many reasons that were driving Andrée to take off was a determination to prove Ekholm wrong. More than anything, Andrée wanted to show the world that his idea worked, but Strindberg realized he had to resist the pull of Andrée's ambitions and think only of his own. Banishing all thoughts of home and yearnings for Anna, he looked Andrée in the eye. 'I think we ought to attempt it,' he said.

Andrée pursed his lips, looked once again at each of his companions in turn, and then headed back to the boat, followed by his puzzled partners.

On board the *Svensksund*, he went directly to Ehrensvärd, the captain. The previous year, Captain Hugo Zachau of the *Virgo* had dictated the terms, ending the expedition when he needed to return to Gothenburg. This year, Andrée was determined that he should control all events.

'We have discussed in some detail whether to launch or not,' he said. 'My companions insist on going ahead and, as I have no valid reason to object, I must agree to it.' Raising his voice so that the men who had gathered round could hear, he shouted, 'We have decided to start.'

Andrée looked at his watch – it was 11.22 a.m. – and turned to Ehrensvärd. 'Will you send all hands on shore to begin the work of dismantling the balloon house?'

Under a clear sky streaked with a few high clouds, the harbour hummed with activity. The protective canvas wall was raised along the south side of the balloon hangar, while its wooden north side was partially dismantled. The draglines, so vital to the success of the flight, were laid out along the shore to help direct the balloon eastwards immediately after the launch, so that it would avoid the highest point of Amsterdam Island, directly across the bay from Dane's Island.

Strindberg released several small hydrogen balloons to gauge the windspeed and direction, took pictures of the preparations and packed his equipment in the balloon basket. Nearby, a reporter from the *Aftonbladet* secured the thirty-six carrier pigeons to the two-storey gondola, each packed in its own basket. To the reporter, Strindberg appeared to be caught between excitement and dismay that the *Eagle* was preparing to launch. Several times he hesitated and looked out to sea before returning to the packing of his equipment in the balloon basket. For the first time, Strindberg was facing the possibility that the flight might not succeed. Until then, he had believed fervently that the *Eagle* would reach the Pole and that he would return safely to Sweden, but Andrée's hesitance in front of Frænkel, Svedenborg, Ehrensvärd and himself had sown a seed of doubt in Strindberg's mind. What if I do not return? he thought. It would mean my beloved Anna would be distraught and I would never see her again. He considered asking Andrée if he had any doubts, and if so, advising him to reconsider the flight, but to do so would show Andrée that he had broken faith with the dream of flying to the North Pole. Ashamed of himself, Strindberg dismissed the thoughts from his mind.

Noticing Strindberg's low morale, Svedenborg suggested that they return to the *Svensksund* to fetch Strindberg's belongings and to synchronize their watches before the launch. As they entered the galley, breakfast was being served; Strindberg and Svedenborg were persuaded by Ehrensvärd and the expedition doctor to join them at their table.

'Let us open a bottle of champagne,' Ehrensvärd insisted, picking at the cage around the champagne cork. There was a loud bang as the cork hit the roof and the champagne fizzed over the edge of the bottle. 'Here take a glass,' he said, thrusting a flute into Strindberg's hand. 'Now let us all drink to the success of the *Eagle*'s flight. The next time we meet, you will be famous for being one of the first three men to reach the North Pole!'

Strindberg took a sip. The bubbles prickled in his mouth, but they failed to raise his spirits. Instead, the alcohol depressed him and he found the excited chatter of the other people at the table an irritation that soon drove him back to shore.

Meanwhile, Frænkel and Andrée were making do with beer and sandwiches, eaten in the balloon hangar while completing final preparations for the launch. Ballast bags were handed down over the balloon's netting and the massive envelope rose within the hangar. For the first time, the carrying-ring was off the ground and the top of the *Eagle* could clearly be seen poking out of the roof of the hangar. Outside, the wind gusted, catching the top of the swollen envelope and slamming it against the sides of the building.

'The *Eagle* is losing gas every time it hits the side of the hangar,' engineer Stake shouted to Andrée. 'It has probably lost nearly five thousand cubic feet already.'

'Don't worry. We won't need it,' Andrée shouted back, as behind him Strindberg worked hard to photograph the last minutes of countdown before the *Eagle* was launched.

'Strindberg and Frænkel! Are you ready to go?' Andrée cried.

It was the instruction Strindberg had been waiting for with a mixture of dread and acute excitement. Suddenly filled with a fresh fear that he might never see Anna again, Strindberg walked over to his friend Machuron, handed him the films he had exposed earlier and embraced him tightly.

'Promise me you will give these to Anna,' he said, pressing a bundle of letters into his friend's hands. His face was streaked with tears. 'Tell Anna I love her,' he begged, his voice cracking. 'And tell her I shall write to her every day.'

With this, Strindberg joined Frænkel in the basket, which had been lowered into a pit at the centre of the hangar's base. Above it, the *Eagle*'s balloon was swaying back and forth, occasionally knocking against what remained of the hangar's wooden walls.

Andrée was the last to board the basket, having handed Ehrensvärd a telegram addressed to the King of Sweden.

He took a deep breath before climbing into the wicker gondola to join Frænkel and Strindberg on the observation platform.

'What does the telegram say?' Frænkel asked Andrée.

'At the moment of their departure, the members of the North Pole expedition beg that your Majesty should accept their humble greetings and the expression of their deepest gratitude,' Andrée replied.

The atmosphere within the balloon hangar tightened as the three men completed final adjustments within the gondola.

'Don't be uneasy if you receive no news from me for a year, possibly not until the following year,' Andrée shouted out. Around him, the crew and the closest comrades of the three balloonists held onto the ropes that secured the *Eagle*, knowing they might never see the three men again.

On Andrée's order, Frænkel and Strindberg cut the ropes holding a ton and a half of sand in ballast sacks to the carrying-ring. The basket lurched upwards by about three feet and the hangar fell silent. The eyes of the world were on this rickety shed at the northern tip of civilization, as the three aeronauts listened for a gap in the gusting wind.

Silence. For a few precious seconds, the wind died down. Their chance, the moment for the *Eagle*'s launch, had finally arrived.

'*Attendez un moment. Calme!*' Machuron shouted.

A few seconds passed, then Andrée's voice: '*Kapa allt!*' Cut all!

Light flashed on the swords of three of the *Svensksund*'s sailors. The blades came down as one to slice through the last three ropes holding the carrying-ring in place. The *Eagle* surged towards the top of the balloon hangar as the ground crew cheered. The three aeronauts answered with the shout, 'Long live old Sweden!'

It was 1.45 p.m. The first flight to the North Pole was at last underway.

Then disaster struck. A gust of wind caught the *Eagle*, smashing it against the side of the hangar. For a second, Strindberg thought the envelope would rip, but the *Eagle* bounced back and began to rise again. A moment later, the bottom of the basket cleared the top of the balloon hangar and the *Eagle* was free.

Frænkel began to hoist the *Eagle*'s sails, and again the balloon reeled. A downward gust of wind swept off the mountains behind the bay, careered down the cliff and caught the *Eagle* at its most vulnerable moment. The balloon dipped and twisted. Meanwhile, Strindberg took photographs from the observation platform on top of the gondola, unaware that beneath him the ground crew were running frantically towards a steam launch, expecting to have to rescue the aeronauts from the freezing sea.

The *Eagle* rose slightly, but as it reached the middle of the harbour, it surged downwards again, towards the water. On board, Andrée and Frænkel pulled Strindberg from his camera.

'Quick! Empty ballast! We're going down!' Andrée shouted to Strindberg. 'We need to force it to rise!'

The *Eagle* touched the water briefly, lifted off, splashed down again and dragged through the water at speed. Inside the gondola, water gushed over the equipment and provisions. On top of the observation platform, the three men gripped the ropes, their knuckles as white and taut as their faces, as the *Eagle* jerked, almost throwing them off balance.

'My God. What was that?' Strindberg cried out at one point. It felt as if the ropes had caught on an obstacle below the water. Like his two companions, he was convinced the *Eagle*'s flight was about to end before it had really begun.

Before anyone had a chance to answer, the gondola dropped under water, only its top third remaining above the surface. Panicking, Andrée screamed out more orders: 'More ballast! Empty more ballast!'

For a few more hair-raising seconds it appeared the

expedition was over, then to the relief of the rescue party and those on board, the *Eagle* rose out of the water and began slowly to climb to its cruising height, heading northwards across the bay. Eight sand sacks, a total of 450lb of valuable ballast, had been emptied, the gondola had been drenched and the three pilots' confidence had been shaken, but at last the *Eagle* was on its way.

CHAPTER EIGHT

THE VOYAGE

ARCTIC OCEAN

11 July, 1897

ELEVEN MINUTES AFTER LAUNCH, THE *EAGLE* PASSED OVER Hollander Naze, a spit of land about a mile north of Virgohamna. After the years of preparation and the months of waiting, Andrée was relieved that at last they were airborne. He basked in the quiet silence, remarking to Frænkel that all he could hear was the creak of the wicker basket and the occasional click of the shutter on Strindberg's camera. As he looked around he realized that it was an almost monochrome landscape. Only the blue sky above had any colour; below him, the water was black and the ice-covered ground was white. In the distance, the granite mountains were dark and topped with snow. It was as if they were entering another world, one in which the absence of colour made everything seem more real, more vital and more acute, like the photographs Strindberg was taking from the observation platform.

But something was missing, Andrée thought. There was

no quiet slosh of draglines towing through the water. And the *Eagle* was trailing no wake behind it.

'We have lost the draglines! They are gone!' Andrée shouted.

Frænkel and Strindberg interrupted their sightseeing to peer below the *Eagle*. Andrée was right; only three short lengths of rope hung where the draglines should have been.

In all the panic of the launch and the subsequent plunge into Virgohamna bay, no-one on board had noticed that two-thirds of each dragline had been left lying on shore. After laying the ropes out, no-one had checked the screw couplings, which had only a few turns of thread so that the lower sections of dragline rope could be jettisoned at the slightest tug of resistance.

'The screws were tight when the ropes were coiled on the ground, but when we pulled them out along the shore the coils must have twisted open, and that was enough to unscrew the couplings,' Strindberg suggested.

Andrée realized his colleague was right, but snapped back at him. 'That's of little use now. The *Eagle* is no longer a dirigible airship; instead it is a balloon like any other. It is everything I wanted to avoid. Now it can be steered only by the vagaries of the wind.'

Memories of General Greely and Admiral Markham's mocking remarks at the International Geographical Congress in London came flooding back to Andrée. Not to check the draglines was a catastrophic mistake. They had surveyed the bay, taking depth soundings, and they had measured the height of surrounding mountains, but they had not checked Andrée's trump card. The draglines that Andrée had told the world would guarantee victory where other balloon flights had failed were lying impotent on the shore of Dane's Island. The only consolation was that if the balloon had not lost its draglines, their added ballast would have dragged the gondola under water when it hit the bay shortly after launch.

Perhaps they had been complacent; perhaps Andrée had

realized the futility of their mission and failed to apply his usual meticulous care to every aspect of preparation. Crammed onto the observation platform, the three men now had no choice but to make the best of a poor situation. Although the ring was too cramped for Frænkel and Strindberg to mutter anything about Andrée under their breaths, their thoughts were in unison: was there any point in continuing the mission when they could not steer the *Eagle*? Only their loyalty to Andrée, their relief at having taken off and the excitement about what might lie ahead – and the attendant glories should they return home safely – stopped them from voicing their concerns.

'What about the sails?' asked Frænkel. 'Is there any point in leaving them in place?' He looked up at the sails, hoisted shortly after the launch, when the *Eagle* had cleared the balloon hangar. They hung limp, flapping loosely in the wind.

'No,' Andrée replied urgently. 'They are of no use now, and if the wind catches them we might be blown towards the high peaks on Amsterdam Island. Get them down immediately until we find a way of reinstating the draglines. Without them, we will be truly at the mercy of the wind.'

The *Eagle* twisted three-quarters of a full turn as the ballast lines, attached to the leeside of the carrying-ring, touched lightly on the water.

'Quick!' Andrée shouted. 'If we do not lower the sails, we will turn to the left and hit Amsterdam Island!' While Strindberg and Andrée lowered the sails, Frænkel scrambled up the ropes above the carrying-ring and swept the canvas sheets aside.

The panic was academic. With 450lb of sand ballast dumped and the 1,160lb weight of the lower two-thirds of the draglines missing, the *Eagle* soon climbed to 1,800ft, the water surface falling far out of reach of the ballast lines and the draglines, had their lower two-thirds not been left behind. Already the *Eagle* was out of control.

Andrée looked at Frænkel and Strindberg. Frænkel was

taking their position from nearby landmarks, while Strindberg was rooting around in his pockets, obviously looking for some personal item when he should have been attending to the *Eagle*.

'You seem completely unaware that at this high altitude the hydrogen is forcing itself out of the *Eagle*'s lower safety valve,' Andrée said. 'The higher we rise, the more we will lose. There is nothing we can do to stop it, and it means that the *Eagle* will not fly for as long as I projected.'

Strindberg snorted. 'And to think our concern was all about how much gas would leak through the seams. However much that might have been, it would have been less than we have lost already through flying so high.'

As Andrée jutted out his chin in defiance, a frosty silence enveloped the observation platform. Strindberg brooded. Once again, he thought, Andrée was unwilling to accept responsibility for any failings. It was the same in 1896: Andrée would not accept Ekholm's criticisms of the *Eagle*. Now it appeared Ekholm had been wise to resign.

Frænkel nudged Strindberg in the ribs. 'What about your note for Anna? Did you not arrange with Machuron that you would scribble a last few words from the balloon and drop it over Hollander Naze?'

Strindberg came to his senses. The note! He had joked with Machuron that it would be the first polar airmail, carried not by pigeon but by his fair hand in the *Eagle* and collected by Machuron to send on to Anna. He'd been searching in his pockets for the scrap of paper he had kept especially for the purpose, when Andrée had rebuked him for not paying attention to the hydrogen escaping from the balloon. Now he had missed his chance to drop it on Hollander Naze, as arranged with Machuron.

'You're right; where is it?' Strindberg replied, searching through his pockets again. He found the paper carefully stowed in a buttoned inner pocket, tugged it out and on it dashed off a few brief endearments. He placed the note inside a tin, then dropped it overboard. From what he could see, the *Eagle* was now over Vogelsang Island, seven minutes and several miles further on from Hollander Naze, but his view was obscured as the balloon had turned to the east and risen to 1,850ft, where it was about to disappear into the grey Arctic fog.

Strindberg was devastated that he had forgotten to post his note at the correct place. He felt the fog was not only enclosing the *Eagle*, but also clouding his memories of Anna. With every mile that they flew deeper into the cloud, Anna's smile seemed to fade. He wished only that he had taken a picture of his beloved with him and that he could tell Andrée and Frænkel of his heartache with the same ease with which he could speak to Machuron.

Hoping that his friend had remembered to drop the tin containing the note to his love, Alexis Machuron stood on the shore of Dane's Island, watching the *Eagle* disappear out of sight for ever.* Peering into the distance, he noted the last sighting of the balloon in his pocket diary: *For one moment then, between two hills we can see a grey speck over the sea, very very far away. And then it finally disappears. Our friends are now shrouded in mystery.*

It was silent and bitterly cold inside the cloud. The clammy mist was only a degree above freezing, but the balloon maintained a good speed of more than twenty miles an hour – fast enough, according to Machuron's calculations before launch, to reach the Pole in two days, and the Bering Strait, between Alaska and Russia, in six days. Such predictions were wishful thinking. Four minutes later, the hydrogen cooled so much that the *Eagle* sank to less than ninety feet above the water, low enough for the short remaining stubs of the draglines to drag along the surface.

'Look, it works!' Andrée shouted. His companions seemed unimpressed; they were more concerned with

---

* Machuron scoured Hollander Naze in vain for Strindberg's note to Anna. To this day, the tin has not been found on Vogelsang Island.

pulling their jackets closed against the cold, damp air. 'The *Eagle* has slowed and the wind is streaming past us. The draglines would have worked! See how the wind is ruffling the flags and would have filled.'

Andrée was right, but Frænkel thought it was not the time for celebration. 'Yes, but we cannot spend the entire flight in cloud and at this height. We need to construct new draglines.'

The balloonists immediately set about splicing the lower parts of one of the eight 200ft ballast lines onto what remained of one of the draglines. Hunched over the ropes for more than two hours, they worked in silence as the heavy fibres tore into their sore, bleeding hands.

'This is thirsty work,' Strindberg said. 'We need to drink.'

'The altitude will have made us thirsty, too,' Andrée replied. 'Frænkel, go below and find something to drink.'

Riled at being ordered around, Frænkel climbed down the rope ladder and returned a minute or so later, clutching a large bottle of beer.

'I hope we will not return to high altitude,' he said. 'It will dehydrate us and we are certainly not prepared for it. We have claret and beer, but what little fresh water we have, I believe Nils has earmarked for making coffee.'

The three men stopped their work briefly to down the bottle of beer in three grateful gulps before returning to the ropes. The *Eagle* flew steadily north-northeast, with the cloud closing in all around as they laboured, hoping in vain that they might construct a line that would make the *Eagle* steerable at an altitude above the clouds.

All too soon, the beer took its toll. 'Watch out below!' Strindberg shouted from the observation platform to Frænkel, at work in the gondola. 'You are about to be showered!'

Frænkel ducked as Andrée and Strindberg relieved themselves over the side of the platform.

In the late afternoon the *Eagle* glided out of the cloud into the sun's warming rays and began to rise again. At

4.54 p.m., it passed over the edge of the polar icecap at an altitude of 1,600ft, far out of reach of the hastily constructed 400ft dragline. Frænkel watched a seagull flying nearby as behind them the peaks and fjords of Spitsbergen disappeared in a light mist. Once again, the *Eagle* was a free-flying balloon, unable to be steered. But the gas in the envelope was slowly cooling as the mist obscured the warmth of the sun and the balloon descended back towards the ice. Forty minutes later it was flying north-northeast at 760ft.

The three aeronauts were thrilled by their glimpses through the mist of the intensely blue sea and the ice, but their attention should have been elsewhere: the *Eagle* had lost a considerable amount of gas. More than 116 cubic feet of hydrogen had escaped during its last excursion to high altitude. Now that clouds were obscuring the sun and the gas was cooling, the *Eagle*'s ability to remain aloft continued to diminish, but the three pilots seemed unconcerned. They released four carrier pigeons – the loss of this ballast had a marginal effect on the altitude – and then tucked in to their first meal, a flask of noodle soup and sandwiches packed by the cooks on the *Svensksund*. They ate in near silence, interrupted only by the creaking of ice, the whistle of the valve above their heads leaking hydrogen and occasional tweets of birdsong.

At around 7 p.m., the faint mist thickened to a fog beneath the *Eagle*. Had all gone to plan, and had the full length of the draglines still been attached to the balloon, the *Eagle* would have been flying lower and fog would have enveloped it, but Andrée still appeared unconcerned. His relief at having at last got underway had given way to euphoria that the *Eagle* did not crash immediately after take-off. Now, not having slept properly for several days, Andrée was exhausted.

With the Swedish flag hanging limp as the *Eagle* moved along at the same speed as the wind, Andrée climbed down the rope ladder to the tiny bunk in the gondola below. 'I have not slept for days,' he told Frænkel. 'I shall sleep now and will take over the first night watch later on.'

While the *Eagle* flew free above an endless sea of white cloud, Andrée struggled to write an optimistic communiqué. It avoided all mention of the fact that the direction of the *Eagle*'s flight was no longer within his control. *Our journey has until now gone well*, he wrote. *We are still moving ahead at a height of 250m in a direction that was initially 10 degrees east of north, but latterly directly northeast. Four carrier pigeons were sent off at 5.40 p.m. Greenwich time. They flew towards the east. We are now over the ice, which is very broken up in all directions. Weather magnificent. In best of humours, Andrée, Strindberg, Frænkel.*

Strindberg and Frænkel kept watch in the bright sunshine, recording their position at regular intervals, while below them Andrée resigned himself to a deep sleep. The *Eagle* changed direction again, heading east-northeast and rising to 2,200ft, soon punishing Frænkel and Strindberg for their complacency in allowing it to fly too high. The higher they flew, the more hydrogen escaped from the envelope and the less weight the *Eagle* would be able to support once it returned to a proper altitude. By 9.43 p.m., the *Eagle* had sunk to 1,600ft and was skimming the top of the clouds.

'Look how we fly on the clouds as if they were a bed of feathers,' Strindberg shouted. 'Is this not exhilarating?'

'Yes, but we are in danger of falling into a vicious circle of descent,' Frænkel replied. 'The deeper we sink into the clouds, the further we fall from the warmth of the sun. And the closer to the cold ice, the harder it will be for the *Eagle* to rise.'

The two men knew that with every degree drop in temperature, the balloon would sink 1,200ft. After a short consultation they agreed to jettison eighteen pounds of sand and buoy number 4, containing Andrée's note, but not before Strindberg added a few words, which were as far from the truth as Andrée's had been: *Above the clouds since 7.45 p.m. GMT.*

Brought to their wits by an expanse of broken ice glimpsed through a gap in the cloud and realizing that dumping the sand and the buoy had had no effect, they cut off the lowest rungs of the rope ladder and threw them over the side too. The balloon rose only slightly as a result, so they removed another six rungs from the ladder and jettisoned them with buoy number 7, adding a short note written in panicky haste by Strindberg: *This buoy was thrown from Andrée's balloon at 10.55 p.m. GMT on the 11th of July, 1897, at about 82° latitude and 25° longitude east from Greenwich. We are floating at a height of 600 metres. All well, Andrée, Strindberg, Frænkel.*

Again, dumping the ballast had no effect. Sixteen minutes later, the balloon had sunk to 1,490ft, forty feet below the clouds. The temperature plummeted to 0.6°C – a fraction above freezing. Through occasional breaks in the cloud they could see high-altitude clouds streaming northwards, but as the *Eagle* entered 12 July, caught in an eastbound air stream, a reconstructed dragline touched the ice.

'Andrée will be pleased. His dragline is back on the ice,' Frænkel said dismissively.

'Yes, but to what effect? The wind is too slow for the sail to work,' Strindberg answered. 'Anyway, I have now realized the design fault of the *Eagle*: the draglines and ballast ropes are too close to the sail; they should be to its stern. The result is that the draglines make the *Eagle* twist, turning the sail out of the wind so that it cannot be used to steer the balloon.'

'We should have tested the *Eagle* before we came to Dane's Island,' Frænkel said. 'Imagine using a new, unproven design on a flight of this nature.'

Using a plumb line and taking their position from blocks of ice, Strindberg and Frænkel calculated their speed and height. They were flying at almost seven miles an hour at heights between 65ft and 330ft – much too low. At one in the morning they jettisoned a further twenty-six pounds of ballast, but the *Eagle* sank further, until the ballast ropes dragged on the ice, slowing their progress even more.

As a black bird passed in the distance, they considered their dilemma. If they remained at their current altitude, the balloon would ice up, slow down and sink further. However, if they jettisoned ballast to rise above the clouds, the gas in the balloon would warm and they would rise out of control to an altitude where the balloon would lose hydrogen. With less gas in the envelope they would eventually sink back below the clouds, back to where they were now, but this time with hundreds of pounds less ballast and many cubic feet less hydrogen. So far, this seesaw journey had lost them more than a ton of lift.

The fog thickened as they considered their options. Unable to come to a decision, they simply stared out at their gloomy surroundings. Visibility was soon reduced to one mile, and at 1.26 a.m. the balloon stopped dead, every bit of it saturated by the sodden air. They threw another buoy overboard – to no effect – and woke Andrée, as arranged, at 2 a.m.

'We have come to a standstill,' Strindberg said with a shrug. 'It's your turn to stand watch.'

While Andrée took over, Strindberg and Frænkel clambered down the rope ladder into the gondola. The wicker basket was cramped and afforded little protection from the elements. Condensation dripped from everything and the blankets on the bed were heavy with dew. Already there was a smell of rotting fibres, which Strindberg could not help but think was redolent of failure. The two men crawled onto the bed side by side, wondering how they would manage to sleep in this poky, damp cell. Despite the discomfort, however, they were soon asleep, exhausted by the tribulations of the previous days.

For five hours the balloon inched slowly north-north-west, then west. The dragline was impotent; the poorly positioned ballast lines twisted the balloon so that the sail could not catch the wind. At one point, the *Eagle* even moved backwards and the sail forced it down, towards the ice. During this time, Andrée spotted several birds, including a fulmar that circled the balloon. It was a bad sign; they should be further from land. But although the mission was in distress, Andrée's attention was elsewhere. The *Eagle* was drifting directionless and at a fraction of its intended speed, but Andrée was mesmerized by the hardness and smoothness of the ice below. *The snow on the ice is a light dirty yellow across great expanses, the same colour as the fur of the polar bear*, he wrote in his diary. *Pressure ridges rarely break the ice. A horse and sledge could drive over it if the surface were hard. No land in sight, although the horizon is unclear. It is indeed a wonderful journey through the night. I am cold but will not wake the two sleepers. They need rest.* A little later, he spotted a pair of walrus directly below him. *One of them became frightened; the other not*, he noted.

As the temperature hovered barely above freezing point and the *Eagle* continued to drift westwards at about sixty feet above the ice, still Andrée seemed unconcerned, as if he had given up hope of completing his mission. Maybe he had never wanted to take off in the first place. Certainly he had indicated as much a few months before to Gurli Linder.

Two weeks before he sailed out of Gothenburg bound for Dane's Island, Andrée's beloved mother Mina had died. It was not unexpected; Mina had lived to an old age, but her death still left Andrée devastated. Rarely a day had passed since the death of his father in 1870 without Andrée either speaking with or writing to his mother. The sudden loss of his father when Andrée was only sixteen had driven him straight into her arms. He became the perfect son, devoted to his mother's happiness, and Mina came to depend heavily on his support and love.

A few days after his mother's funeral, Andrée met Gurli Linder on Djurgarden Island, on the edge of Stockholm's city centre. He suggested they went into Skansen, an outdoor museum and zoo. As they walked around the parkland, stopping to look at buildings from Sweden's rural past, Andrée told Gurli of his grief and sadness.

'Since Mother's death, all my personal interest in the expedition has gone,' he admitted, running his finger along a fence in front of an eighteenth-century wooden chalet with grass growing on its roof.

Gurli had never seen Andrée this depressed. It was as if all his optimistic ambition had died with his mother the previous week.

'I leave for Gothenburg in a few days,' Andrée said. 'Naturally, I am interested in following my idea through, and my feelings of responsibility for my companions are unchanged, but I feel no joy. The only link that connected me to life is severed.'

Gurli looked down at Andrée's hands. His knuckles were white as he gripped the fence. He had spoken of feelings she desperately wished he had for her. Near them, on a patch of dirt clinging to a stone wall, a single African violet grew. Gurli reached out and nipped it off with her nails.

'Look at this,' she said, holding the delicate velvet petals up to Andrée. 'It has already died, but if I put it in a vase on my dressing table, for a few days it will remind me of what it looked like a few moments ago, when it was still alive. We have to use whatever we can to remind us of the best moments from the past.'

Andrée looked at the flower. Such sentimentality was wasted on him; already he was looking at the flower as a scientist, examining its petals, sepals, anthers and ovary. He shrugged.

'You must carry something to the Pole to remind yourself of your mother,' Gurli said. 'From now on, I shall always place a violet beside your portrait at home in memory of you and this day.'

The *Eagle* again came to a standstill as Strindberg woke

and then climbed up to the observation platform shortly before 6 a.m. Using the ingenious stove designed by Ernst Göransson, Andrée's engineer friend, Strindberg made breakfast. Carefully he lowered the stove down from the balloon until it dangled twenty-six feet beneath the gondola, sufficiently out of range not to ignite the hydrogen in the balloon above. Then, using a remote device, he lit the stove's spirit flame and let the coffee boil for eighteen minutes, after which he blew out the flame by puffing down a long rubber tube that ran down to the stove. Then he hauled the coffee pot and stove back to the gondola.

'This coffee should do you good. You look exhausted,' Strindberg told Andrée, whose eyes were like red stains in his waxy face.

'I did not sleep properly for days before the flight,' Andrée replied, looking at his companion.

Strindberg, too, did not look like the proud man who fewer than twenty-four hours earlier had boarded the *Eagle*. Already the cold, the dry air at altitude and the sheer stress of the flight were taking their toll. Strindberg was unshaven and dishevelled from sleeping pressed up against Frænkel, but of most concern to Andrée was that his companion appeared clearly depressed at the thought of how long it would be until he might see Anna again.

'Aah, the coffee is good. I can feel it opening my eyes,' Andrée said, licking clean the tongs Strindberg had used to open a tin of condensed milk. While Strindberg bustled in the corner, converting a barrel from a night stool to a day chair, Andrée tucked into his breakfast of cheese and sardine sandwiches, and gazed once more at the featureless expanse of white ice and grey cloud.

A fulmar swooped past. Pointing at the bird, Andrée shouted to Strindberg, 'We are still not out of range of that gull's nest in the cliffs of Spitsbergen.' The fulmar circled again, then landed on the *Eagle*'s netting, before depositing its droppings on the two men.

The rest of the morning passed relatively uneventfully.

The temperature dropped below freezing as the *Eagle* started to move again, this time to the west. Strindberg and Andrée released another batch of carrier pigeons shortly after 11 a.m., and at midday they spotted a vivid red stain on the ice, probably the blood of a seal killed by a polar bear. But their prospects worsened in the afternoon, when drizzly rain and a fine fog enveloped them. With the temperature still struggling to pass freezing point, they knew it was the worst that could happen to them; in such sodden conditions the rain could not evaporate. It froze into the balloon, the netting, the gondola and any exposed fabric, swiftly increasing the weight of the *Eagle* until, at 3.06 p.m., the *Eagle* bumped twice against the ice.

'Jettison anything that is not essential cargo,' Andrée shouted to Frænkel and Strindberg.

First to go were the heavy knives they would have used to cut the draglines, had they not been left coiled on the shore of Dane's Island. Then they discarded fifty-five pounds of sand and some rope. It was not enough. Ten minutes later they threw an iron anchor and a small block overboard. It was still not enough to lift the *Eagle* off the ice. Half an hour later they released a ballast line and threw a spade over the side. That had little effect.

At 4.51 p.m., they abandoned the polar buoy, a tacit admission of defeat, but still the *Eagle* did not rise. It was laden down by dampness, which had saturated every piece of fabric and rope. Impregnating the guide, ballast and net ropes in tallow and petroleum jelly to make them water-resistant had not worked. The ropes had absorbed moisture and had frozen, causing the *Eagle* to slam repeatedly against the ice as it headed slightly south of west. At 5.14 p.m., the balloon bumped and dragged across the ice eight times in rapid succession, and the three Swedes knew that their ambitious expedition was over.

At least let us eat in peace, Andrée wrote in his diary. But his plea was ignored. At 6.35 p.m., as the *Eagle* hit the ice again, Andrée wrote in his diary of *incessant fog and collisions every fifth minute*, adding, somewhat disingenuously, *humour good*. Maybe the cold roast chicken they shared for their dinner put them in a good mood; otherwise, there was little reason for them to be in high spirits. By 9.30 p.m., the *Eagle* was slamming forcibly against the ice every other minute as it flew southwest, parallel to the route it had taken up from Spitsbergen. *Paid visits to the surface and stamped it every 50 metres*, Andrée wrote, wondering how much more his exhausted companions could take and when the incessant banging against the ice would shatter their resolve. Fortunately, a reprieve soon arrived at 9.53 p.m., when the *Eagle* came to a standstill and did not move for the rest of the night.

Everything drips and the balloon is heavily weighed down, Andrée wrote, admitting defeat for the first time. *We could throw out ballast and the wind might, perhaps, carry us to Greenland, but it is our fate to be content with standing still. We have had to dump much ballast today and have not slept nor been allowed a respite from the repeated bumping against the ice. We probably could not have stood it much longer. All three of us need a rest. I sent Strindberg and Frænkel to bed at 11.20 and I intend to let them sleep until six or seven o'clock, provided I can manage to keep watch until then. Then I shall try to get some rest myself.*

As the balloon twisted on its creaking, frost-encrusted lines, Andrée worried that he might drive Frænkel and Strindberg to their deaths by working them too hard, but his concern for his comrades was short-lived in comparison with his contemplation of his place in history.

It is quite strange to be floating over the Arctic Sea, the first to have floated here in a balloon. How soon, I wonder, shall I – we – have successors? Will we be seen as madmen or will others follow our example? With the silence broken only by the scraping of the draglines on the snow and the flap of the sails in an occasional puff of wind, Andrée continued to write. *I cannot deny that we are, all three, filled with a deep pride. We can face death freely, having done what we have done. It is perhaps the sign of a strong individual who cannot bear to live and die like an ordinary man in the ranks, forgotten by future generations. Is it this, which is ambition?*

As 12 July passed into 13 July, the *Eagle* swayed, twisted, rose and sank throughout the night, but it did not fly any further towards Andrée's ambitious goal of the Pole. *It wants to escape but cannot*, Andrée wrote, watching the *Eagle* struggle like an animal in its death throes. He blamed the windspeed, which had fallen to less than five miles an hour, but he was unaware that the *Eagle* was anchored to the ice. When the balloon had swung around to the south, a rope had become firmly wedged beneath a block of ice.* Even when the wind increased at 3.15 a.m., the balloon remained at a standstill.

Not a living thing has been seen all night, no bird, seal, walrus or bear, Andrée noted in his journal as the clock slowly ticked around to 6 a.m., when Strindberg woke. During the night, the damp cold had penetrated the entire gondola, including the men's clothing and their bedclothes. Like his two companions, Strindberg was dressed in light, formal clothing, worn in case they found land at the North Pole and were met by foreign dignitaries. But he had now begun to feel the cold, and pulled on a pair of thick wool and hair socks over a pair of thin wool ones. On top of these he wore a pair of fur-lined snow boots, describing them as *warm and pleasant footwear* in his almanac.

By the time Strindberg had emerged from the gondola and clambered up onto the observation platform, the fog had lightened. For more than three hours, Andrée and Strindberg chatted amiably while taking measurements of temperature and windspeed, until they came to an agreement that Frænkel had slept more than enough, and Strindberg descended into the gondola to wake him.

---

* Had this not happened, the *Eagle* would probably have been blown straight back to Spitsbergen during the night.

Around 11 a.m. the *Eagle* somehow worked itself free of the ice block, starting with a jerk that almost threw Andrée and Frænkel off the observation platform. It then continued its slow, haphazard flight.

'Our only hope is to jettison everything necessary to ascend to a higher altitude,' Strindberg told Andrée and Frænkel, but they overruled his suggestion and the *Eagle* continued to fly at a low altitude at about seven miles an hour.

Frænkel prepared lunch, a cumbersome affair as he had no fresh water with which to wash the crockery and utensils. The entire meal of 'Hotch Potch Potage' – a soup – and chateaubriand was cooked below the balloon on Göransson's cooking apparatus. It evidently went down well: *a good and invigorating meal* Strindberg called it in his almanac, washed down with King's Special Ale, followed by chocolate biscuits, and biscuits dipped in raspberry syrup. As they digested this heavy lunch and amused themselves by spotting polar bear tracks, the temperature dropped even further. All around them, icicles hung from the rigging and the ropes and cloth were white with hoar frost.

After lunch, at 1.08 p.m., they released another four carrier pigeons, but even this went wrong. The birds settled on the instrument ring and the draglines, reluctant to venture into the fog. Eventually, with a little encouragement from Andrée and Frænkel, the pigeons flew off in the direction of home across an expanse of smooth, flat ice, frequently broken by leads of open water. Andrée's long vigil ended at 2 p.m. With his energy spent and his spirits low, he climbed down into the car for a sleep, but his rest was short-lived. Within minutes of lying down, Andrée was shaken awake by the *Eagle* slamming repeatedly against the ice with the most violent force yet. He clambered up to the observation platform, where he discovered Strindberg had wedged himself between the carrying-ring and the *Eagle*'s envelope with his notebook in hand in order to write to his love, Anna.

Up in the carrying-ring it is so confoundedly pleasant, Strindberg wrote. *I feel so safe there and so at home. Up there, the bumps are felt less, which allows me to sit calmly and write without having to hold on. In the carrying-ring, the vibrations from the draglines are felt to some extent – they are not felt at all in the gondola – but the bumps against the ground are felt much less.*

All three men were exhausted by lack of sleep and the cold. To compound their misery it started to rain, and the drizzle froze to the rigging. Andrée was resigned to failure. Only half an hour earlier he had relinquished his watch and was looking forward to a long sleep. But now, burdened by its rapidly increasing weight, the *Eagle* was spending more time dragging along the ice, colliding with pressure ridges, than it spent in the air. It was impossible to stop the collisions, but, undisturbed, Strindberg took further steps to shut out the bitter cold that was now enveloping the *Eagle*. Over a shirt, jersey and trousers made of thick hunter's wool, he donned a blue army suit and a wool-lined leather waistcoat. A woollen cap on his head and a pair of woollen mittens completed the ensemble.

The *Eagle* was now so heavy with ice that nothing seemed able to lift it. They jettisoned buoy number 9 and a medicine chest; two hours later the balloon was still bumping along the ice, shaking the men's resolve. The disposal of ballast merely meant the *Eagle* rose higher between bumps and hit the ice slightly less frequently, but with such extreme violence that the paraffin containers cracked open, on one occasion causing a fire that was soon extinguished.

Gradually, the *Eagle* turned to the north, but it advanced at a very slow speed and the bumping along the ice continued until 7 p.m., when the violent jarring against the ice caused Andrée to hit his head and Strindberg to be sick.

'I shall climb into the carrying-ring, where the collisions seem less violent,' Strindberg said, but it was no use. As soon as he was ensconced beside Frænkel he was sick again.

An hour later, the three men decided to stake all on a last-ditch attempt to get the *Eagle* to rise above the clouds, where the warmth of the sun would melt the ice in its rigging. There, they hoped, they would have a better chance of continuing their bid for the Pole or heading for land. They dumped six small buoys, a winch, 165lb of sand, the universal barrel seat and various supplies, a total of more than 440lb. The balloon rose, the draglines performed faultlessly, the sails billowed and the balloon flew well, so they threw another 110lb of ballast overboard.

Altogether it is quite splendid! Andrée wrote, but yet again the words written in his diary hid the disappointment he felt at knowing that it was highly unlikely the *Eagle* would reach the Pole. And they were unrealistically optimistic, for the *Eagle* faced yet another dilemma. If the cloud cleared or she rose above it, and her envelope and ropes dried out, the loss of more than a ton of moisture and all the ballast the men had jettisoned would send the *Eagle* soaring thousands of feet into the sky. She no longer had the ballast to fly at a navigable height.

Andrée and Strindberg stood morosely on the observation platform, knowing that their comfortable cruise was unlikely to last. Frænkel was more practical. No longer shaken by the rollercoaster ride of incessant collisions with the ice, he took advantage of the calm and headed for bed at 9 p.m. Andrée moped around, dreading the derision that the failure of his flight was likely to attract from rivals such as Fridtjof Nansen. Strindberg climbed up to the carrying-ring, where he took some readings and put on an extra pair of balloon-cloth trousers and an Icelandic jersey to keep warm while reading Anna's last letter to him. Then, still in the ring, he attempted to fall asleep.

By 10.30 p.m. they were thirty miles north and more than sixty-three miles east of Dane's Island, which they had left nearly fifty-seven hours earlier. Maybe it was wishful thinking, maybe it was the fog, but Andrée reported several times that he had spotted land. In fact, it was only the reflection of clouds in the ice or refractions, the Arctic equivalent of desert mirages. *No bird is seen or heard and so I suppose there is no land near*, he wrote. He did, however, spot a large polar bear swimming in a lead of water about a hundred feet below the balloon shortly before it entered a dense cloud of fog and hit the ice again.

The *Eagle* bounced from hard ice pans into leads of water, rarely rising above surface level. At 11.30 p.m., the dragline they had fashioned from the ballast ropes broke, and with it ended any faint remaining hope of steering the balloon. Fortunately the ice was level, but it was also divided by dozens of leads. Andrée spent the first hour of 14 July examining the surface carefully, looking for somewhere safe to end the farcical flight. Some time after 1 a.m., one of the carrier pigeons returned. It made no difference, for all three men knew their voyage was doomed.

For the last hours of its life the *Eagle* headed almost directly east while Andrée and Frænkel battled with the sails, attempting to use them to steer the balloon to a safe landing site. The sails were useless, though, and at 5.28 a.m., while the balloon was ascending, they finally surrendered, letting the gas out of both valves. Nine minutes later, they were down, but they could not abandon the *Eagle* immediately; instead, they had to wait another hour and a half for enough gas to escape from the envelope to be sure the balloon would not take off again once they abandoned it.

At 7.19 a.m., exhausted by the cold, shattered by the bumping along the ice and battered by the wind, they jumped out of the gondola, relieved at last to be back on something that resembled firm ground. Andrée's dream of flying by balloon to the North Pole was over. Technology had not triumphed over nature. Once again, the Arctic had proved a formidable opponent and the North Pole remained unconquered, its mystery intact. Since taking off from Dane's Island, they had flown – or been dragged along the ice – three hundred miles in sixty-five hours. The nearest land was now 216 miles to the south across open water and broken ice split into thousands of floes by the force of ocean currents.

For Andrée, the failure was made all the worse by the fact that they had not ventured as far north as Nansen, who had reached 86°14′ North on foot the previous year. 'We have not even beaten Albert Markham, who so ridiculed me when I unveiled my plans at the International Geographical Congress,' he told Fraenkel and Strindberg forlornly. Indeed, Markham's record of 83°20′ North in 1876 and Lieutenant James Booth Lockwood's trek to 83°24′ North during General Greely's expedition of the first International Polar Year of 1882 were both safe.

'But our place in history is assured,' Strindberg pointed out. 'It has been the longest flight ever made by man and no-one will forget that we made the first attempt to reach the North Pole by balloon.'

Nevertheless, Andrée's dream lay in tatters on the ice. Typically, he showed little emotion, recording his thoughts with the objective detachment of a scientist: *Worn out and famished, but we have seven hours' hard work ahead of us before we can recuperate. The polar ice wears out the ropes more than our experiment shows.*

CHAPTER NINE

THE FLIGHT

ARCTIC OCEAN

29 May, 2000

I WAKE WITH A START AT 8 A.M. ON THE SECOND DAY OF *Britannic Challenger*'s flight. I've had an hour's much-needed sleep but I feel disinclined to repeat the experience. In the short time my eyes were closed, the sun heated the gas inside the envelope – we call it solar gain – and the balloon ascended to 9,500ft. Very frightening. Fortunately, I had my oxygen mask strapped to my face. If I had not woken up, the balloon would have continued to rise and I could have veered into a different wind stream, taking me off the track to the north. My course through the weather patterns is so critical that the slightest departure from Luc Trullemans' instructions could end the mission.

I immediately vent a lot of helium to reduce my altitude. At first I am nervous of pulling the wrong rope and I am not sure how much effect each rope will have. I pull the white-flecked rope for a second to see what happens. Then I tug it for two seconds. Each time I can feel a lurch as the helium escapes from a valve at the top of the envelope and the basket drops. Whereas Andrée's roller-coaster ride from the ice to above the cloud and back was uncontrolled, for me losing helium is not a problem as long as I have sufficient ballast to compensate when I want to increase altitude later.

Having unwittingly scooted up to 9,500ft, I am determined to make sure any unscheduled change of altitude does not happen again. I dig out my second alarm clock and strap it to my ear inside my balaclava and hood. The other is beside me in the basket. The alarm clock strapped to the side of my head is uncomfortable, but I need it to make sure I wake every hour to check the course, altitude and speed.

Like any conscientious workman, I don't like to blame my tools, but in this case I am really being let down by the autopilot. It performs its most important task well: ensuring that I don't crash into the ground. But it's designed to be used by pilots who are *compos mentis* and it is incapable of reacting when the balloon rises too high, only when it flies too low. When the balloon dips below a preset altitude, the autopilot fires the burners and sounds an alarm. Crude, but effective – the balloon rises and the pilot knows all about it. However, the autopilot is completely ineffective when the balloon rises beyond the height at which I want to fly. The only way to reduce altitude is to release hot air or helium by tugging on one of *Britannic Challenger*'s ropes, and that is something the autopilot is not designed to do.

Of equal concern is that the rise in altitude has indeed steered the balloon on to the wrong track. I am heading nine degrees east of north. I call the control centre on the Iridium satellite phone and Clive Bailey tells me in no uncertain terms that I need to descend quickly to find a more northerly track. As *Britannic Challenger* descends, I note the track every few hundred feet. Then I call the control centre with the readings. By this time, Brian Smith has relieved Clive Bailey, who is exhausted after a night watch. Brian Jones has departed only a few hours into the mission for a more pressing engagement in America, leaving Clive Bailey to take over as flight director.

'I've got three-five-seven degrees at five thousand two hundred feet. Then it's three-five-zero degrees at five thousand one hundred and three-four-zero degrees at four thousand eight hundred,' I tell him.

At first glance, the difference in the tracks does not appear to be great. But it is a variation of seventeen degrees across some four hundred feet of altitude. Such a difference in direction at the current position – six hundred nautical miles from the North Pole – would steer me more than 183 miles in the wrong direction, so it is imperative that I pick the right track and stick to it.

'I suggest you take a track of three-five-zero degrees until we get the next meteorological update from Luc,' Brian says.

I am learning fast that although I am not totally at their behest, I am very dependent on Luc Trullemans and the control centre. They analyse my position and have full access to the meteorological reports. They advise me on the best course to take. I make the final decision, but I know that as the journey goes on and I become increasingly exhausted and disorientated, the control centre will call most of the shots.

Early this morning I passed over the northern tip of Spitsbergen, about fifty miles east of where Andrée took off from Dane's Island. I'm glad I made it as far as Andrée's starting point. Now I have to clear the open water below me. I can see it only through an occasional gap in the cloud, but ditching at sea is my biggest fear.

The water below looks black and deadly. I can hear the wind howling, whipping spray off the crests of the freezing sea five thousand feet below me. I have never been a strong swimmer and the thought of trying to survive in water so cold that it is dotted with icebergs is terrifying. The makers of the immersion suit claim it will protect me

Chile, 1999. Preparing for my flight across the Andes and Rune's aborted high-altitude parachute jump.

© The Daily Telegraph/Stephen Lock 1999

On the way to the North Pole, April 1998. After 600 miles of misery Rune Gjeldnes and I finally reached the top of the world and I completed the Adventurers' Grand Slam.

© The Daily Telegraph/Paul Grover 1998

TOP LEFT: *The Birmingham team: Clive Bailey is on the left and Brian Smith on the right.*

TOP RIGHT: *Longyearbyen fire station – our pre-launch headquarters.*

BELOW LEFT: *The burghers of Longyearbyen lend a hand during* Britannic Challenger's *inflation.*

BELOW RIGHT: *Fully inflated and ready for take-off.*

The view from Britannic Challenger *shortly after take-off, surrounded by 6,000ft peaks.*

All photos courtesy David Hempleman-Adams

The midnight sun, pointing the way to the Pole as I pass over the northern tip of Spitsbergen. Ahead of me lies the Arctic Ocean and the Polar Icecap.

RIGHT: *My favourite view from the top of the world.*

CENTRE: *Grabbing a short sleep en route to the North Pole.*

BELOW: *The Pole at last! Celebrating mission accomplished with a bite of Biltong.*

The beginning of the end. For half an hour after

splashdown, Britannic Challenger *dragged me on a*

rollercoaster ride through water, across ice and

slamming into pressure ridges.

ABOVE: *Echoes of Andrée and the* Eagle *as* Britannic Challenger *finally comes to rest* 132 *hours after taking off from Spitsbergen.*

A frantic rush as the helicopter crew packs up the envelope and basket...

...and bundles it into the waiting helicopter.

Both photos © David Burges

Safe in Longyearbyen, Bill Haynes, the man with the vision to support the record bid, cracks open the champagne.

© The Daily Telegraph/David Burges 2001

from the cold for up to three hours, but I am not convinced that it will be enough in such extreme conditions. The shock of landing in iced water could be too great to endure. And if I did survive the landing, I would lose the feeling in my hands within seconds, making the task of opening the life-raft impossible. At best, I would last an hour in the water, probably less, and that would not be long enough for a helicopter to fly from Longyearbyen to rescue me.

At 2 p.m., Brian calls on the Iridium phone. 'David, are you eating and drinking enough?' he asks.

'I've got no appetite for my dehydrated food. It makes me retch. I'm still on the munchies – sandwiches and soup. And I'm drinking plenty of water.'

'What about the autopilot? Can you rely on it?'

'It's like a woman, Brian. Temperamental, expensive and doesn't do what it's told.'

Brian laughs. I know what I've just said is sexist, but this is not the place for political correctness. I've always been convinced a good joke in adversity does more to maintain morale than any amount of gung-ho bluster. Brian instantly knows what I mean and he can tell that my spirits are high. And when the inevitable moments of crisis come, humour will lift the spirit more than any amount of cajoling bravado.

'Anything else to report?' Brian asks.

'Yes.'

'What then?'

'Do I really have to tell you?'

'It would be best if I know everything, David.'

'Really everything?'

Even over the crackle of the phone I can hear an exasperated sigh in Brian's voice. 'Yes. Really everything.'

'Well, I've peed down my leg.'

'What? Can you repeat that?'

'I'd rather not.'

'You've peed down your leg, have you?'

'Yes.'

193

Brian laughs again, and I can hear him shouting to other people in the control centre, 'He's peed down his leg. Yes, David. He's pissed himself.' Then he comes back on the phone. 'David, why?'

'What else am I supposed to do in my immersion suit? When I need to go, I can't get it off in time.'

There's more laughter at my expense, but the control centre team don't know the half of it. Stuck inside the rubber immersion suit, my body is dripping with sweat and swollen like a sausage bursting against its skin. In fact, I am so soaked by my own perspiration that I barely noticed it when I urinated down my leg.

Brian comes back on the phone. 'Well, I expect you'll be pleased to hear that, according to the thermographs, you are now flying above the icecap. You can take your immersion suit off.'

I whoop with the relief of it.

Flying *Britannic Challenger* has turned out to be easier than I was anticipating, even with the problematic auto-pilot. The hardest adjustment to make is that a Roziere balloon is much less agile and needs less attention than a hot-air balloon. The helium cell at the centre of the en-velope provides most of the buoyancy; the hot air that warms it is needed only for fine adjustment. And as the flight is taking place under the constant sunshine of the Arctic summer, I have to fire the burners only occasionally to compensate for cooling at night.

My sole objective is to stay on course, but at times that involves a considerable amount of intricate flying to locate the altitude where the wind stream is blowing in the direction I want to go. It's made more difficult by the lack of controls. To go down, I release hot air or helium. To go up, I release ballast or fire the burners. It sounds simple, but the skill is to know when to use which method. Helium is vented from a valve at the top of the balloon by pulling on a white rope with flecks. Pulling a black rope closes it. All the valve consists of is two steel plates and a spring – and I have still not recovered from discovering that this little contraption costs ten thousand pounds. In addition, there is the helium chimney, which on a tug of the red rope releases all the helium in the inner cell of the Roziere balloon. High up in the envelope is a hot-air window, opened by pulling a red and white cord, striped like a barber's pole. Pulling another black rope closes the hot-air window. Then there are two other ropes, which are used only to land.

In the heat of midday, the warmth of the sun and the burner idling at its lowest setting are sufficient to increase the volume of the helium, causing *Britannic Challenger* to rise slowly above its track. Instead of turning off the burners, as some people do, I vent some helium or release some hot air. Turning off the burners is too risky in this environment. During the coldest time of the day, I close down everything and fire the burners – rather than release ballast – if I need to increase altitude. This is when the autopilot works best of all.

If I was making the same journey in a hot-air balloon I would have to fly it constantly, but I spend a lot of time sitting on my coldbox, which is covered with a sheet of Styrofoam to keep my backside warm, drinking soup and taking in the sights. The view from *Britannic Challenger* is stunningly beautiful, and because the air is much warmer than I anticipated, I spend a lot of time gazing in awe at my surroundings. Provided I stay below 5,000ft, it is about −10°C under the canopy I have pitched like a tent over the basket. Outside the canopy it is about −15°C; cold, but bearable, and nothing like the kind of acutely cold temperatures I feared.

Luc has advised me to aim for 7,000ft so that I can pick up a track of 350°, but I ignore his advice. I am happy with my course of 355°, especially as I am at 5,500ft, where the air is considerably warmer. Fortunately, I know Brian agrees. 'Now that you've got the autopilot halfway working, why don't you stick to three-five-five and get another hour's sleep?' he'd suggested at our last hourly communication.

Getting to sleep is proving to be difficult. I slept well for several weeks in the basket while it was on the ground, but I cannot get comfortable in it in the air. The basket is cramped, I am too unsure of the autopilot to relax, and the periodic roar of the burners keeps me awake. I have slept for no more than an hour since launching almost twenty-four hours ago. So far, I have managed to keep going on nervous energy, but I don't know how much longer I can go without a decent sleep. I don't want to be nodding off just as I approach the Pole.

Despite the lack of sleep, the cold and the discomfort, I realize how fortunate I am to have the opportunity of flying in a balloon to the North Pole. Few people get the chance to indulge their dreams, and I am very lucky to be one of them. The view is truly magnificent. Most of the time I am far above the clouds, but occasionally I dip down far enough to surf along the top of them – an exhilarating experience, just as Nils Strindberg found out when the ill-fated *Eagle* slowly made its way down to the ice. Below me, everything is white; above me, the sky is deep blue, streaked with the wispy mares' tails of high-altitude cirrus clouds. It is stunning, but the view is best of all when the clouds part for a while and I can glimpse the ice below, bringing to mind my three attempts to reach the North Pole on foot.

The first time was in 1983, when, as an eager and inexperienced twenty-six-year-old, I learned the toughest lesson of my adventuring career. Feeling desperately lonely – I was the only person attempting the North Pole that year – I waved goodbye to the Twin Otter airplane that carried me to Cape Columbia at the tip of Ellesmere Island in the Canadian High Arctic and bedded down for my first night on the ice, determined to complete the 413 nautical miles in forty days. I would need to average eleven miles a day. The folly of that target soon became apparent when, at the end of day one, I had covered just one mile. Every advance of ten yards was a momentous achievement. I had to haul my sledge across blocks and reefs of ice that intersected one another and traversed the ice pack as far as I could see. It was like dragging several hundred pounds across a shifting obstacle course with crumbling barricades that tumbled as I attempted to climb across them. In three days, I managed only five miles. Six weeks later, when I fell off a fifteen-foot ridge and cracked two ribs, my mission was over.

I did not dare return to the North Pole for another fourteen years. By that time, I had walked to the South Pole and the North Magnetic Pole, sailed to the South Magnetic Pole and climbed the highest mountain on every continent, including Mount Everest. Only then did I dare to contemplate what for me was the toughest challenge of all. And again the Arctic beat me and my companion, Rune Gjeldnes, with whom I tried to make the journey unsupported.

The next year, on 28 April 1998, Rune and I finally made it to the top of the world. After fifty-five days together on the ice, Rune had become a brother to me. He had saved me when I slipped through the ice, nursed my frostbite wounds and cooked the meals every night. When he was down and unmotivated, I had egged him on. Together we were an excellent team.

Now I wish I had someone like Rune along with me. Someone to talk to, someone to share the navigation while we take it in turns to sleep. At this moment, Rune is far below me, crossing the Arctic unsupported by walking from Siberia to the Pole and on to Canada. It is a mammoth undertaking, which he is sharing with his friend Tore Larsen. Thinking of the two of them dragging their sledges across the ice makes me regret not taking Clive Bailey or Gavin Hailes along with me. They both asked me, but I turned them down because two people would not fit in the basket. Now I feel selfish, doing it all on my own, especially as they have put in so much time and effort. My only reservation is that Clive and Gavin have no cold-weather experience. I may be a novice balloonist and they may be much better pilots than I am, but the problems I anticipate will be cold-weather problems rather than flying problems.

My mind was made up for me when Ranulph Fiennes returned from the North Pole, shortly before I left for Spitsbergen, with severe frostbite on several fingers. He had sustained those injuries in temperatures warmer than I may face on this flight, but at least when you are in a tent you can turn on the heater and sit it out. Or you can head back to the huts on the landing strip at Ward Hunt Island, as Fiennes did. In a balloon, there is no going back. You are at the mercy of the wind. You have to be able to endure the cold and know how to avoid picking up frostbite injuries. It was the cold that debilitated Andrée, Strindberg and Frænkel. For all their ballooning experience, they were not able to cope with the fearsome conditions the Arctic can throw at you. Nansen or Johansen would have been able to cover the distance on foot that Andrée faced when he ditched the *Eagle*, but Andrée was unable to because he was neither physically nor mentally prepared for the slog of trekking across the ice to safety.

The control centre breaks my reverie. I have brought along several books to while away the time, but I've not had a chance yet to get bored; Clive and Brian call me every hour with instructions and usually nag me to take in plenty of calories.

'What are you eating?' It is the cool polite voice of Brian Smith, a former British Airways pilot; a voice soaked in authority.

'Blimey. For Christ's sake, give me a break, Brian.'

'No. I need to know what you're eating, David.'

'Nothing. I can't stomach it.'

'What do you mean, nothing? You need to keep the calories and the water up. You dehydrate faster at altitude than at ground level.'

'I'm dizzy and I can't face the dehydrated food. Maybe it's the altitude. I'm on ginger biscuits, chocolate, hard-boiled sweets and loads of pork scratchings. I just don't feel hungry and I can't bring myself to cook, let alone eat, the Arctic brew.'

I do feel a bit weak, but as I am not moving much I shouldn't need a vast intake of calories. My biggest concern is the airplane, which is meant to be chasing me to shoot some footage for a television documentary.

'What about the chase plane, Brian?'

'It's too late. You're out of range of the plane and the helicopter.'

I am very disappointed by this news, not for myself but for Patrick O'Hagan, a reporter for HTV who has waited in Spitsbergen several weeks for this flight. Now he cannot get the shots he needs.

'What's your position, track, height and speed, David?'

'Hang on a second. You're nagging me so much that I haven't had a chance to check. Give me a break.'

'We're only doing our job, David. I'm just checking,' Brian replies.

I've had enough. I know the nagging is necessary, but it's getting on my nerves. I decide it's time for revenge. After the end of the comms broadcast, I change the code on the Argos, the electronic beacon that sends out a signal from which a satellite network can calculate my position to an accuracy of about a hundred metres. There's also a dial to set one of twelve pre-arranged codes, which I can use to send messages back to the control centre should all other means of communication fail. For example, code 5 indicates 'injured but can carry on' and code 4 signals 'technical problems – will have to land'. When everything is going to plan, the code alternates from 11 on odd hours to 12 on even hours. I set it to 0 – 'cold-weather problems'.

'What's going on, David? You've changed the Argos code,' Brian demands at the next hourly comms broadcast.

'I'm only doing my job, Brian. Just checking,' I reply.

* * *

By the end of the day, the autopilot is working better, I've almost emptied a tank of propane and one of the Iridium satellite phone batteries is exhausted. I spend the evening checking the pipes for kinks and putting chemical warmers called 'hotshots' on the pipework and burners to prevent them frosting.

Clive tells me to get some sleep, but I find it impossible. The roar of the burner and the motion of the basket keep me awake, but worst of all, the basket is very cramped. I try moving the ballast and my kit around to make more room, but there is not much space and it tilts the basket to one side. However I rearrange my chattels, the basket remains on a slope, which leaves me feeling very exposed even though the basket is waist-high. I now realize the basket is too small and flimsy for the flight, but it was the only second-hand basket on the market and I could not see the point of spending fifteen thousand pounds on a new basket when a used one was only a thousand.

To save the Iridium phone batteries, I use the radio and patch through Iceland Radio and Stockholm Radio to the control centre.

'Congratulations David,' says Brian. 'You've passed eighty-two degrees and fifty-five minutes north.'

We both recognize the significance – it was the most northerly latitude that Andrée reached. Fortunately, I am sailing at 5,000ft, sandwiched between a dense blanket of cumulus cloud beneath me and wispy cirrus above. At this point, Andrée was far below the cloud ceiling, bumping along the ice, probably aware that his dream would soon be over.

Passing 82°55′ North is a major milestone for me. Although there are 425 nautical miles to go, for the first time I have a feeling that this mad caper is going to be a success.

'It's feeling good, Brian. I cannot believe how well it's going,' I say. 'I don't want to overstep the mark, but can you start investigating the options for the pick-up?'

I ask Brian to call Dave Maloney at the Polar Shelf Institute in case we need a helicopter with an under-sling for a pick-up in Canada. And should I end up in Siberia, Genardi Oparin, who speaks fluent English but swills vodka like water, and Alex Eyturchin will sort out the logistics. Then, as if to punish me for my hubris, an acrid stream of smoke trails out of one of the navigation gadgets.

'Shit, Brian. The lithium battery in the autocom tracking system is spouting white smoke.' I grab the autocom, open the back and prise the battery out of it. It continues to smoulder and there's a sickly smell of burning plastic. 'It's okay now, Brian. What do you think caused it?'

Brian tells me he doesn't know, but will investigate. In the meantime, I have to rely on the global positioning system, or GPS, for tracking.

The next major event is the first time I manage to go to the toilet properly in the air. I have been dreading it, and I do not pass my first stool until I've been flying for more than thirty-six hours. Simple as it may seem, having a shit in a cramped, open basket at five thousand feet above the ground amid temperatures of −10°C is no laughing matter. Strangely, going to the toilet is the one topic more than any other that fascinates the many television, radio and newspaper journalists I speak to from the balloon. There's no mysterious science to it. All I do is stretch a plastic bag across a bucket and place my customized toilet seat on top of it. The seat is covered in fur, not for comfort or to satisfy some strange fetish, but to stop my backside sticking to the plastic in the extreme cold. When I'm finished, I chuck the plastic bag over the side and hope there are no polar bears directly below me. Except for the sand from the ballast sacks, it is the only item I plan to dump on the trip. I believe the High Arctic should be left as it is found, and I intend to carry everything else home.

I wake up after ninety minutes' fitful sleep, disorientated and confused. I am losing track of time because of the twenty-four-hour sunshine. I have to refer to my logbook to determine that it is day three of the flight, Tuesday 30 May. Even then I am confused and cannot work out if it is morning or afternoon.

I assume it is morning, and breakfast on the oranges I bought in Longyearbyen shortly before take-off. With the ginger biscuits they have become my staple diet. I store them hanging over the side of the basket, which has left them semi-frozen and particularly refreshing.

After breakfast I switch propane tanks. Two are almost empty. I am concerned that if I do not monitor the fuel consumption carefully, the tank connected to the burners will run out of fuel and I'll not be able to relight the flame. To avoid this, I switch tanks when they are still about ten per cent full.

I've been wearing the oxygen mask while I sleep. After my unplanned excursion to 9,500ft, I can afford to take no chances. I strapped it on before sleeping, but it is only now that I realize no oxygen was passing through; the flow meter reads zero. Fortunately, I have some bottles of compressed oxygen, which will buy me time in an emergency, but the fact that the liquid oxygen is not working is a problem. It cost a fortune to ship it in a large dewar flask to Longyearbyen, and it should have been enough to last ten days to two weeks. Without it, the length of time I can fly at a high altitude is severely limited. I pray that the weather patterns do not change and that I can catch a low-altitude track all the way to the Pole, otherwise the mission may be over.

To make matters worse, the autopilot is still not working as it should. I tell Clive at the next hourly comms broadcast.

'I think we've got it sussed, Old Man,' he says.

'Really, Boy? What's the verdict?'

'If you look back over the last couple of days, it's worked fine at night, when there's less solar gain. It screws up during the day, so the answer is to use it only at night. You'll have to fly the balloon manually during the day and sleep at night.'

It's not what I want to hear. I'm already exhausted. I've had fewer than three hours' sleep since I took off from Longyearbyen more than forty hours ago. I don't think I can fly it manually throughout the entire day. I'm becoming frustrated, and I tell Clive as much.

'Suit yourself, Old Man. You're the one who has to fly it. What do you want to do? Come back?' he replies.

He's got a point. There's nothing for it but to get on with it. I decide to blast the autopilot in the hope it will lock in to a chosen altitude at some point. I check the track and speed as *Britannic Challenger* ascends to 10,000ft, noting the direction the balloon heads at every hundred-foot interval. Then I head back down to 4,000ft, listening to the airliners on my HF radio, while I wait my turn to talk to Iceland Radio.

'Hello, this is Speedbird zero-five-four.'

It is a British Airways flight. I listen to the pilot talking to Iceland Radio, and when the chance comes, I cut in. 'This is Golf Bravo Yankee Zulu X-ray.' To the British Airways pilot I sound like any other jet cruising across the North Atlantic. I ask him to relay my position to Iceland Radio.

'Go ahead, old man,' comes the clipped reply.

'Altitude: four thousand feet. Speed: six knots. Over.'

'Could you repeat that please?'

'Altitude: four thousand feet. Over.'

'Please repeat again? Did you say forty thousand feet?'

'No, four thousand feet.'

'And what's your speed?'

'Six knots.'

'Can you repeat that please? Six zero zero knots?'

'No, six knots.'

The British Airways pilot is slow to catch on, but then he realizes that I am the balloonist he has been briefed about in his Notice to Airmen. Now he doesn't want to get off the radio.

'How's it going, *Britannic Challenger*?'

'Very well. But I can't chat. I don't have the battery power.'

The pilot gives me a few words of encouragement, passes on some weather information and wishes me luck. Then it's silence again.

At about 5.30 p.m., the readout on my GPS system passes a critical milestone: I am now north of the 85th latitude. This is the point of no return, marked by a thick red line on my map. If I ditch now, I will be out of reach of rescue aircraft. Like Andrée, I will have to haul my sledge across the ice to within the range of an airplane or helicopter. Even then, there is a chance a rescue operation might not be able to pick me up as the ice is approaching the point at which it is too thin to take the weight of an aircraft. In that case, I will camp on the ice until one of the summer icebreakers that routinely head for the North Pole passes by.

Clive calls to tell me to ditch the lithium battery that was smoking. He explains how to rig the autocom and the Iridium phone to a lead acid battery by using a car cigarette lighter socket. I fit the parts together, and to my amazement it works. I then drift off into a semi-sleep.

'Come in Golf Bravo Yankee Zulu X-ray. This is Iceland.'

I hear it faintly in my sleep, but assume it's a dream.

'Golf Bravo Yankee Zulu X-ray. Come in. This is Iceland.'

Again I ignore it. I wish it would shut up. Then it occurs to me: that rings a bell – it's me. I grab the HF radio and answer Iceland Radio's call.

'Urgent. Instructions to change track to zero-one-zero immediately,' Iceland Radio tells me. Then they patch me through to the call centre. I hear Clive's voice. He sounds tense.

'Old man. I'll read you the email from Luc,' he says. 'AVN12Z shows some dramatic changes in situation. Please say to David to climb to take an imperative track of zero-one-zero degrees from now. This is very urgent. Luc.'

I slam on the burners to full power, dump the smoking battery and empty three ten-kilogram bags of sand over the side. *Britannic Challenger* surges into the sky with such force that my knees buckle for a moment.

Clive is still on the radio. 'You've got thirty minutes to find the track, otherwise you'll do a U-turn. A new weather front is coming in and it'll take you straight back to Spitsbergen if you don't take a heading of zero-one-zero degrees to avoid it.'

As *Britannic Challenger* ascends, I measure the wind direction at each height. Over the course of nine hundred feet I find eight degrees of difference, but it is not enough. I started on a course of 350°; I need to change track by twenty degrees further east.

Britannic Challenger continues to rise. At 4,960ft I find a track of 008 degrees. Still not enough. At 5,200ft the wind direction has veered back to the west. It's 004 degrees, so I fire the burners again. At 5,480ft the track is 015 degrees.

'It's all over the place, Clive,' I radio to the control centre via the Iceland patch.

The sky is like spaghetti junction with streams of wind heading in different directions at different heights like a succession of flyovers stacked over a road. I need to find the stream heading 10° east of north, or 010 degrees, which is like trying to leap onto a flyover above you that you know is carrying traffic in the direction you want to go.

'I'm going to head back down to five thousand three hundred feet. Maybe it will be zero-one-zero degrees there. I'll call you in half an hour, when everything has stabilized.'

Forty-five minutes later I'm on a track of 010 degrees, cruising at 7.4 knots at an altitude of 5,060ft. The day is saved, and maybe there's a chance of some more sleep. But just as I'm nodding off half an hour later, Clive is back on the radio.

'We've had another message from Luc. It's more urgent

than the last. He says there's been a dramatic change in the wind patterns to the west of the balloon. The message is too long to go into in detail. He says you must maintain a speed of at least eight knots, preferably ten knots, for the next ten hours. If you go any further west than twelve degrees east, the stream will pull you back to Spitsbergen. Luc suggests you climb to ten thousand feet.'

I look at the GPS. I'm at 85°48′ North and 12°20′ East. It's on the borderline – only a third of a degree between success and failure. I don't want to fly at 10,000ft as I'll need oxygen and I'm in short supply. Again, I start the painstaking process of recording the track and speed of *Britannic Challenger* for every fifty-foot change in altitude.

An hour later, at 11 p.m., I radio the control centre. 'I'm tracking on zero-two-zero degrees and eight knots. I can get nine knots at a higher level, but the track is zero-three-zero degrees.'

Clive replies: 'Zero-two-zero degrees at eight knots is better – I hope I'm right about this. Luc's message says to maintain zero-one-zero to zero-one-five degrees until midnight.' He reads from the email: 'Then from midnight until 6 a.m. Zulu time, the tracks must veer between zero-one-five and zero-two-five degrees. From six a.m. until midday, the tracks between zero-two-five and zero-three-five degrees will be fine, but he will confirm that tomorrow morning.'

'So there's not much chance of a quiet night,' I reply.

' 'Fraid not, Old Man,' comes Clive's reply. 'How are you feeling?'

'Tired and full of wind,' I say.

'Well, point your arse out of the basket, let rip and see if you can get nine knots then.'

I'm too exhausted to laugh. The longer this flight goes on, the less sleep I am getting. I've been in the air for fifty-four hours and I've spent no more than four hours snoozing.

'Anything else I can do for you before I go?' asks Clive.

'Yes. A soft bed, please, and a pizza with anchovies and extra cheese to go.'

CHAPTER TEN

THE TREK

ARCTIC OCEAN

14 July, 1897

ANDRÉE, FRÆNKEL AND STRINDBERG STOOD ON THE ARCTIC ice and stared at the *Eagle*, which lay like a beached whale, defeated and deflated. All around them stretched a merciless, unending expanse of snow, ice and open water. In places, the warm summer sun had partially melted the centre of an ice floe, leaving a polynya, or pool, to be traversed. In other places, the floes had parted to leave leads of water, some a few feet across, others up to a mile wide, criss-crossing the landscape. Through this maze of ice rubble, pressure ridges and water, the three men knew they must find their way either to civilization or to their deaths.

They were hungry, exhausted and dejected, but there was plenty of work to do before they could rest. First, the *Eagle* had to be made safe; then they had to prepare their first camp. Andrée immediately issued orders, assigning to Frænkel the tasks of keeping a meteorological journal, erecting the tent and running the camp. Strindberg was put in charge of preparing all meals, keeping track of their provisions and compiling a logbook of astronomical observations. Andrée took it upon himself to be responsible for navigation and reconnaissance, to hunt for food – he shot his first polar bear five days after the *Eagle* landed – and to record their plight in his diaries. *Our days start with boot greasing*, he wrote later. *I reconnoitre after the tent is tidied up and the table is set, Frænkel takes meteorological observations and cleans weapons, cuts sandwiches and lays the table. Nils does the boiling and frying – we eat bear steak two times a day. Frænkel is housekeeper, Nils the cook.*

It took a week to unpack their provisions from the *Eagle*, to assemble the boat and the sledges, then to strap their equipment to each sledge and to consider their meagre options. The cold, however, was a shock for which they were completely unprepared. They had very little protective clothing; a few thick jumpers and sturdy boots, but nothing to stop the icy wind cutting through to their bones. The ice and snow made lashing the boat and equipment to their sledges all the more difficult and slow. To prevent frostbite they had to stop work every half an hour or so to warm their hands in the shelter of the canvas tent, or in the lee of the boat, which they had turned on its side to block out the wind.

All three struggled to come to terms with their circumstances, although Strindberg was relieved that the perilous flight of the *Eagle* was at last over. 'All it would have taken is one spark during one of our collisions with the ice and we might all have gone up in flames,' he told his two companions over dinner in the tent one evening. 'We were lucky that the short fire near the end of the flight did not end in disaster.' But his relief at landing safely was tinged with doubt that they might never reach land across the ice. *Maybe we should have fought harder to get the Eagle above the clouds*, he thought. *Then we might have reached land in a matter of days, not the weeks or months it will take us on foot.*

The men soon lost track of time under the midnight sun. There was little difference in temperature or in the brightness of the sky from one part of the day to another, so for the first week at least they fell into a general pattern of sleeping during morning hours, waking in the early afternoon and working through the late afternoon and night. Eating dinner, the main meal of their day, at breakfast time, they argued for hours about the best way forward. Andrée spent much of each day climbing onto the *Eagle*'s wicker gondola to search repeatedly, and in vain, for land on the distant horizon. All he ever saw was a mess of pressure ridges, formed when the ice floes ground against one another and the softer ice broke apart into huge blocks of rubble that were pushed up to form barriers of ice, like giant white hedges.

By 21 July, Andrée had come to a decision. 'Our best option is to head southeast for Cape Flora,' he told Strindberg and Frænkel. At Cape Flora, an island in the archipelago of Franz Josef Land, a depot of food had been left for the expedition. 'I know from Nansen that it is possible to survive winter on the islands,' he added, as they ate a hearty supper of meat from a polar bear shot by Andrée two days earlier.

Looking down at Strindberg's hand, tending a pan that was frying some more meat over the Primus stove, Andrée was shocked at how dirty his friend had become.

'I hope you washed before preparing our dinner?' he asked.

'Washed?' Strindberg replied. 'I washed myself the day before yesterday. All that's left is the kind of dirt that sticks on all by itself.'

Andrée looked at Frænkel and Strindberg's faces. If my face is anything like theirs, he thought, it must have the same lines of dirt engrained deep in the skin, the greasy residue of a week's sweat. Unable to wash properly, the men stank of sweat, urine and the natural oils that had caked their hair to their heads, made their moustaches clog and hang like thick flannels on their lips, and attracted filth to their skin like iron filings to a magnet.

After dinner, Strindberg settled in their cramped tent. Squeezed between Andrée and Frænkel in one large sleeping bag, he wrote deep into the night to Anna. *Most dearly beloved, I am writing to you after a week's delay. I beg your forgiveness for the anxiety I have thus caused you, but I am sure that I am laying down the foundations of our future happiness. When we enjoy the sweetness of our union, we shall think back to these hard times when we were apart and our joy will grow.* He described in detail the terrifying moments before the balloon took off from the wooden shed at Virgohamna. *My thoughts turned for a moment to you and my cherished ones at home. How would the journey go? I asked myself. How fast my feelings came, but I had to restrain them. I asked Machuron, who was standing nearest to me and whom I found very affable, to pass on my love to you. I know there were tears on my cheeks, but I hid them by checking that the camera was in order and standing ready to throw out ballast. Goodnight, my darling.*

The three men slept for most of the day and woke in the late afternoon. After an early-evening breakfast, Strindberg continued his letter to Anna. *It is almost seven o'clock in the evening and we have just packed our sledges. We are ready and will start out from where we've landed. Let us see how hard it is to reach Cape Flora. The sledges are so heavy to haul. Yes, we are off now!*

It was foggy when the three Swedes began their long trek towards Cape Flora. Each sledge weighed over four hundred pounds, a weight each of them soon discovered they could not drag on their own. Andrée's sledge alone had four planks for crossing gaps in the ice, three bamboo poles, a carrying-ring, a boat hook, some tarpaulin, a sack of private possessions, an eight-pound tin of boot-waterproofing grease, a hose, a large vice, a shovel with a spare handle, a grapnel and rope, and three baskets stuffed with medicine, food and equipment. In total it weighed more than 464lb. Frænkel and Strindberg's sledges were just as heavy with equipment, food, drink and, in Frænkel's case, the canvas boat*.

'It's no use,' Frænkel said after a short while. 'I am the strongest and I cannot pull my sledge for much longer. We shall have to work out some sort of relay.'

They knew Frænkel was right. They decided to harness themselves to one sledge, drag it a few hundred yards, release themselves from the harness, return to the second sledge, tie themselves to it, drag it to the first one and repeat the process with the third sledge.

'This will mean a very slow journey to Cape Flora,' Strindberg said. 'At a stroke we have increased the distance we must walk by a factor of five.'

'We have no choice,' Andrée replied, leaning forward to take the harness on the first sledge. 'Now let's set off.' As one they took the first step.

'Watch out!' Strindberg yelled, jumping into a knee-deep pool of melted ice water as the sledge slipped into a polynya. He grabbed the sledge, holding it steady long enough for Andrée and Frænkel to drag it onto the next ice floe.

'The day is saved,' Andrée shouted.

'But not my letters to Anna, or my only portrait of her. They are soaked.'

Strindberg was devastated. He had taken but a few steps on the ice and already the sack containing his most precious possessions, the only links he had to his beloved Anna, were damaged. There was no way of drying the sack's contents there and then, so he stuffed the sack under the tarpaulin that covered the sledge and prepared, once again, to haul it across the ice with his two companions.

Later that night, Strindberg wrote to Anna again.

Now your Nils knows what it is to walk on the Polar ice. We had a little accident at the start of our journey. The first sledge slipped to one side as we were crossing from

---

* For a full inventory of equipment and food, see Appendix Two on page 320.

*the first ice floe and fell in, and we succeeded in pulling it
out only with the greatest difficulty. I waded into the
water to my knees and held the sledge firmly so that it
would not sink. Andrée and Frænkel then crossed to the
next ice floe and together we managed to lift the sledge
onto it. The terrible thing was that my sack, which was on
the sledge, is wet inside. And it is in there that I have all
your letters and your portrait! Yes, they will be my dearest
treasures during the winter.*

*After we had pulled the sledge up again, we navigated
our way across some ice floes interspersed with leads of
water. We crossed these by pushing the ice floes together.
It was slow work pushing the larger ones, of course.
Eventually we came to a large field of ice that we
wandered across with our sledges for two or three kilometres . . . Well, my dear, what will you be thinking of this
winter? This is my only concern . . .*

Strindberg continued to think of Anna, so far away, and
of how much he was missing her. He wondered what she
was doing, whom she was with and who might see her
languid smile. But he could not reminisce for long. After a
brief lunch, Andrée exhorted Strindberg and Frænkel to
press on. They had a long night's walking ahead of them.

At the end of the trek, the explorers pitched camp on an
ice floe covered in pressure ridges and Strindberg prepared
supper. *We have encamped on a picturesque piece of ice
and have pitched our tent*, he wrote to Anna before he
went to sleep that night. *Inside, we have our sleeping bag,
in which all three of us are now lying side by side. It is a
squeeze, but the camaraderie is good. There is much I
should write about, but now I must get to sleep.
Goodnight, my darling.*

When they woke, Andrée, Strindberg and Frænkel took
several hours to eat breakfast, break camp and strap their
possessions to their sledges. It was cold enough to freeze
the edges of the polynyas and again they encountered
wide stretches of open water, which they crossed by laying

213

the sledges across the boat. After nine hours they stopped, having covered no more than two miles. Strindberg made a foul-tasting soup from peas, rusks, stock cubes and meat powder which he described as a 'scanty dinner', eaten with some butter to increase their calorie intake.

The next day was even worse. The ice was criss-crossed with small crevices and leads, and it was snowing lightly. They struggled to drag and push the heavy sledges across the highest pressure ridges they had encountered so far. All day they battled with a succession of strength-sapping walls of ice, some of them many times higher than the men themselves, interspersed with fields of ice rubble blocks that jarred their joints and threatened to rip the sledges apart. Having to make three journeys to drag their sledges across the treacherous terrain made the task all the more exhausting. For the first time, they considered dumping some of their equipment and food to lighten the loads on their sledges.

Towards the end of the third day's trek, as the clock moved into the early hours of 25 July, they stopped and shouted four loud hurrahs to mark Anna's birthday. Half an hour later, shattered and famished, Strindberg sat down and wrote tenderly to his love. *We have just stopped for the day after drudging and pulling our sledges for ten hours. I am really rather tired, but before I go to sleep, I wanted to say a few words to you. First and foremost, I must congratulate you, for on this day your birthday begins. Oh, how I wish I could tell you myself that I am in excellent health and that you need not have any fears on my behalf. We are sure to arrive home in the course of time . . .*

In Gothenburg, Johan Oscar Strindberg and his family had invited Anna, who had last seen Nils on 17 May, to stay with them. She and the rest of Nils' family had been devouring newspaper accounts of the expedition's departure from Dane's Island. From the letters conveyed by the *Lofoten* and Alexis Machuron, Anna knew how much Nils was missing her. Every morning she woke in the hope that the letter Nils had promised to throw from the *Eagle* would arrive. At breakfast, her first question was always to ask Occa if Machuron had forwarded the letter yet. Every day, Occa had bad news, and after a few weeks Anna stopped asking and gave up hoping. By then she knew the letter would never come, and although she had the utmost faith in Nils, she began to fear the worst.

On 15 July, four days after the *Eagle* was launched from Dane's Island and the day after it came to a final halt on the ice, a Norwegian sealer, the *Alken*, was passing within a few miles of the northern tip of Spitsbergen when a strange-looking bird landed on its mast, pursued by two ivory gulls. The skipper, Ole Hansen, was dragged out of his bunk at around 1.30 a.m. to inspect it.

'You've woken me to look at this fowl? It's nothing more than an Arctic grouse,' he said, unimpressed at being woken during the middle of the night. 'Give me my gun.'

Captain Hansen climbed up the *Alken*'s rigging and shot the bird, which fell overboard.

'Back in the water, where it belongs,' he said with a grunt as he returned to his cabin. 'And don't let me catch any of the deck hands fishing it out of the water for its meat. It's not worth it.'

The *Alken* continued its journey until the next day, when she pulled alongside another sealer and Hansen shared a few titbits of hunting information with the skipper of the other boat. Gradually, he came to an alarming realization.

'So you mean that bird was not an Arctic grouse at all, but one of the carrier pigeons from that Andrée's expedition?' he said incredulously. 'I didn't even know the mad Swede had taken off.'

The two mariners continued their conversation for a short while. As the *Alken* drew away, Hansen shouted to his first mate. 'Get me the ship's log. I want to know where I shot that bird.' When his first mate gave him the location – 80°44′ North 20°20′ East – he issued another order. 'Full speed ahead to that position.'

Half a day later, two boats were lowered from the *Alken* to search for the body of the carrier pigeon. Amazingly, one of them found it. Hansen examined the pigeon and found a brass cylinder strapped to one leg. On the outside of the cylinder some instructions were inscribed in Norwegian: *From Andrée's Polar Expedition to the Aftonbladet of Stockholm. Open the cylinder from the end and take out two letters. The handwritten note is to be wired to the* Aftonbladet *and the one in shorthand is to be mailed by the first post to the newspaper.*

Hansen found only the handwritten letter, written on paraffin-soaked parchment. *From Andrée's Polar Expedition to Aftonbladet, Stockholm. 13th July. 12.30 midday. Lat 82°2′ Long. 15°5′E. Good speed to E.10°south. All well on board. This is the third pigeon-post. Andrée.* The shorthand report, which was intended to provide material for a full account of the expedition so far, and which Anna had hoped would carry personal news from Nils, was missing.

Like Anna, Strindberg spent every spare moment yearning to see his fiancée again. *How very much all this occupies my thoughts during the day,* he wrote on the evening of her birthday. *I have plenty of time to think, and it is so delightful to have such pleasant memories and such happy expectations of the future!*

But thinking back to those precious times spent together was becoming increasingly painful for Strindberg. Every reminder of his past happiness – the sight of Anna as she spun the pointer for the balloon dance, a remembrance of her soft lips as they kissed – made the misery of his current existence and the uncertainty over his future all the more acute. Like Andrée and Frænkel, he clung on to whatever recollections of better times he could muster from the recesses of his memory, but Strindberg felt that for him it was different.

He had a more certain future to look forward to, but also more to lose if his dreams of a life back in Anna's arms did not come true.

After making his companions a dinner of cheese sandwiches, biscuits, coffee and syrup – Andrée and Frænkel teased the last drop from the bottle by washing it out twice – Strindberg continued his letter to his love while sucking a caramel, a *real luxury*, he told her.

We have stopped here for the night on an open place. All around us is ice, ice in every direction. Hummocks, walls and fissures in the sea alternate with melted ice – it's all everlastingly the same. It is snowing now, but at least it is calm and not especially cold. At home I expect you have warmer, summer weather.

It is strange to think that not even for your next birthday will it be possible for us to be together, as perhaps we will need to winter here for more than one year. We are moving onwards so slowly that we may not reach Cape Flora this winter, but be forced, like Nansen, to spend the winter in a cellar in the earth.

Poor little Anna, in what despair you will be if we do not return next autumn. I am tortured by the thought of it, too, though not for my own sake. I do not mind if I suffer hardships as long as I come home to you eventually.

That night was one of terror. Lying in their fragile canvas tent, huddled in their single sleeping bag, Andrée, Strindberg and Frænkel listened and shivered as pans of ice, some hundreds of feet across, smashed and ground against one another as the huge currents of the Arctic Ocean twisted, ebbed and flowed beneath them. They were in the midst of an icequake. Around them the world crashed and rumbled; a scraping sound like a fierce wind rushed at them as huge blocks of ice fell from newly formed pressure ridges; and every now and then, the ice snapped with a bang like a rifle shot as a pan of ice split. It was impossible to sleep. Would the surface they were lying on be overturned and buried in rubble as a pressure ridge was forced thirty feet up? Strindberg feared most of all that the ice would split apart, dropping them, inside their tent and sleeping bag, into the freezing ocean beneath them.

At times like these, Strindberg closed his eyes and tried to drown out the present by thinking back to his life in Stockholm. He saw the day when he went cycling on his velocipede with Gustav Lang and then visited the Peters and Wallings after lunch. He thought of the days spent at the university, poring over his books or teaching undergraduates. But most of all he dreamt of Anna. However hard he tried to think of other things and other people, Anna's kind face with its warm, lazy smile always pushed itself to the front of his mind.

Exhaustion and injuries were starting to bite, but worst of all was the frustration of fighting against the ice rubble and pressure ridges for between ten and sixteen hours at a time, only to cover a mile or so each day. The three men seldom talked about their plight, preferring instead to grit their teeth and keep on slogging through the terrible terrain. Often, when they had to lift one of the heavy sledges over a pressure ridge higher than themselves, Andrée would steal a look at the faces of his companions to search for signs of surrender. So far, there had been none, but he could not help wondering how long their will to live would triumph over their growing fatigue. Then, he knew, their morale would break, and the petty arguments that could lead to their demise would begin. He hoped only that they reached civilization before that day.

The next day the explorers took a new approach to dragging their sledges across the ice, seeking out smooth ice along the edges of leads of open water. This, they hoped, would help them cover a greater distance, but their experiment did not last long.

'Quick! Help!'

Frænkel turned to see Strindberg, walking along the edge of a lead, lose his footing and shout for assistance.

'Hold on!' he shouted, shaking the sledge harness from his shoulders. Beside him, Andrée was doing the same. Strindberg was up to his shoulders in the icy water, still attached to the sledge the three men had been dragging along a smooth edge of a lead. He was near the edge of the ice floe, but unable to pull himself out of the water. Any protrusion of ice that he grabbed came away in his hands. Probing the thickness of the ice gingerly, Andrée and Frænkel crept to the edge of the lead and dragged Strindberg, frozen and shaking with fright, out of the water and onto the ice.

'Take your clothes off. We'll wring them out,' Andrée suggested as Strindberg shivered beside the sledge, searching for replacement clothing. Pulling on some knickerbockers, he set off again, attempting to overcome his shock by talking loudly to his companions about the seals and gulls they had spotted.

Every day, Andrée scanned the ice and sky for wildlife, and often took core samples of the ice. Determined to rescue some scientific credibility for his expedition, he made copious notes of the sparse flora and fauna he spotted. *Cod's head. Cranium. In a gully we found a small fish. It was unafraid but surprised to see us. I killed it with a shovel. Sample number nine*, he wrote on one occasion. For the rational scientist in Andrée it was one way of coping with the uncertainty of his future. It was also a way, Andrée hoped, of silencing critics such as Rear-Admiral Markham and General Greely, who, he had to admit, had been correct in predicting that his plan to reach the Pole would turn out to be an idealistic dream. They had also said there was no scientific benefit in trying to fly to the Pole; the samples he collected, Andrée thought, might prove otherwise.

Strindberg, too, was increasingly at pains to present his journey in a favourable light, even though he was coming to realize that Anna and his family might never read his letters. Later that day, when they came upon a very wide lead of water and Andrée and Frænkel headed off in search of a crossing point, Strindberg took the opportunity to sit beside the sledges and write again to Anna.

The weather is pretty bad – wet snow and fog – but we are in good spirits. We have been talking all day, Andrée of how he entered the Patent Bureau and so on. He and Frænkel have gone ahead on a reconnaissance tour, I have stayed with the sledges and am now sitting writing to you. It must be evening at home, and like me you have had a pleasant day.

Here one day passes like another: pull and toil at the sledges, eat and sleep. The most delightful hour of the day is when I am in bed and can allow my thoughts to fly back to better and happier times, when we were together. For now, our most pressing concern is where we shall winter. I can see the others coming back so I shall stop writing and continue our plodding with the sledges. Au revoir, my beloved.

The next morning, Strindberg woke to find tracks outside their tent indicating that a large polar bear and cub had passed by their camp during the night. Although Andrée and Frænkel were excited by the paw prints, taking them as a welcome sign that a vital source of food was nearby, for Strindberg they were a frightening reminder of their precarious grip on life.

Footsore, fatigued by the weight of the sledges and frustrated by their slow progress, the three explorers decided after breakfast to dump almost half of their equipment and food. Urging each other to be ruthless in dumping as much weight as possible, by the time they had finished their sledges were almost two hundred pounds lighter, and with newly repaired runners. A good task finished, they filled their stomachs with as much of the dumped food as they could eat. *Great indulgence in food after making reduction*, Andrée noted in his diary.

After lunch, Strindberg shot his first polar bear; they

found the meat to be much better if it was soaked in sea water for an hour before eating. The following day, Frænkel added to the tally by shooting a particularly bold bear that had not been scared off by a whistle and hunting horn. The skin was removed carefully to repair the sleeping bag, which was shedding its reindeer hair everywhere. *Lose one, you find a thousand*, Andrée had joked about the hairs, which were turning up in their food, stuck to their clothes and slicked onto their greasy, filthy skins.

With all the extra bear meat to carry, the explorers dumped more of their meat powder and bread on 28 July, and washed down some honey and biscuits with a bottle of champagne before resuming their trek shortly before midnight.

For the first time since they had landed on the ice, the temperature dropped significantly below freezing so they wrapped sennegrass, used by Laplanders for insulation, around their feet before putting on their outer socks and freshly greased boots. Andrée also greased his hands with whale blubber to protect them from the cold. With the wind behind them, he was optimistic of covering a large distance that day.

'The northwesterly wind ought to help push the drift of the ice floes southeastwards, towards Cape Flora,' Andrée shouted as they set off.

But his hopes were soon sunk by a succession of fourteen leads of open water. To cross the widest they had to strap each of their sledges in turn to the boat and ferry it across the open water. It was a lengthy and perilous operation; they paddled cautiously, taking care not to let the weight of the sledge unbalance the boat, and had to make the journey between ice floes three times to convey each of the sledges. Their fortunes did not improve once they were back on solid ice: severe rubble blocked their way along the entire route that day.

The pressure ridges and rubble subsided only towards the end of the next day's trek. Wearing snowshoes for the first time, they came to a large pan of ice, smoother than any before. This they nicknamed Parade-ice, pronouncing it 'paradise'. For several hours they made good headway, enjoying the relative relief the level ice gave their jarred and weary limbs. It was bliss, Strindberg thought, not to be trying to gain a foothold on tumbling blocks of ice rubble while yanking his sledge across a broken landscape. Several times he and his companions had sprained ankles, twisted their knees and pulled muscles while clambering over pressure ridges; walking on a smooth, flat pan of ice really was paradise in comparison. But the easy going did not last. At the end of a sixteen-hour trek they came to the widest lead they had yet encountered. And the day after that was much the same: exhausting slogs across rubble alternating with treacherous open water, the backbreaking toil made worse by the ocean currents beneath the ice.

'We must head southeast to reach Cape Flora, but the sea is carrying the ice to the southwest,' Andrée observed, looking up from his calculations. Frænkel recorded their position every day and made most of the meteorological observations, but as expedition leader, Andrée reserved the right to navigate their course. 'To counteract the drift and still head southeast towards Cape Flora, we must walk directly east,' he decided, so they set off in a new direction, hoping they could walk faster than the ocean current could push against them.

It was a day on which all three men had their own personal miseries. Andrée slipped into a pool of melting snow water, Frænkel contracted snow-blindness and Strindberg realized he had become so grimy he could no longer shift the dirt. Their only relief from this wretched existence came at the end of the day, when Strindberg reported that some of the food on Andrée's sledge had been ruined when he fell into the water.

'What's damaged then?' Frænkel asked.

'The Mellin's Food,' Strindberg replied, referring to a gruel made from a milk-substitute baby food. 'Our dessert.'

'Very good! We had better eat it then,' Frænkel said, sounding distinctly more cheerful than before.

While preparing their food, Strindberg attempted to get one of his hands clean, but four weeks of sweat and grime just would not shift and he gave up after scrubbing long and hard with a wet sock. Nevertheless, as Andrée noted with characteristic detachment, the difference between Strindberg's half-cleaned and dirty hands was *like that between a Caucasian and a black man.*

On the last day of July, they set off in a dense fog that prevented Andrée from finding the best route. It was a whiteout, the bewildering environment every polar traveller dreads, when the clouds and the ice beneath the feet meld into a single featureless expanse of whiteness, without depth, contours or shade. Carefully they edged their way forward, frightened that at any moment they might unwittingly step on a section of ice that was too weak to take their weight. It took six hours to cross ten leads of water; then they came to a succession of pressure ridges that continued for more than a mile. When the hummocks and rubble abated and the terrain flattened, the snow was deeper than ever before. At times it was too much for Strindberg, and his knees would buckle beneath him as he slumped, exhausted, into the snow, briefly enjoying his collapse for the respite it offered from the backbreaking trudge, before hauling himself back onto his feet to continue the endless march. *5 a.m. start. We tramped on our knees through deep snow*, Andrée wrote in his diary. *Nothing but tramp-tramp on our knees. The discoverer of the attractions of collapsing: Nils. Ever since the start we have been in very difficult terrain.*

At 6.40 p.m., they were relieved to fall into their tent and curl up in the sleeping bag, but they were soon shaken out of the joy of their rest when Strindberg revealed his astronomical measurements. Despite their long labours, Strindberg told his companions, the ocean currents had carried them further west that day than they had managed to walk to the east. *This is not encouraging*, Andrée wrote with considerable understatement, *but we shall continue our course to the east for some time more, or at least for as long as there is still some sense in doing so.*

After climbing into the sleeping bag with Andrée and Frænkel, Strindberg again wrote a few words to his love. *It is some days since I last chatted to you. Since then the situation has worsened considerably,* he began, before describing how they had dumped almost half of their provisions to lighten their sledges, and explaining their difficulties in crossing the leads.

Nils had in fact given up writing of how he missed Anna. Dreams of their shared future had been replaced with descriptions of the cold realities of survival. The time had passed for gentle words. He was too tired and too dejected to continue to hope for the better and happier future he had written of only a few days earlier. As he wrote his last words that evening – *and then we unpacked in order to leave some of the provisions and equipment here* – he no longer had the energy to think of home. He was weary, more so than he had ever been. Laying down his pen for the last time, he sighed with relief that he would no longer have to pretend to Anna that the trek was a brave adventure from which it was only a matter of time before he returned to her embrace. He tucked the notebook in which he had written the letters to Anna under his head, turned over and fell into the kind of deep slumber that only the truly tired sleep.

During the early days of August, Andrée, Strindberg and Frænkel encountered much better conditions, probably, Andrée thought, because they were moving away from the fiercest section of the polar ocean stream. They still had to battle across rubble fields, but most of the time they were walking across wide expanses of flat, hardened ice, and they covered greater distances than ever before. And on 2 August their luck improved further. About an hour after eating the last of their supply of polar bear meat for breakfast, a bear crossed their path. Frænkel and

Strindberg both missed it, but Andrée dropped it with a single shot to the breast. Although it was old – Andrée later wrote that the cooked flesh was *as tough as galoshes* – they removed its kidneys, tongue, ribs and some fillet, leaving the carcass to the gulls in the hope it would entice another bear to follow them on their trek.

The weather had also begun to improve considerably, and by 4 August, for the first time since they left the *Eagle* on the ice a fortnight earlier, Strindberg was able to make an accurate astronomical assessment of their position. This time, it was bad news. 'Since leaving the *Eagle*,' he told Andrée and Frænkel, 'we have covered thirty-three miles in a south-southwesterly direction. And in the last four days the drift has been so strong that we have veered almost eight miles to the north-northwest.' Their efforts had come to nothing. Strindberg's measurements showed that after several days of dragging their sledges for more than four miles each day, they had wound up further north than when they had started out.

Andrée spent the next few hours scanning the horizon with his binoculars, hoping to sight land, but he could see nothing but ice. Early that morning, he gave up hope of reaching Cape Flora. *We can overcome neither the current nor the ice, and have absolutely no hope of doing anything by continuing our march to the east*, he wrote in his diary. *We therefore intend to start our next hike towards the Seven Islands, which we hope to reach in six to seven weeks.*

It was extremely discouraging. They had spent their best energies attempting to walk southeast; now they were slightly south-southwest of their starting point and about to reverse their course. Their disappointment was not alleviated by the knowledge that the smaller depot of food on the Seven Islands might not be enough to see them through the winter. But Andrée felt they had no choice but to head that way.

CHAPTER ELEVEN

THE DOWNFALL

ARCTIC OCEAN

4 August, 1897

'WE ARE RUNNING OUT OF FOOD,' SAID STRINDBERG, LOOKING up from the inventory in his logbook. Beside him, crouching in the shelter of the upturned boat, Andrée and Frænkel were finishing their breakfast of cocoa and polar bear. They had suspected as much; the few scraps of meat Strindberg had served them were insufficient sustenance for a day's hiking on flat terrain, let alone the morass of pressure ridges, ice rubble and leads that lay between them and the Seven Islands. 'Bread, in particular, is in short supply, and of the one hundred and ninety-five pounds of provisions we are dragging on our sledges, many offer little nutritional value,' Strindberg added, reeling through the list. The coffee, salt and soup tablets contained few, if any, calories, and the luxuries such as chocolate, port and whortleberry jam were good for morale but would do little to bolster their strength.

Winter was approaching fast, and with it came the cold and permanent darkness the three men feared more than anything. Already the temperature had dropped to −2°C and their route was awash with pools and leads of open water that Andrée wrote they could negotiate only by crawling between islands of ice *on all fours as if we were still in the spring of our youth*. One of the leads they encountered was a mile wide; it took them four hours to raft across it on an ice floe.

When they stopped walking eight hours later their spirits were dented even further when Strindberg prepared a meagre lunch of some small scraps of bread, butter and biscuit, not enough to replenish their energy ahead of another seven hours to be spent dragging their heavy sledges across the ice. At most, they were managing to cover three and a half miles in twelve hours, and that was on relatively flat ice; usually it was much less. With about 130 miles to trek in a straight line to the Seven Islands – and possibly twice or three times as far against the drift – their lack of progress was slowly, but steadily, chipping away at their hopes of ever reaching land again.

And so it continued for another week. The ice deteriorated, the temperature dropped to −8°C, the wind blew in their faces, increasing the distance they had to walk by pushing the ice against them, and they were forced to adopt starvation rations. Rain, snow and sweat soaked their clothes and their boots began to fall apart. All three men became ever more exhausted, Frænkel relied increasingly on opium to control frequent bouts of diarrhoea, and the reindeer hair on their sleeping bag continued to shed. *A little reindeer hair in the food is to be recommended*, Andrée wrote, as usual trying to make the best of their plight. *While removing it one is prevented from eating too quickly and greedily.*

By 11 August, however, Andrée was less optimistic. *First thing in the morning I fell into the water and so did my sledge. Nearly everything became wet through. Strindberg ran into Frænkel's sledge and broke the boat with the grapnel. All the sledges turned somersaults several times during the day. Mine twice turned completely upside down. The terrain was terrible. All imaginable difficulties happened and when the evening came, we were not at all happy.* Despite the hardship, their tent was often a scene of cosy domesticity, Strindberg darning clothes and Frænkel oiling guns before the three of them crawled into the sleeping bag together.

But their stock of meat was dwindling fast, as Strindberg pointed out, even though they ate polar bear only every other day. This dire situation was not helped when Frænkel and Strindberg failed to shoot a large polar bear that crossed their tracks and, later on, a seal that was basking on the ice. When they could, they ate ivory gulls, and they celebrated passing south of the 82° line of latitude by sharing a small tin of sardines and an almond tart.

On Friday 13 August, they finished their last pound of polar bear for breakfast and set off knowing that they must find some other source of protein soon. An attempt to shoot a seal came to nothing, and a small fish that Andrée caught was not enough to satiate their bottomless hunger. Then, just after they crossed a lead, their luck turned.

'Three bears!' Andrée shouted to Frænkel and Strindberg.

They set off in hot pursuit, knowing from previous experience that they needed to be crafty to track them down.

We hid behind a pressure ridge and waited, Andrée recalled, *but no bears came. Then I volunteered to be bait and crept forward across the flat ice, whistling softly. The female bear noticed me and advanced towards me, sniffing. I turned away from her and lay down in the snow. I was soon too cold to lie still, so I shouted to the others that we should take the bears by surprise. Almost immediately the female bear approached me again, but was stopped by a shot that missed her. I jumped up and shot again. The fleeing bears stopped in their tracks.*

Another shot, fired by Strindberg or Frænkel, rang out.

It wounded the female bear at a distance of about eighty metres. She roared and turned to flee, Andrée took careful aim, and with a single shot killed her. His fourth shot dropped one of her cubs. Frænkel hit the other bear, wounding it and eliciting a blood-curdling roar. The final shot, by Strindberg, brought the beast down.

There was great joy among the group, and we cut our bears into pieces with satisfaction, Andrée wrote that evening. It took all day to strip the bears of their hearts, brains, ribs, kidneys and tongues, and load 138lb of fresh meat onto their sledges, enough to last them for twenty-three days. *We have been butchers all day,* Andrée continued in his diary. *I have been trying to do some tanning to get skin to mend the sleeping bag. The skin from the front legs seems to be the most suitable, as it is the thinnest.*

That night they had a feast. Strindberg made a soup of polar bear meat and fried the heart, brain and spare ribs. They ate this with bread and wholemeal wheat biscuits. *At 6.30 a.m. we went to our beds after having washed our hands and eaten ourselves full!* Andrée concluded, satiated at last.

When they woke at 4 p.m., they continued their feast with a cooked breakfast of bear meat and kidneys, a gull that Andrée had shot the previous day, and some biscuits, bread and coffee. The rest of the day was spent sleeping off their indulgence and repairing the sleeping bag, their coats and spectacles. Andrée made himself a waterproof coat and bandaged Strindberg's injuries: a cut and swollen hand, and a boil on his upper lip.

After Andrée had finished nursing his wounds, Strindberg listed proposals in his logbook for improvements he hoped would ensure their next polar balloon expedition was a success. *The draglines to be sheathed with metal; the car to be positioned inside the carrying-ring; the hydrogen to be somewhat heated by boiling water in the car and condensing the steam in a sheet-iron vessel in the balloon; the balloon to be made of the same cloth about 6,000 cubic metres in volume.* Even with the prospect of a long, frozen winter on the ice ahead of them, and the very real possibility that they might again run out of food, Strindberg remained convinced they had a chance of returning to Sweden and embarking on a third attempt to fly to the Pole.

The next day both Andrée and Strindberg had diarrhoea, but although the attacks were long and painful, they again ate massive portions of fried polar bear, bear soup and boiled bear that evening. The feast finished on 16 August, three days after they shot the polar bears.

While they were resting, the weather deteriorated. To protect themselves against the biting wind and driving snow, the three men pulled on leather jackets and 'baschliks', checked woollen caps with earflaps that tied under the chin, and which were worn over thinner wool caps. The skies cleared the next day, enabling Strindberg to take their position. Again, he had bad news. 'The current has dragged us twelve miles southeast in the last six days.' Ironically, the drift was in the direction of Cape Flora, their original destination, now abandoned. But they knew it was still out of reach.

'We must take a more westerly course to reach the Seven Islands,' Andrée replied, 'and hope that with every step we counteract the drift sufficiently to result in us heading to the southwest.'

Outside the tent, though, the ice was a mass of tiny, constantly moving floes which stymied any attempt to move in a particular direction. *We have not even advanced 1,100 yards*, Andrée wrote after a long and frustrating day spent strapping each sledge in turn to the boat, paddling it across open water, then returning to pick up the next sledge and repeating the process until all three sledges had been individually ferried to firm terrain. *The ice here is terribly pressed together and shattered into small floes. We ferried across five stretches of open water before midday, that is in four and three-quarter hours, and had to do so again immediately after eating. We must be near the sea as the ice is so divided*. The fast-flowing unpredictable currents convinced Andrée that land was nearby and he scanned the horizon frequently in hope, but spotted only more ice extending in every direction.

That night, as Andrée was repairing his trousers and Strindberg was cooking their dinner, there was a noise outside the tent. Looking through a crack in the opening of the flaps, Andrée saw a bear directly in front of him. Unflustered, he continued to sew.

'Look! Here's another bear for us,' he said nonchalantly to his companions.

Frænkel grabbed the gun he had been cleaning and crept out of the tent. Directly in front of him was the bear, about to attack. As it lunged towards him, Frænkel squeezed the trigger and dropped the beast with a single bullet. Then, as if shooting a bear was an everyday occurrence, he turned back into the tent to finish his work and eat his dinner. Later, when they inspected the dead animal, they discovered it was the largest and finest male bear they had killed so far. There was plenty of meat on the corpse for the gulls even after they had removed twenty-two pounds of the best cuts.

The next day, they emerged from the tent into another whiteout. The thick clouds above them, the falling snow and the ice beneath them merged into one. Unable to distinguish between ground and sky, every step they took was frightening. Andrée wrote:

The terrain is exceedingly tiring, the new snow preventing us from seeing the bumps, which constantly gave the sledges unexpected jerks. The freshwater pools, not yet frozen, forced us to make many detours. I am quite done for by the day's work.

I do the scouting. It is very difficult, as I often have to clamber a long distance among ice rubble and over pools and along leads. The worst are the freshwater pools, which turn in innumerable windings, real labyrinths. I usually throw my gun over my shoulder when I go off, and Strindberg and Frænkel stay behind, waiting and shivering. Sometimes they scout in one direction and I in the other.

We are often forced to make dangerous crossings. The sledges capsize, or become stuck, hanging over a chasm. 'Lie still!' we shout to the person pulling the sledge who by this time has fallen over. So he lies there, supporting the sledge, until we can come and help him.

Often they laboured all day to cover a mile or less, battling to haul their sledges across a hellish landscape. The skill was in knowing how to adapt their methods to the constantly changing terrain beneath their feet. Sometimes the sledges had to be pulled at great speed across a fragile stretch of ice that was about to give way. At other times, a more gingerly approach was needed and the sledges had to be moved slowly, then carefully swung on their axes while balanced precariously on the top of a pressure ridge or ice boulder. Frequently they had to use spades and hatchets to cut a path through the blocks of ice, or completely unload the sledges and then relay cargo across the most impassable stretches of ice. At other times, they ferried their sledges across water, balanced on the boat for several hours at a time, sighing with relief at reaching the far shore safely, only to step out onto ice that was too weak to take their weight. Immediately, their sledges would lurch back into the water, and all their equipment and provisions would be soaked through.

With every step taken and ridge climbed, they knew their battle against the ice was becoming more desperate as the strength was sucked from their muscles by hunger and fatigue, but still they continued to grind towards the west, their hopes pinned on reaching the Seven Islands before winter set in.

On 21 August, they gave up cooking polar bear meat for lunch and took to eating it raw. *The kidneys, seasoned with salt, tasted like oysters*, Andrée wrote. *We hardly wanted to fry them. Raw brain, too, is very good.* But it was a considerable risk: they knew that polar bear meat often contained trichina larvae, a parasite that was killed only by cooking the meat for several hours. If the meat was infected, the larvae would spread throughout the body and sap the men's strength, causing nausea, vomiting, diarrhoea, fever, swellings and acute muscular pain. If enough larvae collected in the heart muscle, trichinosis could be fatal.

That evening, just as they were erecting their tent, three more bears attacked them. Frænkel and Strindberg shot one each, and Andrée hit the third, but it escaped, wounded. Again, they scavenged the best parts from each animal. For dinner, Strindberg attempted a new recipe, mixing the bears' blood with oatmeal to make a blood pancake, which he fried in butter. He was even more adventurous for their late-night supper, concocting a cake made of Mellin's Food, water and yeast, and a soup from the algae they had found stuck to the ice. Andrée was very impressed. *The soup should be considered as a fairly important discovery for travellers in these regions*, he wrote, his eye as ever on posterity.

The knowledge that the flight of the *Eagle* would be regarded as a failure by the academics and polar explorers who had scorned his ambitions at the International Geographical Congress in London still burning inside him, Andrée was more than ever determined that his expedition should return with some valuable scientific data. He continued to take meticulous, detailed and remarkably detached notes of any wildlife he encountered. *Young ivory gull; weight 1lb (full grown), was shot by me*, he wrote. *It had black tips to its big tail, to its wing feathers and to its shorter covert feathers. Some of the feathers along the upper side and the sides of the neck were tipped with grey. The head was grey-black around the base of the beak, around the eyes and along the front of the head. The beak was black. The young ones seem to cry with a 'pyowt pyowt' sound. When the mother is anxious or is giving a warning signal, she makes a sound like 'pyirrrrr' with a harsh, emphasized r. The young gull was white underneath, but it had the same colour feet as the older birds previously caught.*

On the ice, the litany of misery continued. The next day it became even worse. *There can scarcely be found a couple of square yards of ice which do not present evident traces of pressure, the entire terrain consisting of an endless field of large and small ridges,* Andrée complained. The temperature had remained consistently below −7°C, enough for most of the leads to freeze over, but this created a new problem as the fresh ice covering the leads was pushed up into pressure ridges by the movement of the ice floes. Even so, there was the occasional compensation. *We walked through a magnificent Venetian landscape with canals between lofty pressure ridges on both sides. We even spied a water square with an ice fountain and stairs down to the canals. Divine!*

But while Andrée was enjoying the scenery, his compatriots were in pain. While crossing a pressure ridge, Frænkel pulled his sledge so hard that he dislocated his knee, and Strindberg complained of a pain in one toe that made walking difficult and which they feared might be the first sign of frostbite. They did not mention their deepest dread − that it might be the first symptom of trichinosis.

A day later, Frænkel was suffering from severe diarrhoea and muscular cramps, a situation that did not improve when he fell into the water two days later. Strindberg's pain spread to his foot, and Andrée joined Frænkel in suffering several bouts of diarrhoea. Nevertheless, they managed to cover around four miles each day, possibly because Strindberg had increased their rations to more than three pounds of polar bear meat a day after they spotted more bear tracks, prompting Andrée to joke, 'It seems that we have wandering butchers' shops around us.'

Over the next days, as August began to give way to the much colder days of September and the sun touched the horizon for the first time, the health of all three men continued to decline. Andrée and Frænkel took morphine for stomach pains and swallowed opium to control their diarrhoea. The temperature plummeted to −20°C, and with the wind gusting at speeds up to twenty miles an hour, the wind-chill made the frosty air feel twice as cold. At night, they huddled close together in the tent. *The temperature is falling. With each degree we creep deeper into the sleeping bag*, Andrée wrote. By day, they struggled to steer their sledges on a straight course across the rubble as the cold froze the ice and snow into crumpled blocks as rigid as steel. Even Andrée's resolve was being broken.

On the night of 29 August, he wrote wistfully of his yearnings for the comfort and security of Sweden. *Tonight was the first time I thought of the delights of home*, he noted, struggling to grip a pencil in his shaking, mittened hands while his thoughts were with Gurli Linder, lying warm in bed, an African violet as always in a vase beside his portrait on her dressing table. *Strindberg and Frænkel, on the other hand, have spoken of it for ages. The inside of the tent is covered in ice and the double-thickness groundsheet feels stiff when it is being rolled up. I sweep it clean every morning and evening, before and after the cooking.*

Although he had given up writing to Anna, Strindberg's thoughts, when they weren't consumed with the harsh realities of basic survival, were also with his love. Gradually he was having to face the fear that had hung unspoken between the couple since the day of their engagement. With every day that passed, Strindberg knew that the dark thoughts he and Anna had not dared to voice – 'It is bad enough to be a widow, but to lose your love before you have married is possibly worse' – were closer to coming true.

The next day, as Andrée was sweeping the tent shortly after they pitched camp, Strindberg shouted a warning. 'There's a bear on top of us!'

Ten paces in front of them stood a huge male polar bear. Frænkel seized a gun and, without hesitating, fired a shot. The wounded animal ran off, pursued by Frænkel. Three more shots rang out. Frænkel had killed the bear, but it had fallen into a broad lead. Andrée ran to the water's edge and hauled the bear towards the ice using a grapnel. Then he lassoed the animal around its neck and a front leg. While Strindberg yanked with the boat hook, Frænkel and Andrée dragged the beast onto the ice. Exhilarated by the hunt, Andrée took a photograph of Strindberg and Frænkel looking like triumphant big-game hunters as they stood beside the slain animal. They removed sixty-six pounds of meat and strapped it to their bodies to prevent it freezing; rationed at four and three quarter pounds of bear a day between them, they reckoned it should last them another fortnight.

On 3 September, the three men stopped at a new challenge. Standing on a thin peninsula of ice, they were surrounded on three sides by a vast expanse of open water. There was nothing for it, Andrée decided, but to take to the sea in the boat. *We loaded everything on it and rowed for three hours at a good pace towards the Seven Islands*, he wrote later. *With a rather solemn feeling we began this new way of travelling at 1.50 p.m., gliding slowly over the mirror-like surface of the water between large floes loaded with giant boulders of ice. Only the shriek of ivory gulls and the splashing of the seals when they dived and the abrupt orders of our coxswain broke the silence.*

At last they were moving at speed, much faster than they had managed across the ice. It was glorious. As they drifted along the meandering leads, they dreamed of continuing their journey all the way to the Seven Islands in this blissful manner. The eternal dragging of the sledges had exhausted them, and the thought of covering greater distances with less effort was very seductive.

But at 5 p.m. their joy ended. Trapped in an enclosed bay, sealed shut by the movement of an ice floe behind them, they heaved their boat back onto the ice floe, transferred their belongings to the sledges, and resumed the backbreaking trudge westwards.

The fourth of September began with a celebration. It was Strindberg's twenty-fifth birthday.

Andrée woke his friend with a bundle of letters from Anna and his family, and ordered extra rations to be cooked to commemorate the day. Then he handed Strindberg the gold locket he had been carrying since Anna gave it to him the day before they left Gothenburg. Inside it was a picture and a lock of her beautiful hair.

Tears welling up in his eyes, Strindberg examined the locket in silence. For almost four months he had not seen Anna or heard her soft voice; if only in all that time he had known that a lock of her hair and a picture of her fair face was so close to hand, it might have made the yearning slightly less acute. He fingered the snippet of hair and sniffed it warily. Anna's faint scent and the silky smoothness of her golden curl instantly carried him back to their last precious weeks together, when he would stroke her hair as he cupped the back of her neck while they kissed.

He didn't need to express his joy to Andrée and Frænkel; they could see it for themselves. For the first time in weeks, Strindberg did not speak of how much he was missing Anna and home. Instead, his face beamed with complete contentment.

It was a real pleasure to see how happy he was, Andrée wrote that evening, but the rest of the day did not continue as well for Strindberg. *Nils marked his birthday by falling very thoroughly, sledge and all, into the soup*, Andrée confessed. Dressed in clothing that was rapidly freezing to his drenched skin, Strindberg became a sorry sight. His companions had had to pitch the tent, dry him off and help him change his clothes, a process Andrée described as a *very troublesome and time-wasting business*. Worst of all, most of the bread and biscuits and all of the sugar on the sledge were destroyed. Strindberg attempted to rescue the damaged food by adding the dissolved sugar into the coffee and chocolate, and by making a chocolate-pancake mix with the sodden biscuit, but his efforts were in vain.

Determined not to allow the accident to spoil the festivities, the explorers celebrated Strindberg's birthday over the most sumptuous formal dinner they could prepare with their limited resources. After dinner, Strindberg made a speech, thanking Andrée once again for the locket, a present that was as unexpected as it was welcome. Then they retired to an uncomfortable night – their blankets, which had been on Strindberg's sledge, were still wet through. Andrée, in particular, complained of the cold, as he had to lie wrapped in one blanket instead of his usual two.

Despite efforts to change their sleeping habits, the three men continued to sleep through daytime hours and trek during the night. But as September progressed and darkness returned to the Arctic, it meant that they increasingly trekked or boated through a cold, miserable gloom. Ultimately it was of little consequence, they reasoned, for it would soon be dark around the clock.

Three days after Strindberg's birthday they made a sail from a piece of tarpaulin, the handle of the shovel and the table. They hoped it would help them increase their daily mileage when they took to the water in the boat, but it was not enough to overcome the fiercest drift they had so far encountered. From 6 to 9 September, they moved backwards by eighteen miles. It was as if they were on a giant conveyor belt, the ice moving faster beneath their feet and sledges and the water flowing quicker under the boat than they could manage to forge ahead to the west. Instead of heading southwest towards the Seven Islands, they were heading slightly east of south.

They were also running out of polar bear meat, and even more worryingly, of cartridges for their guns. 'Pull the trigger only if there is a good chance of hitting two birds with one shot,' Andrée ordered when Frænkel and Strindberg were shooting at gulls.

To make matters worse, Frænkel's foot continued to deteriorate, and by 9 September, he could no longer pull his sledge. That night, Andrée nursed Frænkel and wrote in his diary:

> *I drained a blister of pus, bathed it and dressed it. I hope it will heal. We can hardly manage if he is not full strength. Our diarrhoea seems to have abated. Yesterday I had my first motion in four days. It was normal in amount and consistency. Frænkel has frequent motions and the consistency seems to be rather fluid, but he no longer complains of stomach pains.*
>
> *Strindberg and I take it in turns to go back and fetch Frænkel's sledge. This taxes our strength. We could not manage more than six hours' march, especially as the terrain was extremely difficult. Just when we stopped, I fell in the water. An ice floe that to all appearances appeared solid and onto which I jumped, proved to consist of nothing but ice sludge that gave way when I landed on it.*

Andrée had thrown himself onto his back and floated face up until Strindberg and Frænkel fished him out of the water with a pair of oars. He was very embarrassed. *I had no idea that ice sludge can appear in so many varying forms,* he confided later that evening. *It usually consists of thin cakes pushed up on top of each other. These naturally have a certain ability to float and to stick together, but they can bear little weight.*

For the next eight days the explorers wrote not a single word. On 17 September, Andrée explained why.

> *Since I last wrote in my diary, a great deal has changed. Trudging onwards with our sledges, we realized that the newly fallen snow was slowing our progress. Frænkel's foot injury prevented him from pulling his sledge and forced Strindberg and me to take it in turns to go back*

and pull his sledge too. Strindberg has also injured his foot.

Our meat is almost finished and the ice is becoming ever more difficult to cross. But our biggest problem is that the current and wind continues to push us into the jaws of the sea between North-East Land and Franz Josef Land. We have not the slightest chance of reaching North-East Land. On the 12th and 13th, while halted by violent westerly winds, we were forced to concede that we must spend the winter on the ice. Our situation is not particularly good.

It was a considerable understatement. Exhausted, weakened, and with two men injured, they faced months of permanent darkness and crushing cold with broken equipment and inadequate, worn-out clothing, and with insufficient stocks of food to last the winter.

Their first task had been to find a suitable ice floe on which to spend the winter floating on the Arctic Ocean. On 14 September, they set off in their boat, and found a floe that was large enough to house an ice-hut. Using blocks of ice and snow to build the walls and roof, they sealed their home from the cutting wind by throwing water over it until it froze into the cracks between the blocks.

The next day, Andrée shot a seal. Realizing that this could be their last fresh meat for some time, the explorers ate it all, leaving only the skin and the bones to attract gulls. They even ate the stomach and intestines, including the empty crustacean shells they found in the seal's guts. Like polar bear, the seal meat was extremely unpleasant. It was blubbery, hard to chew and saturated with fish oil, but Andrée was so hungry that he insisted it was palatable. *Every part of the seal tastes delicious fried*, he proclaimed. *We are especially fond of the meat and blubber. I dearly hope we shoot several score of seals to save ourselves. The bears appear to have disappeared and we shoot gulls to supplement our meat. They are delicious birds but they are costly in ammunition. Food must be found soon and in quantity if we are to have any hope of holding out for a while.*

Ever the resourceful engineer, Andrée turned his attention to devising other methods of supplementing their diet with protein. He had already made fishhooks, baiting them with polar bear meat and cutting a hole in the ice to reach the water, but so far he had failed to catch any fish. Now, he adapted the tea strainer and some balloon cloth into a net, with which he hoped to catch plankton or anything else edible in the water. *If the experiment works it could improve our situation*, he commented. Unfortunately, he soon realized that the water beneath their ice floe was not rich in food, a discovery that did little to improve their chances of survival.

Frænkel's foot is better now, but is unlikely to be healed for another few weeks. Strindberg's feet are also bad, Andrée went on to report. *Our humour is fairly good although we joke and smile rarely. My young comrades are coping better than I dared to hope. Yesterday, our courage was bolstered by the discovery that we drifted 36 miles further south over the last three days. Maybe we will float sufficiently south to be able to feed from the sea, and maybe it will not be as cold at sea as it is on the pack ice. He who lives will see.* Andrée then came to the reason why he had picked up his pen again having not written for more than a week. *This is a special day for us. We sighted land for the first time since 11th July. It is undoubtedly New Iceland.** *Landing however is out of the question, for the whole island seems to be a single block of ice, edged with glaciers.*

On 18 September, they celebrated King Oscar's silver jubilee with a gala banquet, meticulously prepared and documented in his logbook by Strindberg. The day was noteworthy for two other reasons: exactly four months

---

* In fact it was White Island.

earlier they had sailed from Gothenburg on the *Svensksund*, and they had now been trekking across the ice for just over two months.

With the Swedish-Norwegian union flag flying above their tent, they began their celebration with a starter of roasted seal and ivory gull fried in butter and seal blubber. The main course was seal liver, brains and kidneys, accompanied by bread and butter, and washed down with a bottle of wine. For pudding, Strindberg had mixed chocolate with Mellin's Food gruel, biscuits and butter to make a cake, and prepared a gateau *aux raisins* with raspberry syrup sauce. They toasted the King with a bottle of 1834 Antonio de Ferrara port wine and then sang the national anthem. They finished the celebration with more wine, biscuits, butter and cheese.

The next day, their culinary prospects improved further. *Today we added to our food store so it may well last well into February*, Andrée wrote in his diary. *I shot two seals and a great seal. I cannot describe how glad I felt or how pleased my companions are now that we can see our chances are so much improved.* They spent most of the day cutting up their booty, conserving the blood so that Strindberg could make blood pancakes, using two parts of seal blood to one part seal fat, half a spoon of flour, a pinch of salt and a pinch of dried yeast. *The pancake does not produce that loathing that Strindberg and I felt the first few times we ate seal meat and blubber*, Andrée admitted, although Strindberg could not cook the pancake the next day as the Primus stove refused to work; his subsequent attempts to cook over seal blubber lamps came to nothing. Instead, he dug the unburned fat out of the makeshift burners and offered it to his companions, cut in slices and laid on bread. 'It tastes splendid,' said Andrée, once again attempting to make the best of a dire situation. 'It tastes just like bacon and bread. I like it.' But Strindberg's bread and blubber open sandwiches did not stop Andrée from attempting to relight the Primus stove. For hours he bent over it, until at last he succeeded with some difficulty in getting it to boil a soup of seal meat, seal blubber, Mellin's Food gruel and water, in which Andrée noted *the seal meat seems almost to melt away on boiling and after a few minutes is extremely tender and delicate.*

Eager to return to building the ice-hut, Strindberg left Andrée and Frænkel to finish their unpalatable meal. He was soon interrupted. 'A bear!' Strindberg shouted out to his friends eating in the shade of the tent. Panicked by the sudden appearance of the huge animal, both Andrée and Strindberg took a shot and missed, but Frænkel calmly took aim and killed the beast with a single bullet. *Great joy! A great and magnificent bear*, Andrée enthused. *We have increased our food supply to last into April, the end of winter, and obtained a splendid skin. The bear is the polar traveller's best friend ... We now have so much meat and blubber that we are finding it difficult to protect it from other bears during the night. We pile it up near the edge of the tent and fence it in with all manner of things. The problem of keeping our house in order has become a burning issue here in the cold.*

The bear had solved their food crisis, but the prospect of spending winter holed up on the ice was denting morale. The sheer physical strain of hauling their sledges across the ice and battling the elements had left the men with little energy or impetus for conversation as they sank into the communal sleeping bag at the end of the working day. For weeks they had exchanged words only when necessary, silently united in their agony. A few days earlier, Andrée had written that the three of them rarely smiled or joked; now, with the daily treks ended and only the ice-hut to build, the prospect of a cold, dark and lonely winter approaching had driven a wedge between the men. After ten weeks' struggle on the ice, they were living with the consequences of Andrée's blind refusal to respond properly to any criticisms of the *Eagle*. Strindberg and Frænkel bickered with Andrée, blaming him for their predicament; in turn, Andrée was resentful that their naïve optimism before the launch had pushed him into ignoring his concerns about the prospects for the flight.

During the last two days the weather has been very pleasant, Andrée wrote that evening, *but on the other hand the days have not passed without the beginnings of discord becoming evident among us. I hope that this seed will not germinate and grow.*

Over the next days the ice floe drifted along the east side of White Island until it was within a few miles of its southeast tip; the three men spent the time completing the ice-hut. Polar bears scavenged every night, swimming through the icy water or leaping from floe to floe, attracted by the smell of the stock of meat. Andrée chased one of the marauding bears in his socks, but did not manage to shoot it. *The night bears seem to be a kind of thief bear*, he wrote. *The one that visited us yesterday night dragged our big seal away twice. We would have lost it had Strindberg not frightened the animal into dropping his booty.* But the biggest problem, as ever, was the ocean currents. *The floe our hut is built upon is diminishing fast as ice pressure brings the island shore ever closer*, Andrée wrote on 29 September. *We cannot escape the island. Last night we moved into the hut, which we christened 'Home'. We slept in it and found it rather nice, but it will become much better when we have the meat inside, out of the reach of the bears.*

At 5.30 a.m. in the morning of 2 October, disaster struck while Andrée, Frænkel and Strindberg lay asleep in the hut. With a deep rumble, followed by a crack like a whip, the ice floe they were camping on split into dozens of pieces. *We heard crashing and roaring as water poured into our hut*, Andrée wrote. *We rushed outside to find that our splendid large floe had splintered into many small floes, and that one of the splits ran directly along our outside wall. The remaining floe was only eighty feet across and one wall of the hut might be better described as hanging from the roof rather than supporting it. Our future prospects have been greatly changed.*

With 'Home' in tatters and the ice floe they had hoped to spend the winter on shattered, they had no choice but to lie in what remained of their hut that night. *The day had been rather tiring*, Andrée admitted. It must have been. Their belongings, including the meat from two bears that they hoped would last them for four months, were scattered across several floes and needed to be collected.

Luckily, the weather was beautiful so we could work quickly, wrote Andrée in the last entry that can be clearly discerned in his diary. *None of us lost courage. With such comrades as I have, one should be able to manage under any circumstances.*

CHAPTER TWELVE

THE POLE

ARCTIC OCEAN

31 May, 2000

AT 10.40 A.M. ON DAY FOUR, I OVERTAKE ANDRÉE. *BRITANNIC Challenger* has now been in the air longer than the *Eagle*. It is only a statistic – nearly sixty-five non-stop hours aloft – but for me it is quite some milestone. I am already much further north than Andrée managed; now I feel I am on my own, no longer tracing the steps of my hero but venturing into virgin territory. Nobody has flown for this long in the Arctic Circle or this far north. It is a strange feeling; so much achieved, but so far still to go. I pat myself briefly on the back and then remind myself that the nearer I get to the Pole the more I have to lose should I fail.

I am dog-tired. I've snatched a few hours of sleep here and there, but nothing substantial. I am aware of the deterioration in my handwriting when I write my position in my logbook, but the brief naps I've had are insufficient to make me capable of improving my spindly scrawl.

The autopilot is playing up again. Since last night, when

Luc instructed me to find a new course to the Pole, I have had to fly the balloon manually. The track I was flying along at that time brought me close to a position where the balloon could have been sucked into an anticyclone that would have sent me scooting back to Spitsbergen. I had to change direction abruptly and maintain a speed above ten knots. It has been fiendishly difficult, like flying the balloon through an intricate vertical maze of overlapping, unpredictable winds. Up a bit, check course and speed. Up a bit more, check course and speed. Down a lot, check course and speed. Further down, check course and speed again. Then a quick mental calculation to determine the altitude at which I was closest to the ideal course and speed. Once I have worked it out, I head for that altitude, keeping my fingers crossed that the winds at that height are still heading where I want the balloon to go. I cannot afford the smallest mistake. A few degrees too far west and the wind will drag *Britannic Challenger* into a weather pattern from which it will be impossible to escape.

I am around 150 miles from the Pole and the temperature has started to plummet. So far, it has been relatively warm, maybe −10°C at worst, much warmer than I was anticipating. There is no wind-chill as I am flying with the wind, so the cold has been no worse than if I was at the top of a sun-baked ski slope in the Alps. For most of the flight I have been more concerned about sunburn than frostbite, but now the cold is beginning to sink its teeth into me. The thermometer reading has dropped to −30°C, draining the warmth from my bones. Although not nearly as bitter as when I walked to the North Pole in 1998, it feels a lot colder as the basket is very cramped and I am unable to move sufficiently to generate some warmth in my limbs. It feels as though my muscles are freezing up, becoming solid around my bones. At times like this, I have the sensation that life itself is draining from my body and the blood has stopped pumping through the veins in my fingers. I have terrible cramps in my calves. There is nothing I can do but roll up like a ball on the floor of the basket, pull my feet towards me to alleviate the cramps and wiggle my fingers and toes to fend off frostbite.

Then Clive comes in for an hourly comms, patched through Iceland Radio.

'How's it going, Old Man?'

'I'm bloody cold, and I've got killer cramps, Boy, but otherwise not bad,' I reply. 'The autopilot is still playing up, but it's done so at the same time as it did yesterday, so I'm assuming it's solar gain. I'm at twelve thousand feet and the liquid oxygen is still not working. Other than that, things are okay.'

'I've got good and bad news from Luc, Old Man.'

'Give me the good news first.'

'He says you're on a good track but he wants you to come down to below ten thousand feet and find a track of zero-four-zero. You need to slow down.'

'That's very welcome. It's bloody freezing up here. What's the bad news?'

'He doesn't think he can get you directly to the Pole. There's a low pressure stuck directly over it.'

'Oh shit. That sounds bad. Is there a Plan B?'

'He's working on it. Maybe you'll have to fly past the Pole, to the east of it, and then double back to get close.'

It sounds good to me. I'll jump through any hoop in order to get to the Pole. 'As long as he gets me to the last degree,' I tell Clive. Competition balloonists have told me that would qualify as reaching the North Pole, but if Luc can get me any closer, so much the better. 'I've finished two tanks of fuel and there's only twenty per cent left in the third, but it's looking good. I've still got plenty of fuel and ballast.'

'Good. Good. Now pay attention, Old Man. I have a latitude and longitude position that Luc wants you to head for. You have to programme it into your GPS receiver and then use it to head there.'

'Boy, you know I can do that. I know how to use the GPS and I'm not too old to learn new tricks.'

'I thought it might be a bit too complicated for an old bugger like you. The way you're behaving, anybody would think you had been flying for sixty-five hours with little sleep.'

'But I have, Boy. It's not easy doing this, you know.' The tiredness has sapped my sense of humour. Then I realize that Clive is pulling my leg. 'It's all right for you, nice and warm in Birmingham, with hot food and drink on tap and a warm bed to crawl into at night,' I say. 'It's brass monkeys up here. This isn't easy.'

'You should try working in the control centre, Old Man,' Clive says. 'Nobody here has been home for four days and hardly anyone has had a shower. It stinks. Most of the people thought they would be back home the day after you took off. Claire Ingrams has only got a lipstick with her and she's not been home since Saturday.'

'I don't smell too good myself, Boy,' I reply.

'Now listen, Old Man. The next twenty-four hours are going to be very busy. Eat, drink, sleep and fart now, because you won't get the chance later on. You need to get some rest so that you are "a lert", which is the technical term for someone who knows what they are doing. In the meantime, slow down and find the track. You need zero-four-zero. Then call me via Iceland Radio.'

And with that, Clive is gone. He and Brian Smith have become my link to the outside world, and at times I feel as if he is with me in the basket, egging me on, encouraging me to grit my teeth when the fatigue is overwhelming. Brian is all calm reassurance, but Clive, it has turned out, is just what I need. Irreverent, lippy and fired up on Red Bull, his eternal enthusiasm keeps me going and his jokes raise my spirits.

By the late afternoon, the blanket of cloud has cleared, giving me the most fantastic sight I could wish for. It is stunning. I crouch on the coldbox in the corner of the basket, looking down at the ice and ahead towards the Pole, thinking about what Andrée, Frænkel and

Strindberg must have seen during their flight. I am much higher than they were at any time during the flight of the *Eagle* so the pressure ridges look like wrinkles on the ice rather than the massive frozen walls of tumbling ice I know them to be from my treks to the Pole.

The sun glints off the ice, making it appear a rich golden disc, broken by wide expanses of glistening water. Flying at eleven and a half knots, 6,700ft above the ice, I am struck by the contrast between my luck and Andrée's fortune. There is little difference between his approach and mine, and my flight has so far been everything he had hoped his would be: an inspiring marriage of nature and technology for man's benefit. We both sought a way to steer a balloon to the North Pole, but used vastly different means. His method might have worked had the guide ropes remained attached to the *Eagle* at the time of departure. I don't have any fancy methods of steering off the wind like Andrée planned; instead, I have a century's worth of meteorological expertise and communications technology at my disposal, which enables Luc Trullemans in Belgium to pick the right wind pattern to direct me northwards across the polar icecap. But other than these differences, our methods are very similar. Indeed, in real terms Andrée spent considerably more money and time than I have preparing for his voyage.

These are humbling thoughts. The margin between success and failure is so very thin; Andrée might easily have succeeded had he had just a fraction of the meteorological know-how that I have. Several times so far during this flight I have felt that I am not entirely alone in the basket. I am not religious or spiritual, but I have an eerie sense that somebody is watching over me, willing me to succeed. Maybe it is Luc, keeping an eye on the weather in Belgium, guiding me towards the Pole by remote control. Maybe Andrée is with me in the basket, willing me to succeed where he failed. Maybe I am just feeling the weight of expectation of my friends, family, sponsors and the control centre in England. Or maybe I want to reach the Pole in a balloon not just for my sake, but also to prove that the man I regard as the boldest adventurer of all time was not some foolhardy dreamer but a man with a vision ahead of his time.

Clive is on the radio again.

'What the hell are you up to? We've been trying to contact you for more than an hour! Neither the HF radio nor the Iridium phone got through to you!'

'Take it easy, Boy. I've been asleep. It's the first decent sleep I've had.'

Having told Clive that I was hallucinating with exhaustion, he suggested that I take a nap from 5 p.m. until 6.30 p.m. It is now 7 p.m. I cannot see what all the fuss is about, and I tell Clive as much.

'Sure you need your sleep, Old Man,' he says. 'But I have to be able to speak to you in an emergency. If I can't get through to you on comms at a prearranged time, I assume the worst has happened.'

'But you said I could turn them off,' I reply.

'Oh . . . did we? Our mistake then, but don't do it again, even if we say you can. From now on we want everything on. Autopilot on! Iridium on! HF on! Stop farting around!'

Clive's bark is worse than his bite. We've got to know each other well enough over the past months to converse in very direct terms without causing offence to each other. I had switched off the HF radio because the transmissions from Iceland Radio kept me awake. It was only after the control centre approved it that they realized their mistake, but at least I've grabbed nearly two hours of sleep.

'Listen up, Old Man,' Clive says. 'I've got some important instructions regarding the bottled oxygen. Elgar Hay and Professor Dennison at DERA in Farnborough say you ought to stay below fifteen thousand feet and use one litre a minute. If you go up to eighteen thousand max, you must increase the flow to two litres a minute.' Standing in the corner of the basket is a

251

large steel Dewar flask of liquid oxygen. I had hoped to rely on it, but it's not working. Using bottled oxygen is difficult, but I may have to depend on it. 'It will last up to forty-three hours at one litre a minute, but that must be via a cannula strapped beneath your nostrils. It is very important that you breathe in slowly and breathe out fast. It'll be easier to speak on the radio with a cannula than with a mask, but there's a problem with sleeping. If you want to go to sleep, Old Man, you must lie on your back and gaffer-tape your gob shut. Then you need to gaffer-tape the cannula directly under your nose. If you've got no tape, you must use the mask and strap it to your face.'

'Blimey, sounds like you want to shut me up, Clive.'

'Quite the contrary, Old Man. I want you to sit still, do nothing and keep gabbing away. You must increase the flow of oxygen if you make any movements, and you won't be getting rid of me. I'll want very regular contact. If you make any unusual comments, if your voice sounds odd or there's any sign of slurring – which also means you'll have to keep off that bottle of brandy I know you've got – then I'll be shouting at you to turn the oxygen up. Got it, Old Man?'

'Yes, Boy. Loud and clear.'

Thankfully I don't need to strap on the oxygen yet. The thought of taping my mouth shut and being constantly monitored persuades me that I am going to do everything I can to stay below 10,000ft, the altitude at which I would normally start to use oxygen.

I have still not had a proper meal. I feel slightly nauseous. Maybe it is the altitude, possibly it's fatigue, but I'm too tired to cook. I'm surviving on ginger nut biscuits, chocolate, pork scratchings and oranges. Not the healthiest diet, but it's easy.

Two hours later, the calm, courteous tones of Brian Smith immediately alert me that he has taken over from the rumbustious Clive at the control centre. Brian passes on Luc's latest weather analysis and suggests that I descend gently to 4,000ft in order to get the track to come round to 360° from the current track of 27°.

An hour after that, Brian is back. 'David, you're slipping too far east. Are you certain you're following the tracks correctly?'

'Sure, Brian. I am bang on track according to the GPS.' The GPS calculates my position by taking bearings from a network of atomic clock satellites. It is meant to be accurate to within ten metres.

'It doesn't make sense,' Brian insists. 'You are off target. I'll get back to you.'

A short while later I hear Brian's voice again, patched through Iceland Radio on the HF radio.

'Tell me, David, what setting is your GPS receiver on? Grid or True?'

'Grid. Why?'

'It should be on True. It makes all the difference.'

Brian doesn't need to tell me. The Grid setting is used when navigating using charts or maps. It works well in most places, but near to the poles it becomes less accurate as the grid lines superimposed on the map are parallel to one another whereas the lines of longitude converge at the Pole. The True setting uses proper positions of longitude and latitude, and is absolutely precise. I let Brian know that I have now switched to True.

'In that case, you need to turn left. I'll speak to Luc to get a new track and let you know as soon as possible,' he replies.

I've learnt from bitter experience that the smallest technical slip-up can make the difference between success and failure. In 1998, I battled for days to get an Argos beacon to work properly. It sent out a signal that was picked up by satellites to confirm my position, but it gave different accuracy readings every hour, even when I was stationary in a garage at Resolute Bay in the Canadian High Arctic. After three days of trying to get it to work, we realized it was transmitting its position in metric measurements, rather than in degrees, minutes and seconds. As soon as we made the adjustment, it worked perfectly. It was fortunate we discovered the fault before we set out, otherwise our base manager, John Perrin, would not have been able to find us on the re-supply. On the same expedition, three of our cooker fuel pumps failed and we could neither cook food nor heat our tent until replacements were dropped in by aeroplane. Other adventurers have had their missions ended prematurely by the failure of some mundane piece of equipment, like the fuel clip on the Breitling Orbiter round-the-world balloon. Costing a mere sixty-nine pence, it leaked, bringing the balloon down in the Mediterranean only hours after launch. Bertrand Piccard, the pilot of Breitling Orbiter II, joked afterwards that maybe he should have bought one that cost £1.50. It's easy to laugh at such errors, but I know very well that the failure of a tiny piece of equipment can end an adventure prematurely.

'Right,' says Brian, back on the radio after a short while, 'Luc says you need to take a track of three-three-zero. I want you to call in every fifteen minutes until we get you back on a sensible course to the Pole.'

Thank God for you boys back home, I think. It's a massive understatement to say I would be lost without them.

Once again, I go through the process of painstakingly noting down the directions in which the wind streams are heading at various heights and then selecting the altitude where the wind is streaming in the direction I want *Britannic Challenger* to go. It takes several hours, but at last I am once again on course, flying towards the remote spot in the sky where Luc has calculated I must head. Since I switched over from Grid to True on my GPS, my tracks and Luc's tracks now match.

The demands of flying with such accuracy have exhausted me, and at 2.45 a.m. on Thursday 1 June – day five – with a clear view of the icecap thousands of feet beneath *Britannic Challenger*, I tell Brian that I am going to try and snatch two hours of sleep. He reminds me to leave the autopilot, Iridium phone and HF radio switched on. For some reason, I also decide to strap on my harness and tie myself to the basket. Then I ensure both burners are switched on, in case one fuel tank should run out of fuel, and turn on the autopilot and the klaxon. Other balloonists have hit the ground while asleep, something I obviously want to avoid, so I set the autopilot alarm to go off if I veer five hundred feet below my chosen altitude of 3,000ft.

It is night, and although the sun is still burning brightly above, it is not sufficiently powerful to cause *Britannic Challenger* to gain altitude by warming the gas in the balloon. In these conditions, the autopilot works beautifully, anticipating changes in altitude ahead by monitoring changes in barometric pressure. At times, it seems almost mysterious to me. While I lie on the floor of the basket, trying to sleep, the autopilot fires two or three short burns for a fifth of a second each for no apparent reason. A few minutes later, when I see the barometric pressure dropping, it becomes apparent that the burns were needed to maintain the balloon's height and direction.

I take a last look at the photograph of Claire and my children stuck inside my logbook, make a mental note to call Amelia, my youngest daughter, who is celebrating her fifth birthday later today, and hunker down on the floor of the basket in an attempt to grab some sleep. The basket is cramped, the floor is uneven and slopes towards my head, and it is too short to allow me to stretch out fully. Nevertheless, within seconds I have slipped into a very deep sleep, exhausted by the long hours awake, the cold, the altitude and the constant stress of flying the balloon.

I don't know where I am, or why I am here. All I know is that an alarm is ringing in my ears and that it is a signal that I must get out quick. I know I am in a position of danger, with my path to safety blocked only by a waist-high barrier. So I swing a leg over it. On the other side, I can see a thick mist covering the floor and hope the ground beneath it is solid. But try as I may, I cannot cross the barrier. I push and strain, but something is preventing my escape.

Then I wake up. I am standing in the basket, with one leg thrown over the side. I still do not know where I am or why there are clouds below me. For a second I think I am in heaven. Only the harness is stopping me from jumping out of the basket, but I continue to jerk at the reins. Then the cold air hits me like a sledgehammer and I leap back into the basket, inhaling with a start as I realize I am floating several thousand feet above the polar pack ice, one tiny step away from plunging out of the basket. I am frozen to the spot, my throat and lungs so tense with fear that my scream comes out like a strangled yelp. Fuck! Shit! My God! A string of obscenities runs through my head, but very little of it comes out in intelligible form.

My hands and knees are shaking so much that I have to grip the side of the basket and lower myself slowly onto the coolbox that doubles as my seat. My God, that was a narrow escape. If it had not been for the harness I would, without a doubt, have stepped out of the balloon into oblivion. I reach for the radio, but the adrenalin coursing through my veins has made my heart beat with such force that I am unable to speak. My voice cannot keep up with my racing brain and the first words I utter come out completely garbled. I try to calm myself, but my breathing is fast and shallow, making me dizzy. Come on, calm down. Pull yourself together. Breathe deeply and slowly, I tell myself. Gradually I get a grip on things. Then the shock kicks in.

I feel frightened, really frightened, like no fear I've felt before. Tears well up in my eyes and then trickle down my face. It is a relief. The fear and tension subside and I am able to pick up the HF radio microphone and call into the control centre. Brian Smith answers.

'Brian, Brian. I tried to climb out of the basket. I nearly lost it completely.'

'You what?' he answers.

'I woke up with one leg over the side. I swear I was about to step right over the side. Only the harness stopped me. I must be more tired than I realized.'

'Christ . . . are you all right?'

'Yeah, I think so; a bit shaky. I've had some close calls, but nothing quite like that. I'll be all right in a while, when my heart returns to my chest.'

'Don't worry about it,' Brian says, and his authoritative, unflustered voice calms me. He runs through some questions. I know he is testing my reactions, so I make every effort to get them right.

For the second time, I have the sense that somebody or something is watching over me. Yet again, luck has been on my side. Every time that something could, perhaps ought to have gone wrong, I manage to snatch success from the jaws of disaster. It is uncanny. Brian suggested I put on my harness – I haven't previously worn it while asleep – and an hour or so later it saves my life. The odds of making it this far were heavily stacked against me when I set off, but I've made it through every challenge along the way. All I can think is that somebody up there wants me to get to the Pole.

'You sound okay,' Brian says. 'Now do all your safety checks.'

The routine relaxes me. I feel fine by the time I have gone through the procedure.

'Have something to eat, David,' Clive advises.

'I don't feel like it.'

'Have a hot drink then. After that scare your blood sugar levels will be all over the place. You'll feel exhausted in a few minutes.'

Then I remember: it's Amelia's birthday. 'Brian, is it Thursday today? I've got to speak to Amelia. If it's Thursday, she's five today.'

'Take it easy, David. It's three o'clock in the morning in Britain. You can call her later. Right now you're only fifty-five miles from the Pole. You've got other things to consider.'

Amelia's birthday. Five years old. It seems like yesterday that she was born, the third of my daughters and still the baby of the family. I think back to what was going on five years ago.

Having had two daughters, I thought I knew it all. I even went into the delivery room with a copy of the *Daily Telegraph* under my arm as I was convinced Claire's labour would take a long time. I was right. Amelia was big, more than ten pounds at birth, but Claire was determined not to take any pain relief. Maybe it was the length of the delivery or maybe it was the pain she went through; whatever the reason, Claire blacked out seconds after Amelia was born. The doctor immediately dumped Amelia in my arms and the midwife hit the panic button. Within minutes the crash team arrived. I was frozen to the spot, watching the doctors feverishly attend to Claire, fearing that my wife was about to die. Panicking about bringing up three daughters on my own, I begged and prayed that Claire would survive. After about five minutes, she came round. The doctors left the room, leaving Claire and me staring at each other, with Amelia between us. I wanted to say something, but I was speechless, overcome with the realization of how precious life is and how fragile our hold on it can be.

Thinking back now to that moment makes me feel extremely guilty. I know where the priorities in life lie, but sometimes I cannot help but ignore them when I go out and court danger. Floating in a balloon above the Arctic pack ice is by far the most dangerous thing I have ever done, and I cannot help but wonder how Claire would feel if she had to bring up three daughters on her own.

Once again I am torn between my life at home, where I rightly belong, and the barren wildernesses that continue to exert such a pull on me. As I glance around the cramped confines of the wicker basket, I spot my skis, brought along in case I crash on the ice and have to make my way to a pick-up point. They are the skis I used in

1998 to haul my sledge to the North Pole and they are still festooned with the doodles that Amelia and my two other daughters, Camilla and Alicia, drew on them. Two years ago, when I was engulfed in a whiteout and the wind-chill had taken the temperature down to –60°C, I would glance down at my skis to look at the colourful pictures of dinosaurs, the sun and flowers painted by my daughters. On some days they were the only burst of colour in the swirling mass of white snow and ice, and they would remind me of home. Every day, as I worked my way northwards, I would look at my daughters' pictures and just think that every mile ground out and every day survived brought me closer to the moment when I would see my family again.

It may seem ridiculous that I put myself through such discomfort and frequent danger when all I often want is to be sitting at the kitchen table, watching my daughters play or helping them with their homework. After all, nobody forced me to clamber into this balloon, to go without sleep and to shiver for days on end above a desolate landscape. But much as I would like to, I cannot find an easy answer to the question of why I do it. Part of it is the camaraderie of working with like-minded people towards a common goal. Part of it is about setting myself a challenge and being addicted to the sheer adventure of it. After all, it beats sitting behind a desk. And if I am honest about it, there is a part of me that wants to prove myself to the world, to say that I have done something that not many other people could do. Andrée thought the same way. He did not want to end his days wondering about what he might have achieved had he followed his dreams. I am like that too.

Fifty miles to the Pole, and I am sandwiched by thick cloud above and below the balloon. As far as the mission objectives are concerned, I have succeeded. *Britannic Challenger* is within the polar ring, the last degree of latitude north of 89°. I could turn around now, but nothing on earth could make me do that. I am determined to get as close as possible to the Pole.

With the sun hidden from view, the temperature drops dramatically, causing the gas valves to ice up. The burner has a yellow flame – it's not a good sign – which continues to burn for a second or so each time the valve shuts. I strap a heat pack to the valve and switch the code on the Argos transmitter to 3, indicating a technical problem.

This is not a time for ignoring superstition, so I dig out the worry beads given to me by Rajiv Wahi, the managing director of Typhoo, who sponsored my trek in 1998 to the North Pole. I am already wearing my lucky Z stone around my neck. Together, I hope, the Z stone and the beads will help me get to the Pole.

An hour later, when I am forty miles from the Pole, Clive picks up the emergency Argos code and his voice comes in crackling on the radio.

'What's the matter, Old Man?'

'I can hardly hear you, Boy,' I reply.

'Tell me about it. The closer you get to the Pole, the worse it will get. We may lose you altogether.'

'Clive, the flame is burning yellow.'

'Don't do anything. I'll call Pete Johnson and see what he says.' Pete Johnson designed the burners. He will know what caused the yellow flames.

Another hour later I am thirty miles from the Pole, and Clive is back on the radio. 'Right, Old Man, pay attention. Luc phoned. You need to find a track of three-six-zero degrees, which should be at five thousand feet. I've spoken to Pete Johnson. He says to switch off the burner with the yellow flames. If you don't, it could melt the ignition leads.'

'I've got that. What about if we lose comms as I approach the Pole?'

'Just stay on a heading of three-six-zero degrees. It may mean you're in the polar region for twenty-four hours. And if you get a latitude reading of ninety degrees north on the GPS, put your right hand over your left shoulder and give yourself a pat on the back.'

Reaching 90° North would mean I was directly over the North Pole. To the millimetre. It's a point on a map, but to all practical intents an impossible place to reach in a balloon. Even on foot, you would struggle to hit the North Pole right on the button because the ice at the top of the world drifts faster than your feet can carry you.

'I'm having great difficulty finding three-six-zero,' I reply. 'The air flow is all over the place, but I'll let you know how I get on.'

The wind slows right down and my speed drops from around eight knots to fewer than three knots. It takes half an hour to cover another two miles, and a full hour to cover four and a half miles. Nevertheless, by midday I am just twenty-one miles from the Pole, staring at the GPS receiver, barely able to believe how close I have managed to fly to the North Pole. Snow crystals are floating out of the hot-air cone near the top of the balloon, streaming down around me like a shower of diamonds. Once again, I have the feeling that somebody is watching over me, willing me on ever closer to the Pole.

I call Clive, but it takes a while to get him to come to the radio. He has been inundated with requests for interviews now that the media can see *Britannic Challenger* has reached the polar ring. Clive is telling everyone that the mission is accomplished, but as far as I am concerned the cake still needs its icing.

'I am at eighty-nine degrees and thirty-nine minutes north, Boy,' I tell him. In my right hand I am clutching Rajiv's lucky beads, wrapped around the radio's microphone. 'What's the game plan now? I could head for Canada; I've made it to the last degree. Mission accomplished and all that, but I don't think it's quite time to head for home. I want to keep going.'

'Well done, Old Man. Don't stop now. We've got interviews to do, so you might as well keep going. Don't be alarmed by large changes in track this close to the Pole, just keep heading northwards and see where you get to.

Check the autopilot is on, the Iridium is on and you have your safety harness on. Remember KISS – Keep it simple, stupid.'

The wind drops again, so I tape the oxygen cannula beneath my nose, fire up the one working burner and climb into the sky. At 11,600ft I find a wind stream that is heading almost directly north and I clamp *Britannic Challenger* on to its track.

Slowly, but with an assured sense of inevitability, *Britannic Challenger* inches closer to the Pole. Luc's forecasting is amazing. At the last moment he made me turn left as if it was a simple crossroads in the sky, and now I am directly on course for the target. I just cannot shake off the feeling that somebody or something bigger than the team and me is willing me to get to the top of the globe, watching above me and ensuring that nothing goes wrong. To fly to the last degree without any major mishap is astonishing, but now, just to turn left and fly directly towards the Pole seems unbelievable.

Hour by hour, I drift closer, flying now at 12,000ft with the oxygen cannula taped below my nose. At 1.10 p.m. there are sixteen miles to go. Brian Smith radios to say, 'You will let us know if you reach ninety north, won't you?' By 1.50 p.m. I am another two miles nearer the Pole.

Then I stop dead. The wind has disappeared. Clive suggests that I descend gently to 9,000ft to try to find a track to the Pole, but it makes no difference. I move no closer. So close, yet so far. Instead, the balloon drifts to the west. An hour later, Clive changes the plan and suggests I ascend slowly back to 10,000ft. I follow his instruction, but *Britannic Challenger* does not budge an inch further northwards.

'Why don't you call it a day, Old Man?' Clive suggests. 'You're closer to the Pole than you ever dreamed you'd get. Luc says you could get closer, but you'd have to go up to twenty-three thousand, and you haven't the oxygen.'

'Yes, maybe you're right, Boy,' I reply, but I do not tell him I'm not giving up yet.

I open the burners and climb to 13,000ft. With my eye on the GPS, I watch *Britannic Challenger* drift slowly northwards. It is as if it is teasing me with what could be. Eventually, less than twelve miles short of the Pole, the balloon stops dead again and I decide it's enough. I am, I work out, more than ninety-eight per cent of the way there. Again, I have the feeling that something or somebody is pulling me towards the Pole, like a giant magnet drawing me in, but this time it's saying that's enough. You've done it. It's time to go home. I have some of the best people in the world looking after me in the control centre and in Belgium, but this has been beyond even their abilities. Something weird has been going on. Someone has been watching over me. Maybe it is Andrée.

Somewhere down there, within sight but hidden by a thick blanket of cloud, I know the North Pole lies, and I whoop out loud with the sheer exhilaration of achieving something that I really thought was impossible. I have achieved Andrée's dream of sighting the North Pole from the air. In fact, I would have succeeded by his benchmark if I had turned around tens of miles further back. There is no mountain or landmass at the top of the globe, as Andrée thought there might be. Instead, there is just a massive ice floe floating above a notional point where all lines of longitude converge and where every direction points south.

I think back to the day, just over two years ago, when Rune and I set foot on the North Pole. Tuesday 28 April 1998 will be etched in my mind for as long as I live. It was the day I finally completed the Grand Slam. For seventeen years I had attempted to reach the North Pole; on that day my dream ended, thankfully in glory. In the midst of a rubble field, with the Arctic sun breaking through the clouds, Rune and I finally reached 89°59′59.4″ North and decided it was as close to the Pole as we were ever likely to get. Physically and emotionally exhausted, our resolve tested to the limits, we hugged each other. According to the GPS we were within fifty-five feet of the Pole, as close as dammit. It was impossible to navigate any closer. A year earlier, Rune had seen me break down in tears when our 1997 North Pole expedition ended in failure. That day he saw me cry again, this time with joy at finally reaching the top of the world.

After hugging and congratulating each other, we looked around. At that moment, it seemed startlingly mundane. The North Pole appeared no different to any of the other stretches of ice, snow and rubble we had crossed in the previous eight weeks. The experience put me in mind of Captain Robert Peary's words on becoming, in 1909, the first man to reach the North Pole, an achievement that is still very much disputed: *The pole at last! My dream and goal for twenty years! Mine at last! I cannot bring myself to realize it. It all seems so simple and commonplace. As Bartlett said when turning back, when speaking of his being in these exclusive regions which no mortal has ever penetrated before, 'It's just like every day.'*

Rune cheered and whooped, and hugged me again for good measure. Then he turned to me and repeated the mantra that had become a ritual every time we pitched camp. 'God save your Queen,' he said, and saluted me.

'And God save your King,' I replied.

By then, we were both getting dangerously cold, so we pitched camp double-quick and crawled inside our tent for a late lunch and a mighty celebration. While he was getting the stove ready, Rune took one last GPS reading. From the outer tent, I heard another loud whoop.

'Look, David,' he shouted, holding his GPS up for me to see.

In the time we had been pitching the tent we had drifted closer to the Pole. According to his GPS we were at 89°59′59.9″ North – within ten feet of the Pole and as close as is humanly measurable to the top of the world. For a few seconds, the world revolved quite literally around our tent. Then, the patch of ice we were sitting on floated off the Pole and we left the scene of our triumph behind.

I am struck by loneliness as I think back to those wonderful moments. Somewhere on the ice pack below, Rune is now completing his trek right across the Arctic ice from Siberia to the Pole and on to Canada. Two years ago, I told him of my dream of flying a balloon to the North Pole. A year ago, he was ballooning with me in Chile. He has been instrumental to my success every step of the way, and how I wish he was here now. This journey to the Pole has been much easier in terms of physical endurance than my trek with Rune, but the stakes have been higher, and somehow the last moments have been harder because I am on my own.

Then I remember it is Amelia's birthday. Twenty miles from the Pole my only concern was to remember to call her, but the demands of trying to fly the balloon have made me forget. I dial the number for home on the satellite phone.

Claire answers, and when she hears my voice she replies as casually as if I was calling from the office. 'Well done, darling. So when do you think you'll be back?'

I tell her all about the flight, but her mind is elsewhere: she is running a party for twenty-five girls from Amelia's school. Then I speak to Amelia, who is clearly pleased to hear my voice but more excited about her birthday party than my achievement.

'Are you coming home soon, Daddy?' she says. 'We miss you.'

We chat for a short while and I sing happy birthday to Amelia. She says she saw the balloon on television, and then she's gone, back to the bedlam I can hear in the background.

I switch off the phone, sip from a bottle of water and eat a block of chocolate and a piece of Biltong. Home, James, I think.

CHAPTER THIRTEEN

THE AGONY

WHITE ISLAND, NORWEGIAN ARCTIC

2 October, 1897

EVENTS MOVED QUICKLY AFTER THE NIGHT OF 2 OCTOBER, when the ice floe split close to the Andrée expedition's laboriously constructed ice-hut. Strindberg wrote only two words in his almanac for 3 and 4 October: *Exciting situation.* Then, on 5 October, he wrote three more: *Moved to land.* They had arrived on White Island. Eighty-six days after they took off from Dane's Island, Andrée, Frænkel and Strindberg had solid earth beneath their feet again and a distant hope of surviving the winter in their hearts. Exhausted and frostbitten, dragging their heavy equipment behind them, the sight of the island, the scrape of their sledges on rock and the relief of firm ground beneath their feet instead of the treacherous, shifting ice, lifted their spirits.

But the situation was hopeless. The coarse gravel, permafrost and ice of White Island offered no shelter and no opportunity to build a warm and safe underground refuge. Nevertheless, on 6 October, they set off in a snowstorm to explore the bare, windswept island. Galvanized by this new chance of survival, they climbed the glacier at the centre of White Island to find defeat staring them in the face. There was nothing but sea and ice all around.

'We shall have to spend the winter here,' Andrée told Frænkel and Strindberg. 'It's our only chance of survival.'

The next day, Strindberg wrote one word in his almanac: *Moving*. Along the shore from where they had first set foot on White Island, they found a spot, higher up and with a few low rocks offering the scantest shelter. This, Andrée declared, was to be their camp, named 'Mina Andrée's Place' in honour of his beloved mother, Wilhelmina, whose birthday it was that day. Then they erected the tent and prepared a meal from the store of polar bear and seal meat they had piled in the boat after rescuing it from the cracked ice floe. Above them, the northern lights twisted and turned, streaming like green and purple rivers across the sky.

Over the next few days they dragged their sledges and the boat further up the shore, towards the camp, unloaded their possessions and packed them in and around the tent. On the ice-covered beach they collected driftwood and whalebones, stacking them in piles nearby. Then they built a secure refuge against the unrelenting snow, wind and ice, propping whalebones along its west side and drift-wood along its north and east faces against a rock wall on its southern side. Across the bone and wood structure, the tent and what remained of the balloon cloth were stretched and secured to the ground to make a roof, weighed down with items of equipment from the three sledges. At last they could stretch out in relative comfort after months spent in a cramped tent. The shelter was many times larger than their tent and had a raised ledge along the rock wall, on which they could all sleep. Best of all, it was weather-tight. With the narrow entrance on its northeast corner sealed shut and the Primus stove on full blast, the shelter could be quite warm and cosy.

After three months' hard, physical work on the ice, it was an immense relief to rest their exhausted bodies at last and give their injuries a chance to heal. Their only concerns were to protect their food store and to ration their fuel sensibly, but there is no sign that the three explorers rested and recuperated. For ten days, none of the men wrote a word in their journals. Then, on 17 October, Strindberg wrote his last entry: *Home 7.05 a.m.* After that, there was silence.

At some point over the next few days, possibly as much as a couple of weeks later, Strindberg left the shelter to gather food for their next meal. Suffering the symptoms of trichinosis, contracted by eating infected polar bear meat raw, and shivering violently because of the cold, he stooped as he staggered against a frigid northerly gale. His woollen jumper, shirt and jacket were inadequate protection against a wind that had blown across hundreds of miles of empty Arctic pack ice until it hit the barren shore of White Island. About ten feet from the west side of the shelter, he found the carcass of one of the seals Andrée had shot while they were floating on the ice floe near White Island. The seal meat he hacked from the corpse looked little different from any of the other seal flesh they had eaten before: under the tough skin it was greasy, its layer of blubber frozen firm by the cold, but beneath the blubber lay the succulent meat. The only discernible difference was that it no longer looked as pink as fresh seal meat; instead, it had turned grey, but otherwise there was no sign of decay.

Strindberg cut several pounds of meat from the dead seal and stumbled back to the shelter with it clasped under his jacket to keep it warm. Once inside, he set about making their meal. Holding the blunt knife in his cut and swollen hand, a symptom of his trichinosis infection, he cut the frozen slabs of seal meat into smaller chunks to make a soup, and into slices of steak for frying.

Attempting to light the Primus stove, Strindberg

discovered that, like the time once before when he had had to resort to cooking over seal blubber candles, it would not light. 'We may not be able to cook tonight. What do you think seal tastes like raw?' he asked Frænkel and Andrée, popping a tiny scrap of half-thawed seal into his mouth. 'We've not eaten it raw like the polar bear meat. Maybe we are missing a delicacy?'

He immediately got an answer. Seal meat was even more disgusting raw than cooked, worse even than uncooked polar bear. The foul taste of rotten fish oozed into his mouth; the seal meat morsel was minute, but sufficiently saturated in fish oil for it to coat his tongue, palate and throat. 'Aaagh!' he shouted, gagging as he spat out the chunk of meat. 'I should have known. Seals eat only fish. It tastes like a fish market that has not been washed down for months.'

While Frænkel mended clothes and oiled the carbine, Andrée tended to the stove, persuading it eventually to produce a sooty, smoky flame. It was sufficient for Strindberg to cook the meal, but the soup, left to stew for several hours, never became more than lukewarm. Strindberg did his best to cook the steaks, but their insides were slightly undercooked when the three men came to eat them with a bottle of wine.

They talked for an hour or so after the meal, until Strindberg, feeling nauseous and complaining that his eyelids felt heavy, suggested they go to bed. As they had done every night for three months, they crawled into the reindeer-skin sleeping bag together, lying like soldiers in a row, side by side on the rocky ledge at the back of the shelter, while the wind buffeted the main wall, causing the canvas tent and silk balloon cloth to bow inwards between the whalebone and driftwood supports.

For the first time since they had arrived on White Island, Strindberg did not complain of the cold. Instead, he said he felt sweaty, with a raging thirst and a sore throat. As Andrée and Frænkel tried to fall off to sleep, Strindberg's condition worsened. He tossed and turned in the sleeping bag. His muscles and bones ached, he said, and he found it difficult to talk with an uncomfortably dry mouth.

'Nisse, would you like some water?' said Frænkel, alarmed at the sudden deterioration of his friend directly beside him. 'I'll melt some snow for you.'

But Strindberg was unable to answer; it was as if his mouth was paralysed. He struggled to open his eyelids. Through slit eyes he could see double visions of concerned friends hovering above him. Summoning all his willpower, he nodded, but found he could manage to dip his head only slightly.

'I think that means yes, he does want water,' Andrée said to Frænkel, who opened the flap at the edge of the tent to scoop some snow into an aluminium saucepan. He heated the saucepan over the Primus stove, adding more handfuls of snow and ice as the snow melted down.

While Frænkel warmed the snow, Andrée kept an eye on Strindberg and noticed he was moaning urgently while fingering his waistcoat. He watched, unable to work out what Strindberg was trying to communicate. Then Andrée realized he wanted Anna's locket, which was tucked in his waistcoat pocket. Strindberg wanted to look at the picture of his fiancée. Andrée pulled the locket out of Strindberg's waistcoat pocket, where he kept it next to the tickets from the exhibition he had attended with Anna the night before their parting. Opening it carefully, Andrée found that the lock of golden hair was still inside; he lifted it out and placed it between Strindberg's fingers. Then he held the locket engraved with the initials N.S. open in front of his friend's heavy-lidded eyes.

Struggling to focus, Strindberg tried in vain to see Anna's picture. His vision was dimming; he found the tent too dark. A noise came from his mouth. Andrée strained to hear it. 'Again!' he said, bending his head so his ear was directly over the young man's mouth. 'Say it again!' Strindberg grunted again and glared with his widely dilated eyes at the seal blubber lamp nearby.

'He wants the lamp so he can see,' Frænkel said from his position beside the stove. 'He wants to see Anna.'

Andrée grabbed the lamp, placed it directly beside Strindberg and held the locket open again, taking care to ensure the glow of the flame caught Anna's photograph well. Strindberg nodded once and sighed gently, his lips breaking into the slightest of smiles. Andrée looked at the portrait. Strindberg had spoken so fondly of Anna's warm smile during those first nights on the ice; by the golden light of the candle it looked even more beguiling than he had described it so many times before.

Then Strindberg closed his eyes and jerked his hand, indicating he wanted the candle taken away. The light made him feel even more nauseous; it burned uncomfortably brightly, causing hallucinations. Andrée removed the curl of Anna's hair from Strindberg's pinched fingers and placed it back inside the heart-shaped locket. Closing it tightly, he pushed it into Strindberg's sweaty fist, wrapping the chain around his fingers. Then he squeezed his friend's fist, as if to say: Grasp this tightly, hold onto it, never let it go.

When the water was ready, Frænkel lifted Strindberg's head gently and held the cup to his friend's parched lips. Realizing that Strindberg was unable to swallow, Frænkel poured the water into his mouth and tipped his head back so that it would wash down his throat. Several times Strindberg jerked, as if he was choking on the water but unable to cough or splutter.

Over the next few hours, Andrée and Frænkel could do nothing but watch as Strindberg deteriorated, sweating and moaning, his legs sometimes writhing like snakes as the paralysis moved down his body. Five or six hours after he had cooked the meal, Strindberg's breathing became short and raspy – the paralysis had reached his lungs. For a few minutes, he fought to breathe, his breath rattling in his chest. Then the rattling stopped as suddenly as it had begun, and Strindberg was silent, lying on his side with his mouth open.

Andrée knelt over the man who had remained loyal to him through two attempts to launch from Dane's Island, the companion who had supported him when Ekholm and many others had claimed the *Eagle* was not fit for flight. He knew Strindberg was the one true friend he had, a friend who had proposed marriage to his fiancée Anna because he was convinced that he would return from the Pole a hero. Nobody had believed more than Strindberg that Andrée's ambitions were not the dreams of a fool seduced by the romance of adventure and hell-bent on making his name, but the plans of a visionary ahead of his time.

Resting his hand gently on his shoulder, Andrée bent over Strindberg, straining to listen for a breath from his friend's mouth over the sound of the wind beating against the shelter. He heard nothing, but he could just about feel Strindberg's soft, shallow gasps caress his cheek. He looked over to Frænkel, widening his eyes and nodding to indicate that their friend was still alive, but not for much longer. Then, with a gentle sigh, Strindberg's chest dropped as he exhaled his final breath, and Andrée realized it was over. Having kept his hopes up for longer than either of his companions, Strindberg would never see Sweden or his beloved Anna again.

'Finished. It's over,' Andrée said, his shoulders slumping as he rocked back onto his heels. 'Help me pull him over.'

The two men turned Strindberg onto his back and crossed his arms over his chest. On his left hand, he wore his engagement ring. In his right hand, Strindberg still clutched Anna's locket tightly.

'We should get him out of here. I'll go and get a sledge,' Frænkel said, the words coming with difficulty. Taking one last look at the man who less than a year ago had been a stranger to him but whom he had come to love as a brother, Frænkel crawled over to where the canvas and balloon silk at the opening of the shelter was flapping in the wind. Pushing the flaps apart, he grimaced and recoiled as a shaft of light entered the tent. 'The light! It is too bright outside; it makes me sick. I shall have to find my snow goggles.'

'I, too, feel unwell,' Andrée replied. Even by the warm light of the candle, Andrée looked waxy and ill to Frænkel.

Pulling a blanket over his head, Frænkel crawled out of the shelter, past the seal from which Strindberg had hewn the hunks of meat only hours previously, and towards the sledges. Rummaging through the boxes spread out on the snow, Frænkel found and pulled on his goggles, then headed back to the shelter. Inside, he found Andrée on all fours, retching with his head close to the ground.

'We'll have to work quickly if we are going to bury Nisse properly. I feel too weak to lift him,' Frænkel said, his voice slurring.

Andrée and Frænkel dragged Strindberg out of the shelter. They grabbed a leg each and gritting their teeth against waves of nausea, hauled him across the ice, his arms remaining crossed on his chest. About thirty feet from the shelter, Andrée turned around and noticed that Strindberg's right arm was trailing on the ground, the locket still wedged in his fist with its chain dangling behind it.

'Take the locket from his hand,' Andrée instructed Frænkel, but Frænkel was bent double, heaving and gasping for air. Andrée prised the locket from Strindberg's hand and tucked it into an inner pocket of his jacket. Then he removed Strindberg's jacket and lifted his right arm back onto his chest, crossing it with the left hand.

'What about a flag? We should wrap Nisse in the flag,' said Frænkel, now standing over Strindberg's corpse. 'It would be the right thing to do.'

But Andrée did not respond. He knew that, like Frænkel, he had neither the energy nor the will to find the Swedish-Norwegian union flag and to wrap Strindberg's body in it. Tacitly, the two men continued to drag their dead friend along the beach to where they knew there was a cleft between two large rocks, about a hundred feet from the shelter.

Too weak to lift Strindberg directly into the cranny between the rocks, they tugged and yanked him into the gap, stopping twice; once because Andrée had a vertigo attack when standing on the lower of the two rocks, and the second time when Frænkel's vision blurred. Eventually they gave up, leaving Strindberg's feet poking out of the crevice. Frænkel took Strindberg's almanac and fountain pen from his jacket. Andrée removed a purse containing a small silver wild boar that Strindberg wore around his neck, added the silver heart-shaped locket engraved with the initials N.S. to it and stuffed it in a pocket inside his own jacket for safekeeping.

With their last vestiges of strength and determination, they collected several dozen stones and dumped them on top of Strindberg's body. Bracing themselves against their nausea and weakness, they stood for a few seconds in front of the Arctic grave, silently offering their companion their final respects. Unable to summon up the energy to erect a cross, they staggered back to the shelter, breathless and disorientated, and collapsed onto the floor.

Andrée grabbed the single-barrelled rifle and crawled up onto the rocky ledge at the back of the shelter. Unable to move any more, he lay shivering and sweating in his tattered clothing. Nearby he had his axe, the fishing line he had made on the ice, and a tin of lanolin ointment. In his jacket was his diary; he intended to write a last note, but his vision was dark and blurred, and he could bear no bright lights.

Frænkel rolled across the ground to the medicine chest and flipped open its lid, grabbing and scattering some of its contents before he slumped onto his back, poisoned, like Andrée and Stringberg, by botulism as a result of eating the grey seal meat.

In these respective positions, the two men died several hours later when the paralysis caused by the *botulinus* toxin reached their lungs, resulting in a slow, frightening suffocation. Nearby, their Primus stove rested on the stone ledge. Lying on the ground was a gilt fruit knife, some cooking utensils and a box containing the expedition's supply of money in case they reached Alaska or Siberia: 160 roubles and eighty dollars in silver and gold.

The three men had lasted more than three months after departing from Dane's Island in a blaze of raw optimism. Outside the tent stood their three sledges, pointing up the slight slope towards the scene of their last breaths, abandoned, half-unpacked by Andrée and Frænkel. One sledge had been unloaded; the other two still carried most of their cargo, including the boat. Gradually, over the next months, they were covered by the drifting snow; then, as the snow melted and set again, they were encased in ice, waiting for the *Braatvag* expedition and a young reporter by the name of Knut Stubbendorff to discover them thirty-three years later.

Andrée's dream perished on the Arctic ice, but the dream of flying to the North Pole did not die with him. Several other attempts were made from Dane's Island, most of them many times more hare-brained than even Andrée's worst detractors had labelled the flight of the *Eagle*.

In 1906, Walter Wellman, an American explorer, transported an airship to Dane's Island, but its engines were poor and the airship was never inflated. He returned the next year to make a flight of fifteen miles and, in 1909 he managed forty miles before mechanical failure forced him to return to Dane's Island.

In 1925, Captain Roald Amundsen, the Norwegian who had beaten Robert Falcon Scott to the South Pole in December 1911, set off for the North Pole with the American explorer Lincoln Ellsworth in two Dornier seaplanes. Forced to land about 120 nautical miles short of the Pole, he evacuated both aircrews on one of the airplanes.

In 1926, Richard Byrd, an American naval officer, announced that he had reached the Pole by flying from

Spitsbergen with Floyd Bennett, an American pilot, but most polar historians doubt Byrd's claim. The same year, Amundsen led another expedition, this time on the *Norge*, an airship that crossed the Pole and flew on to Alaska. Generally regarded as the first definite arrival by man at the North Pole, it meant the Norwegian Amundsen was probably the first to both poles. The American Robert Peary's 1909 journey by dogsled and on foot is regarded with the utmost suspicion as he claimed to have covered forty miles a day in the final stages, a feat that has not been equalled to this day.

Two years later, Amundsen lost his life while attempting to rescue Umberto Nobile, an Italian air force general who, after designing the *Norge*, crashed during his own flight to the Pole aboard the *Italia*, triggering a huge international rescue operation.

Throughout this period, when the North Pole was conquered by air and possibly on foot, the bodies of Andrée, Strindberg and Frænkel remained buried beneath the ice, their fate and location unknown until 5 August 1930, the day when Olav Salen and his fellow hunters from the *Braatvag* stumbled on the remains in the permafrost of White Island.

Two weeks later, Knut Stubbendorff, an ambitious young reporter working for *Dagens Nyheter*, a Stockholm newspaper, was in his cabin on board the *Isbjörn*, a rickety fishing sloop bound for White Island. He had lost a fevered race among newspapermen to meet the *Braatvag* on its return from the island, but in the process he had scored a much more significant victory. Having heard on the radio that the Scientific Commission appointed to examine the Andrée discovery had reported finding only two bodies, Stubbendorff persuaded his editor that he should continue on to White Island in the hope of locating the third corpse.

On the morning of 5 September, after an incident-ridden voyage, Stubbendorff landed on White Island with six men. As soon as they set foot on the tundra they were attacked by three polar bears, all of which they shot.

Much of the snow and ice had melted since the *Braatvag* expedition had departed with the remains of two bodies. The thaw had uncovered another sledge and dozens of items belonging to Andrée, Frænkel and Strindberg. Stubbendorff meticulously recorded them in his notebook, but his most astonishing discoveries were still to come.

Walking on from the cairn erected in memory of Andrée by Dr Gunnar Horn and other members of the *Braatvag* expedition, Stubbendorff discovered most of a human skeleton lying on the ice. A backbone, a pelvis and a thighbone lay together; nearby, Stubbendorff found another thighbone, a kneebone and a foot. He kept walking, scouring the ground carefully before taking each step. A short distance further along the rocky beach, he found an upper arm bone with the rags of a striped shirt still wrapped around it. He kept looking, carefully working out the precise layout of the camp until, towards the end of the day, he found a human skull beside a piece of driftwood frozen in the ice near the other bones.

The next day, thinking that there was little else to be found, Stubbendorff and his men resorted to brute force to dig for further artefacts. While hacking away at the rock and ice, his iron bar suddenly struck against something that sounded brittle and hollow.

'Stop!' he shouted, in case anyone else struck a blow to the ice. Dropping to his knees, he swept away the flakes of ice hacked out by his iron bar.

The young reporter pressed his face to the glassy surface. Deep within the ice, he could make out the faint outline of a head and torso of a man lying on his left side. Stubbendorff buffed the ice with the sleeve of his coat, excited that he had found the very spot where the last of the Andrée expedition members had perished. He paused, and pulled out his notebook. *Inches beneath where I am standing*, he wrote, *a man, once full of longing for life and with warm blood pumping through his veins, slipped into the kingdom of eternal cold.*

He rubbed the surface again; gradually, he saw that the man was lying with his left arm curled beneath his head as if he had fallen asleep in this position. Carefully, he chipped away at the ice, spinning the clock back further and further with every shard of ice brushed aside, until he came to the torso, frozen to the ground in the exact position Knut Frænkel had died thirty-three years earlier.

With the help of the *Isbjörn*'s crew, Stubbendorff delicately slipped his hands under Frænkel to lift the explorer from his frozen grave. The torso, he could feel, would lift cleanly from the permafrost, but Frænkel's head, frozen to a bowl-shaped depression in the rock, refused to budge. 'Pass me your knife,' Stubbendorff demanded. One of the *Isbjörn*'s crew handed him a short dagger, which he gingerly worked into the narrow gap between the skull and the rock, whittling away the ice until the entire torso and head could be lifted in one piece from its resting place and placed in a basket. A day or so later, as Frænkel's body was transferred to a makeshift coffin on the *Isbjörn*, the head fell off.

Over the next three days, Stubbendorff found a remarkable inventory of equipment, including another sledge, balloon cloth, tarpaulins, three pairs of snow shoes, a sextant, a metal box of provisions, a medicine chest, clothing, a sack containing geological samples in copper boxes, two boxes of ammunition and an oar. Most importantly, he found the crucial documentary evidence of the fate of the Andrée expedition: several tin boxes containing reels of exposed film, Frænkel's almanac and his three notebooks, Strindberg's logbook and almanac-diary, and a meteorological journal.

On the final day, the *Isbjörn* hoisted its storm signal flag. A northerly wind threatened to trap the sloop within the ice floes around White Island. The expedition had to evacuate immediately.

While the *Isbjörn* headed for home through the stormy seas, Stubbendorff took to his cabin, where he began to examine the documents. The chance of revealing the exact fate of Andrée, Strindberg and Frænkel was too great a temptation to resist; he knew that upon the sloop's arrival in Tromsö, a Swedish government commission would seize the journals, notebooks and film. Stubbendorff was well aware that in his hands he held the closing chapters of a story the Swedish nation had wanted to hear for more than three decades; it was a scoop no self-respecting journalist could ignore.

Working by the dim light of a torch and a low-powered desk light, Stubbendorff worked around the clock, his intense concentration rendering him oblivious to the severity of the storm that was tossing the *Isbjörn* from wave to wave. Prising apart the frozen documents found on White Island, Stubbendorff allowed each bundle of paper to thaw under the meagre warmth of his desk lamp until the diary pages or letters could be separated from the clothing fragments and other artefacts to which they were stuck. It was a painstaking operation. Stubbendorff allowed each notebook to dry only to the point at which individual leaves could be safely parted from one another with a knife. If he tried to separate the pages when they were still too wet, the leaves ripped like sodden tissue paper, but if left to dry too much, the pages remained stuck together like cardboard, their contents hidden for the rest of time.

For more than twenty-four hours Stubbendorff worked at this, not daring to break his concentration even to eat, let alone sleep. The first document he tackled was Strindberg's almanac, its first pages parting quite easily, although the handwritten text on them could still not be read. Realizing that the pages might stick back together as they dried, Stubbendorff prised each of the precious leaves from the book and dried them separately, each page on its own piece of coarse paper laid on any flat surface he could find.

Stubbendorff's cramped cabin soon stank of rotting paper; it covered every surface. On his bed, across the desk, on chairs, along shelves and even on the floor, the wet pages were arranged in the order he had pulled them from the journal. Those pages that were almost dry he hung on cotton strung like lines of bunting across the narrow cabin, swinging back and forth with the tempestuous motion of the sea. Then, as the flock of silk-thin documents dried, the words gradually emerged. Slowly, the paper lightened and the dark ink appeared, letting the story of the dead men glimmer through, like voices speaking from beyond the grave, telling of the last weeks of the ultimate tale from the golden age of adventure, the last Jules Verne-style voyage undertaken at a time when technology seemed to offer everything to the man who dared.

For thirty-three years, their families and friends had speculated on their downfall. Had the balloon crashed straight into the icy waters, its three passengers dying of hypothermia within a few minutes? For a while, until the North Pole was reached, some people supposed they had indeed reached a landmass, that they were still alive, unable to return to civilization. Others thought they had crash-landed on the ice and attempted to haul themselves back to Spitsbergen only to be cut down by exhaustion, starvation and the cold. Now, Stubbendorff had the answers.

Despite their disappearance and apparent failure to reach the North Pole, the names of Andrée, Strindberg and Frænkel were lionized in Sweden. Like Captain Robert Falcon Scott in Britain, Andrée and his compatriots were mourned by their generation, for whom they came to embody a daring and courageous spirit that ultimately failed tragically in its quest. Theirs had been a disaster as heroic as Captain Scott's, possibly as ill-planned, certainly as foolhardy. And yet there was a grandeur about it, a sense of impossible romance, even in 1930 when their bodies were found.

Echoing Scott's last words – 'Our bodies must tell the tale' – so the remains found among the ice on White

Island began to give up their secrets. While the *Isbjörn* steamed full ahead for Tromsö, the three Swedish adventurers gradually emerged from the mists of time as the writing in their journals appeared in front of Stubbendorff's eyes. They told him of their attempts to survive, of their fears, hopes and experiences, but most of all they told Stubbendorff of their despair at leaving behind those they had loved, women left to mourn what might have been, to wonder what had happened to the three brave men from Sweden.

While Stubbendorff was working in his cabin, a middle-aged woman in Gothenburg was preparing to board a steamship bound for Southampton. After a long visit to relatives and family, Anna Hawtrey was looking forward to returning to Paignton, in Devon, where her husband Gilbert was waiting.

It had been a pleasant August holiday, but for Anna visits to Sweden always awakened memories of her earlier life when she was engaged to a dashing young physicist. It seemed like another lifetime, but the heartache of thirty-plus years ago still lingered.

As usual, she had visited her former fiancé's family, with whom she had lived for some time after her engagement. And as usual, the visit had ended in tearful farewells. With her bags stowed on board the ship and her tickets checked, Anna had tears in her eyes as a breathless young man ran along the quayside and interrupted her final farewells to a friend.

'They have found him!' he panted. Anna recognized the young man as the son of a family friend. 'On White Island,' he continued. 'In the ice. Two bodies, one of them is Nils. He still has his engagement ring on his finger.'

Anna felt faint. Thirty-three years of silence, and now this.

'How do you know? What can you tell me?' she demanded.

The story came tumbling out. How the walrus hunters

had stumbled upon the bodies, what they had found and how the *Braatvag* had now returned Andrée and her beloved Nils to Sweden. The story of the discovery had been in the newspapers, but the family she had been staying with had kept them from her until Nils's discovery was confirmed.

At last, Anna learnt what had happened to her first love, the man she never forgot, who bequeathed to her in his will everything he owned, and whose pictures adorned her home in Devon. The memories came back bright and sharp: those happy times in her youth; the whirlwind romance; the engagement; the long Sunday afternoons in the country and Nils's obsession with photography; his declarations of everlasting love before his departure for Dane's Island; the letters he wrote from Virgohamna and the pictures of him in the newspapers.

She thought back to that first afternoon they had spent together, when Nils borrowed a pony and trap and they spent a magical afternoon in the Scanian countryside. She remembered, too, how Nils had watched her out of the corner of his eye, and how handsome he had looked sitting upright with the reins of the pony in his hand. Later, he had told her in detail of his fascination with her smile, words that she had never forgotten. And then she remembered how he had suddenly reappeared, inviting her to his parents' house, two years after they first met. Most of all she remembered the uncontained joy she had felt the next day, when Nils had taken her to the island of Skeppsholmen, directly opposite the Royal Palace in Stockholm, to propose marriage.

But with those happy memories came painful recollections of the silence, the prayers for a word or a sign as Anna waited with Nils's father, Johan Oscar Strindberg, and his family. For months she had dared not think that Nils might not come back; it seemed disloyal when he had been so adamant that he would return, the Pole discovered at last. But as winter approached, Anna lost faith and slipped into a deep depression. Her biggest fear, that of losing her love before they had even married, arrived to haunt her.

The only indication that Nils might still be alive came within days of his departure from Dane's Island when Ole Hansen, the captain of the Norwegian sealer the *Alken*, reported having shot one of the expedition's thirty-six carrier pigeons. It was carrying a brief note that spoke of 'good speed' and all being well on board the *Eagle*, but there was no message from Nils. Anna clung to those words and to the letters brought back by Nils's friend, Alexis Machuron, from Dane's Island. They were all she had to remind her of her true love.

A year after Strindberg, Andrée and Frænkel sailed from Gothenburg in a blaze of glory, the Swedish government sent out several search parties in the hope of finding the three men still alive on the ice. One even landed on White Island and ventured to within a few tens of feet of Strindberg's grave, but turned back empty-handed.

In September 1899, more than two years after the expedition's departure, the captain of *Martha Larsak*, a Norwegian cutter, found something that reawakened Anna's hopes that Nils was still alive and that maybe he might soon return. It was the polar buoy, found on the shore of King Charles Land, part of Iceland. The plan had been to throw it from the *Eagle* as it flew over the North Pole; instead, it had been jettisoned when the balloon was weighed down with ice and desperately struggling to lift itself above the clouds. The little union flag of Sweden that should have popped up when the polar buoy hit the ice was missing. The copper wire on the upper side of the buoy was torn away and the cork inside it was damaged, but worst of all, there was no message. Newspapers printed speculative reports, but these only made Anna's agony worse.

'It would be better to know that Nils will never return than to be tortured by the thought that he might be out there somewhere, desperately trying to make his way home, or maybe in pain, alone and unable to shelter from the cold,' she told Nils's father one night.

Johan Oscar Strindberg watched helpless as Anna sank deeper into despair. He, too, thought back to happier times, such as the evening when Nils returned from the first expedition to Dane's Island. He had been so proud of his son, despite his apparent failure to take off. Anna was very welcome in his home, but sometimes he thought her presence heightened the feeling of loss, his grief at Nils's disappearance made all the worse by watching Anna's agony. *There are times when she is mourning, but she never torments anyone with her pain and despair*, he wrote in his diary. *How long will it last, if the uncertainty goes on year after year?*

In August 1900, when Johan Oscar Strindberg thought Anna could take no more, another buoy was found, this time on the coast of northern Norway by a wrecker that was scouring the beach. It had been at sea for 1,142 days but still contained the message written by Andrée on the first day of the *Eagle*'s flight: The journey was going well, the note said, the weather was magnificent and all were in the best of spirits; furthermore, the balloon was flying directly northeast and at a good altitude. And at the end of the message was a short note in Nils's distinctive handwriting, although it offered no consolation or warm words of greeting to Anna: *Above the clouds since 7.45 p.m. GMT.*

Again, the newspapers speculated. Anna contracted pleurisy and lay in bed for weeks reflecting on the fate of her beloved. *Her faith is cruel and hurts my heart*, Johan Oscar Strindberg wrote at the time. *I fear that she will never recover and not have the chance to confront her grief and loss, however futile that may be. How much crueller it would be if her Romeo were to return to find his Juliet dead. I cannot believe how brutal life sometimes can be.*

For thirteen years Anna waited before abandoning all hope that Nils would return. Then she met Gilbert Hawtrey, an Englishman. They travelled to America and later settled in England. At last she found happiness again, but Nils was in her thoughts every day.

The best part of a lifetime had passed until that moment on the Gothenburg quayside, when Anna was told that her Nils had been found. The intervening years did not make his fate, once it was revealed, any less agonizing. The young man begged her to stay, telling her there would be a state funeral, but she could not change her plans.

'Tell me how Nils was found,' Anna demanded. 'I need to know everything. Spare none of the details.'

'They found him buried in a cleft of rock under a foot of carefully piled stones. It was an unmarked Arctic grave. It seemed he died first,' the young man said. 'He was dressed in his trousers and waistcoat; in it, they found two tickets to an exhibition in Stockholm.'

Anna gasped. 'They must have been from our last night together. What else did they find?'

'Very little. He still had his boots on his feet, but the bears got to his body. On one of the finger bones was his engagement ring.'

Tears rolled down Anna's cheek. 'Was a heart-shaped locket found?'

'Yes, but in the other man's jacket. In Andrée's jacket,' the young man replied. 'He also had a notebook written by Nils, I believe.'

Turning to her friend and burying her face in her shoulder, Anna wept silently. At last, after all these years, she knew what had happened to her first love. Within a few weeks she would hear from Stubbendorff, who, as she cried on the Gothenburg quayside, was cautiously drying Nils's letters to her. At last, Anna would be able to read the diaries and the letters that told of the dream that had driven Nils away from her, the dream that lay crushed like her love in the Arctic ice.

To Anna Hawtrey, the precise cause of the tragic death of her beloved Nils was unimportant. She had long finished grieving by the time her former fiancé's remains arrived back in Sweden from the Arctic wastes, but she had not forgotten him. The home she shared with her husband

Gilbert at Paignton in Devon was dotted with his photographs. One room in the house was dedicated to Nils; to visitors, it seemed like a shrine.

But Nils was not the only member of the Andrée expedition who had left an unconsummated love behind. In Gurli Linder's Stockholm home there was also a small shrine. It was dedicated to the man who had spurned her secret love for him before he first embarked for Dane's Island in 1896.

Today, as every day, there is a violet beside your portrait, she wrote shortly after Andrée's body was found, referring to the flower she had told Andrée would always remind her of him. *When I smell its perfume all that separates us disappears. Dear August, I see and hear you. But the same question comes back to me. What became of all you were? Do you exist in some other form in the infinite universe? Can my thoughts of love help you in any way? The autumn of 1894 was our happiest time, though we knew deep down inside it was to be our last. I led an unusual double life in those days. But my love was for you alone. It was constant and unfailing, although it was never fulfilled. I can still feel the pain when you told me, 'The expedition will always come first.'*

Then you came to Stockholm, Gurli continued, referring to the state funeral and national mourning that greeted the return of Andrée, Strindberg and Frænkel's remains. *The king himself was there to hold a speech of welcome. I watched with Greta and with Signe. It was so strange. I did not actually feel anything. It was as if it was not you, as if it did not concern me. I saw us both as we were then. All that happened since has become unreal and irrelevant.*

Goodnight, dearly beloved. I am with you tonight. Grant me a few moments of peace and happiness in your arms. Let me know that you love me.

In August 1949, nineteen years after Nils's bones were returned to Sweden, Anna died and was buried in what is now an unmarked grave in the municipal cemetery at

Paignton. Today, there is no headstone or memorial, nothing to indicate that her remains are in any way distinct from those of her husband, Gilbert, with whom she shares the grave.

Having had no children with the man who never questioned her love for Nils or the pain he knew she still felt when she thought of the explorer she kissed goodbye in May 1897, Anna's last will was short. Anna Albertina Constancia Hawtrey, née Charlier, left everything she owned to her husband, but she made one exception.

As the solicitor reading her will came to the end he paused and handed it across his desk so that Gilbert could read his wife's final request. It was simple and direct, but it still took Gilbert by surprise. 'I spent my entire marriage to Anna knowing that had Nils Strindberg returned from the Arctic, or had he never departed for Dane's Island, then I would never have met such a wonderful woman,' he told the solicitor. 'Considering the circumstances that allowed our meeting, I will follow her request to the letter.'

Before she was buried a few days later in Paignton cemetery, Anna's heart was removed. It was cremated and its ashes packed in a silver casket, a larger version of the heart-shaped locket she had given to Nils on his birthday fifty-two years earlier. The casket was sent to Sweden and buried with the cremated remains of Nils Strindberg in Stockholm, where their engagement had begun over half a century earlier. At last, the two young sweethearts who had never forgotten their love for each other were reunited in their homeland.

CHAPTER FOURTEEN

THE HOMECOMING

ARCTIC OCEAN

1 June, 2000

'SO WHAT'S THE PLAN NOW, BRIAN?'

The Pole is in the bag; there's a palpable sense of relief, of anticlimax even, but having climbed Mount Everest, I know this is the moment when things are most likely to go wrong. I've always remembered the adage that more climbers die coming down from the summit than on the way up to it. With their ambition realized and their guard down, they take less care and consequently make mistakes on the descent. It's something I want to avoid.

'I've spoken to Wayne Davidson at the weather station at Resolute Bay. He says there's cloud all the way from the Pole down to eighty-five north on the Canadian side,' Brian says. 'It's academic really, as we don't think we can get you to Canada.'

This is bad news. Having planned on landing in Canada, I've sent John Perrin, my pick-up man, out to Resolute Bay. I know the set-up in the Canadian High Arctic, and it would be easier to be picked up there than

288

in Russia. As for Alaska, I don't think I've got the range or the stamina.

'I've also spoken to Luc,' Brian continues. 'Bearing in mind that it's a very early weather projection, we've got three choices. Plan A: fly south. When the weather clears, land about five hundred kilometres north of Spitsbergen. Plan B: fly on to mainland Russia. 'And Plan C . . . ah.' There's a long pause while Brian ums and ahs. 'Er, I can't remember the third one.'

'So there's not much choice really, is there, Brian?' I say. 'It's Spitsbergen or Russia. Is there no chance of making it to Canada?'

'Only if you fly above twenty-four thousand feet. Given your tiredness and the way the oxygen is playing up, it's not an option.'

Canada would have been ideal. If I could make it to Ellesmere Island, then the Sea King at Eureka could pick me up. On the icecap north of Ellesmere Island, it would have to be a Twin Otter aeroplane; it needs only a hundred feet to land and eight hundred for take-off, but much of the polar icecap has already melted too much to take its weight.

Russia is even more of a problem. I know there is no helicopter cover in the area north of Murmansk, towards Franz Josef Land. If I want a helicopter pick-up, I'll have to land in Siberia, and the chances of returning from Russia with the balloon or any of my equipment are nil; it will all be stolen. Any further west and I'll have to wait for around a month for an icebreaker that I know is taking tourists to the Pole. I have food for ten days in the balloon basket – I've still not managed to eat anything substantial – and twenty-five days of full rations on the sledge. On half rations, I could survive for sixty days on the ice, but it's not something I want to contemplate.

'Looks like it's Plan A then, Brian,' I say. Once again, the winds have decided my fate. 'What's the track and at what height am I likely to find it?'

'I'll get back to you with that one when I've spoken to

Luc again. For the moment, stick to the track you're on. It's fast and you're heading in the right direction.'

As I fly away from the Pole, I look back at it and consider that I could tell people that I had flown closer to, or even exactly to, the Pole. After all, nobody else would know any different. Unlike some of the claims that have been made concerning reaching the Pole, such as Robert Peary's assertion that he reached it on foot in 1909, my declaration would be plausible. But I did not embark on this flight so that I would have something to boast about down at the pub; it is about a personal achievement. I am doing this only for me, and if other people do not understand why I am satisfied with what I have achieved, then that is their problem. I am still unable to believe how close I got; I have been extraordinarily lucky.

Again, I am overwhelmed by a sense that a force is at work that is greater than all the people who have worked so hard to get *Britannic Challenger* to the Pole. At every juncture, luck has gone our way. Taking off from an island plagued by high-speed winds which all but disappeared a moment before launch would be considered luck enough to satisfy most people. Then, for all the communications to start working again, just when their failure was becoming critical, was a remarkable turn of events. To put my harness on just before I fell into a sleep during which I almost walked out of the basket was, again, unusually fortunate. To turn left and fly in a perfect straight line beyond the initial target of the polar ring to within twelve miles of the Pole is, again, another extraordinary piece of luck. Now, to be heading back to where I came from is the icing on the cake.

'Calling Golf Bravo Yankee Zulu X-ray.' Iceland Radio is calling. I respond. '*Britannic Challenger*, a patch from base coming through.'

It's Clive. 'We've spoken to Luc. He says to stick to seven thousand feet; it's a perfect high-speed track to Spitsbergen. You should be home by eight a.m. on Saturday.'

That's fewer than thirty-six hours for the return portion of the flight, more than twice as fast as the trip up to the Pole.

'How are you feeling, Old Man?'

'More tired than I've ever been before, Boy. I've just had an hour's sleep and it's made a bit of difference, but it's still not enough.'

'I suggest you set the autopilot and have another kip. There's nothing much else to do now. What's the weather like?'

'Clear above, Boy, patchy cloud below. I can see the ice; it doesn't look pleasant. I'm going to sleep. Speak to you in two hours.'

Brian wakes me with a call on the satellite phone two and a half hours later.

'David, what's happened? We've not heard from you.'

My head is thick with tiredness, but I immediately come to my senses when I look across at the navigation equipment. The altimeter reads 4,200ft; I was so tired I fell asleep without switching the autopilot on. *Britannic Challenger* has drifted down nearly three thousand feet in that time. Another couple of hours and I would have crashed into the ice. Once again, luck has been on my side and I've snatched the mission from the jaws of defeat.

'Christ, Brian. Thank God you called when you did.' I tell him what has happened.

He is unflustered; his placid voice is calming. 'I'm going to be here all night, David, looking after you, so keep me informed of how you're feeling. Grab as much sleep as you can and when you don't feel like sleeping, you can talk to me.'

The adrenalin has stopped pumping now that the Pole has been bagged; it makes the exhaustion much more difficult to withstand. My thinking is slow and my eyelids feel like heavy curtains about to fall to the floor. I always thought coping with fatigue on the return flight would be the hardest part of the journey, and my prediction was right.

'Luc's off to sleep and the NOAA* computer he needs is down, so he's happy to let you fly through the night. He says the present track is good, but if you want to steer it, descend to turn right, go up to turn left.'

With so much to be sorted out before I can rest, I ignore the callings of my body for sleep and run through various logistics with Brian. I need to make sure the pick-up helicopter has a sling to carry *Britannic Challenger*'s envelope; I have to go through all the pre-landing checks; I'm concerned that people I promised could come to the pick-up – television and newspaper reporters, primarily – will arrive in Spitsbergen before I land. Wanting most of all to keep the cost to a minimum, I suggest to Brian that I head for the ice east of Spitsbergen.

'According to my thermographs, the ice looks good there,' I tell Brian. 'It'll be a short, cheap hop in the helicopter and it'll take me longer to reach, so that gives the reporters time to get to Spitsbergen.'

'What about the polar bears, David? It's the worst area for bears.'

'I'll deal with that problem when I come to it.' I have a rifle that I bought in Longyearbyen, and although I don't want to have to use it, I will if the need arises.

I have encountered a polar bear before. One night in February 1984, a short distance into my solo unsupported trek from Resolute Bay on Cornwallis Island to the Magnetic North Pole, I heard a scratching and sniffing sound outside my tent. It was 2 a.m. and I was exhausted, but the sound woke me immediately. I did not know that I was in Polar Bear Pass, the area with the largest concentration of polar bears anywhere in the world, but I did recognize the sound of an intruder. Unzipping the flap of my tiny one-man tent, I saw a huge adult polar bear twenty-five yards away, staring directly at me.

I grabbed my gun and fired a warning shot, but the bear

---

* America's meteorological office, the National Oceanic and Atmosphere Administration

appeared not to take any notice. Having not eaten for days, the huge animal quite clearly had me in its sights. Compared with seals, the staple diet of the bears dotted around Cornwallis Island, I was tasty fare, and I could see a warning shot was not going to frighten it off its next meal.

The bear took a couple of steps away from me, then swivelled and plodded very definitely and menacingly towards the tent. Although it was happening relatively slowly, there was no mistaking the fact that I was being attacked.

Screaming 'You bastard!' at the bear, I unleashed a volley of bullets. Back in Resolute Bay, the locals had told me to take careful aim and fire off single, well-aimed shots, but with the countdown ticking I forgot any sensible self-control and fired every bullet in the gun at the animal. The bear dropped to the ground. Several of my bullets had hit home, but even then I was not taking any chances. Pumped to the eyeballs on adrenalin, I fired a further two shots into the area behind its shoulder, the only access point to its vital organs, then reloaded the rifle with five bullets and emptied them into the bear's huge white carcass. The bear was a mess, but I had survived.

Once I had calmed down I felt dreadful. The last thing I had wanted to do when I set out was to kill any of the local wildlife, let alone a beast as magnificent as a polar bear. I had no right to be where I was; I had intruded into the bear's territory, not the other way round, yet the bear had drawn the short straw. Feeling very guilty, I radioed back to Resolute Bay and told them to send a plane.

When the Twin Otter arrived, the pilots were amazed. The bear lay a matter of feet away from my tent; it was clear that I had experienced a very close escape. Swearing and cursing at the weight of the beast, the pilots heaved the bear into the plane and ferried it back to Resolute Bay where it was cut up, skinned and ticked off the hamlet's annual quota of polar bear kills. The fell was sold, the meat fed to huskies and I made the newspapers in England as the first Briton to shoot a polar bear for many years.

Flying through the night, I sit on my icebox and think back to that day, making small adjustments to the altitude to keep *Britannic Challenger* on a course of 161° towards Spitsbergen. I also think about poor old Andrée, who deserved to do better. I am very much aware that if Andrée, Strindberg and Frænkel had made the same trip today, an emergency rescue team would have plucked them from the ice shortly after it all went wrong. At worst, they would have had mild frostbite and dented prides.

It is a humbling thought that on any adventure your fate is largely in the lap of the gods; on this flight more so than on anything I've previously attempted. You can plan meticulously, but something else usually determines whether you succeed or not. In this case, it has been the weather and the other members of the team. Working in front of a computer screen in Belgium, Luc Trullemans has effectively flown *Britannic Challenger* to the Pole. While it would be unfair to portray Luc as the organ grinder and me as the monkey, it is fair to say that he could have directed any reasonably competent pilot to the Pole, whereas I would not have got there without his assistance. I paid him well for three months of solid work, and he deserved every penny. Luc has proved to be the single most important element in the mission. Without him, I would not even have taken off.

Everest taught me humility, but this challenge has been in a different league. I don't mean to belittle climbing Everest – it is very hard – but this has so far been nearly a hundred hours of continuous, concentrated effort. I am convinced I could not have done this if I was younger; I would not have had the mental stamina. Having three children has certainly helped, particularly the experience of looking after a sick child through the night and then having somehow to get through the next day. It taught me what it is to be extremely tired, and how to dig deep to find the last reserves of physical energy and mental determination needed to keep going. My children have taught me how to keep going even when I thought I could not continue.

Mid-morning on Friday 2 June, I cross the 85th line of latitude into the comfort zone. On the way up to the Pole, the 85th parallel was the point of no turning back; on the return journey, it marks the beginning of the area within rescue range of Spitsbergen. Even if I am forced to ditch now, the mission will have been a success.

'Well done, Old Man. How are you feeling?' Clive asks.

'Not bad, Boy. I've had some sleep, which has made a big difference. Weather and balloon fine, but I am still not hungry.'

'Keep up the water, sweets and biscuits; you should be eating pasta and drinking three litres of water a day. You've still got a lot ahead of you.'

'In that case, I think I'll come down now,' I reply. 'I'm sick of being trapped inside this tiny basket. I'll come down, and let you come and pick me up.'

Clive is his usual ebullient self in reply. 'If I'd known that you would get gobby, I wouldn't have let you sleep for as long. We should have kept you awake; now that you're thinking for yourself, there's more of a chance of it going wrong.'

'The satellite phone battery is almost spent,' I say. 'What can I do?'

'I've got instructions from Colin Hill on how to jury-rig it to the lead acid battery. That should keep it going for a while,' Clive replies.

I then issue a string of requests and commands.

'You're starting to tell us what to do, Old Man. Let me remind you that we can still drop you in the shit. Best if we do the thinking and you feed the monkey, isn't it?'

I know Clive is right, but I am concerned about the landing arrangements. 'Can you speak to the tower at Longyearbyen? Ask them about the winds, the ice conditions and about the best place to land.'

'David, relax. It's all in hand. The Polar Institute says

the best place to land is eighty-one degrees north, twenty-one east. Failing that, there are three small islands twenty miles directly south of there. One of them is very flat; Nelson landed on it once – by boat, not balloon, of course. I've also spoken to Airlift, the helicopter company at Longyearbyen airport, and told them the sizes and weights of the largest objects – your head excepted. Now I just need clearance from the governor to have you picked up by chopper. Finally, I've spoken to the polar bears and informed them to expect a picnic hamper at eight o'clock tomorrow morning.'

'So what is there left for me to do, Boy?'

'Keep up the good work, get some more rest and prepare for the landing. It'll come sooner than you think.'

Again, the exhaustion comes back to hit me like a warm, damp flannel smothering my face, so I take a couple of caffeine tablets. They make no difference, so I take a few more. Still no improvement; I must be too tired for caffeine to have an effect. Thankfully, I need to do very little for the next few hours. The autopilot is in control and I sit in the basket, trying to doze and wire the Iridium satellite telephone to the lead acid battery. Eventually I get it to work, but there's not much power left in the battery. At least it enables me to answer some requests for interviews.

'Are you disappointed not to have made it to the Pole?' one of the journalists asks.

I'm flabbergasted. 'What do you mean?'

'Well, twelve miles short of the Pole is not the Pole, is it?'

I want to scream, but I have to keep my cool and I tell him that the objective was always to use Andrée's yardstick: within sight of the Pole. That meant inside the polar circle – sixty miles from the Pole – but I did better than that.

'I could have flown closer, but it would have meant climbing to twenty-four thousand feet when my bottled oxygen was not working,' I say. 'This trip wasn't about hitting the Pole on the dot; the challenge was to fly through the most unpredictable winds there are, and I managed that. The last degree is definable in ballooning terms, the North Pole is not. I came within twelve miles and I have no problem with that at all. You would be a stupid man to say you were going to get spot on the Pole. You cannot do it. Even in a hot-air balloon in this country, you do not know where you are going to land.'

What I really want to ask him is if he has ever been to the Pole or flown a balloon. Then he would understand the scale of the challenge. If I had wanted to hit the Pole on the button, I would have trekked on foot instead of flying by balloon, the most unmanageable form of transport imaginable. Even the round-the-world attempts had a massive goalmouth by comparison. They had to start and finish on the same line of longitude, but flying exactly to the Pole and back is like launching from one stick, flying to another stick 708 miles away and returning to the first stick.

I have flown to the bull's-eye of the target, but not hit the absolute centre of that bull's-eye. To fly 708 miles and get within twelve miles of the Pole is accurate to within two per cent. Competition balloonists appreciate how difficult it is to fly with that degree of precision; they have to hit a one-metre bull's-eye from a distance of a few miles, but they can choose exactly where to take off from within that radius. If you told them they had to launch from a predetermined position, waiting for the wind to blow the right way and still hit the target, they would refuse.*

*Which is why the British Balloon and Airship Club later said it was 'an absolute impossibility' to fly closer to the North Pole than I had. Guinness World Records acknowledged I had flown closer to the Pole than anyone before and added it was highly unlikely anyone could repeat the feat. After consultation with the BBAC, Guinness announced that they recognized my flight as the first balloon flight to the North Pole. Initially they had said I would have to come within one metre of the absolute position. Because of the speed of the currents under the ice, that is something that very few, if any, of the people who have reached the Pole on foot can claim wholeheartedly (and even GPS is accurate to within only ten metres at best).

I defy anybody else to fly from Spitsbergen to the North Pole and back, not because they are not capable but because I have been remarkably lucky. At every stage, everything came right, and it's highly unlikely that anybody will ever be so fortunate again. Climbing Everest, trekking to the North or South Pole, sailing around the world, even flying to the moon are not comparable, for one simple reason: they are repeatable. Other people might be able to take off from Russia, fly in a balloon to the Pole and land in Alaska, but no-one else will be able to take off from Spitsbergen, get within twelve miles of the Pole and fly straight back to Spitsbergen. I didn't think it was possible – that's why my pick-up team is in northern Canada – but I've had a staggering run of luck. At every juncture, the right thing happened. I am not a brilliant pilot. Any pilot could have done it, but the luck that went with it made it possible for me. It has been an extraordinary achievement for the whole team. So when a journalist asks me if I am disappointed, all I can answer is that disappointment is the very last emotion I am feeling.

Early afternoon, and Brian is on the radio again.

'Anything to report?'

'Nothing much, Brian. It's been plain sailing. I've just had a crap. First one in days. I had to throw it over the side.'

'Bet that sent you shooting up into the atmosphere,' Brian jokes. 'I've spoken to the weather god. You have to find a track of one-four-zero degrees immediately. Luc says you're veering too far west of Spitsbergen; we need to bring you further east.'

Hoping it will be the last time I go through this rigmarole, I repeat the lengthy process of ascending slowly and noting the wind direction every fifty or hundred feet. I go from 7,500ft to 9,000ft, but cannot find the 140° track, so I descend. Eventually I discover the track at 7,400ft.

Just before radioing the control centre to let them know I'm on course, I drop a drained HF radio battery over the side. It's a big mistake. The balloon shoots up to 16,000ft. Panicking at the loss of ballast, I strap on the bottled oxygen mask and accidentally set off the fire extinguisher. It's a short burst, but I am coated in white powder as I try to vent hot air from *Britannic Challenger*'s envelope. Eventually, I have the balloon under control, and it descends slowly to 9,000ft, where Brian comes in on the radio.

'Golf Bravo Yankee Zulu X-ray, what is your position, height, track and speed?' he asks.

I pass over the details.

'Are you having difficulties finding the track, David?'

'Not exactly. I had it spot on at seven thousand four hundred feet.'

'So why are you now on the wrong heading at nine thousand?'

I tell him about the battery and the fire extinguisher.

'You're a bit white, are you? That'll help you blend in well with the landscape on landing and make it easy for the helicopter to find you. At least it'll keep the bears away.'

'Brian, I'm on my way back down to seven thousand four hundred feet,' I say, a bit too tired to be teased. 'What else do you want me to do?'

'Descend to around five thousand two hundred and maintain that height. Stay clear of cloud and keep it nice and steady, low and slow – your favourite.'

An hour later and Brian is back on the radio. In the meantime, I have made contact with Longyearbyen tower.

'What's the game plan now, Brian?'

'Keep it cool. The distance to go isn't far, about a hundred miles, but you've got about ten more hours to go. Your estimated time of arrival is zero-seven-one-five Zulu, or nine fifteen a.m. your time. Not bad, considering Luc predicted a couple of days ago that you'd land at eight. What a star!'

Not wanting it all to go wrong at the last moment, I strap on my harness and check the autopilot. I intend to sleep, but instead I look over the side at the ice. It has become very fragmented. According to my thermographs, the ice should be in a good condition at this location, but I can clearly see that it is not. I tell Clive of my concerns when he comes on the radio for the scheduled comms at the top of the hour.

'The ice doesn't look good here,' I say. 'If it's as bad as it appears this far north, then I think the ice further south may not carry my weight. I think I should start descending.'

'Funny you should say that, Old Man. We were thinking the same. Our thoughts are that you're not getting any less tired as time ticks on. I'd rather have you on the ground sooner, waiting for the chopper, than in the air for much longer.'

Brian then takes over on the radio. 'How are you feeling?'

'Okay,' I say.

'You need to go through all your landing checks. Clive will run through them with you. Call back with your position when you've completed the checks and you are ready to start the descent. Take as long as you like.'

'Okay. I've got all that. What about the weather?'

'Cloud base is at fifteen hundred feet or better. Visibility twenty kilometres or more. There's a possibility of light snow.'

'Okay. I'll speak to you when I'm ready.'

'Good. We're looking forward to seeing code fourteen on the Argos.'

We all know that code 14 means a safe landing, but now that the end is in sight I don't want the flight to end. I'm looking forward to seeing my wife and children again, and I'll be pleased when life returns to its normal routines, but I know that when I land I'll be waving goodbye to someone who has become a companion and guardian angel on the flight: Andrée.

Sitting on my icebox, tears well up in my eyes as I check my position and realize that for the second time this flight,

I am flying directly over the area where the *Eagle* flew in a loop during the second day of its faltering voyage. Without Andrée, I probably would never have thought of ballooning to the Pole. I feel a massive debt to him, Strindberg and Frænkel, and I hope that I have repaid it in some way by showing that their ambitious plan did work. Andrée and I both made the flight at the same age, forty-three. He was the visionary, and I have been the executor.

Although I have been successful, I doubt my achievement will be remembered for nearly as long as Andrée's misadventure. There's good reason for that, and it seems right to me: Andrée was a genuine explorer, venturing into unknown territory, whereas I can claim only to be an adventurer or sportsman, re-treading old paths in a new way. And as far as polar exploration is concerned, the public prefers tragic failures to triumphant heroes; that's why Scott is better remembered than Amundsen or Shackleton, the two greatest polar explorers of all. If you are successful, then people assume it must have been easy.

Throughout the flight, on a number of occasions I've had the feeling that something or somebody has been helping me. I'm not particularly spiritual or religious, but I've felt as if Andrée has been beside me in the basket, fulfilling my wish for a companion to share the adventure. It sounds fanciful, but I am convinced that Andrée has been willing me on, keeping an eye on me, so that more than a century after his ideas were derided by the establishment and his flight ended in ignominy, I could prove that his vision was right.

Having tied the propane tanks securely to the side of the basket, switched off all oxygen, strapped all my equipment in place, taken down the canopy over the basket, double-checked my safety harness and life raft and put on my immersion suit, I begin *Britannic Challenger*'s descent at 3.42 a.m. on Saturday 3 June by tugging the white-flecked and the red-white candy-striped ropes that vent helium and hot air. For a few moments *Britannic Challenger* does nothing, as if reluctant to leave the skies; then the majestic old dear begins a slow, stately descent.

For an hour, I crouch in the basket, anxiously scanning the ice below. It does not look good. Fifteen minutes pass without sight of a floe large enough to land on. Several times I see a perfect shadow of the balloon against the broken ice. It reminds me of when I spotted the shadow racing across pans of perfect ice towards the Pole. That was a wonderful moment, but this time the sight of the shadow is even better: this time, it means I am nearly home.

An hour and a quarter after *Britannic Challenger* begins its return to earth, I hear the faint clatter of a helicopter's rotating blades, then I spot the rescue helicopter on the horizon, the first speck of colour I have seen in this monochrome landscape for five days. Gradually, I am removing myself from this isolated, solitary existence that I crave so much when away from it, and beginning my reintroduction to the real world.

The next half an hour passes in a blur. Flying at 1,000ft and increasingly aware that I am running out of firm ice to land on, I stand on the candy-striped rope. It's a bit unorthodox, but it is the only way I can keep the hot-air valve permanently open. Soon I am only a hundred feet up, but the ice below me is a mess. Looking for a suitable place to land, I fly on, barely skimming above the ice at ten to twelve knots as I talk to *Britannic Challenger*: 'Come on, old girl. Help me find somewhere smooth, soft and big to put you down gently.'

But my appeal to my chariot comes to nothing; seconds later, the white ground comes towards me with a violent rush as *Britannic Challenger* strikes an ice floe. Wishing that I was experienced enough to flare the basket and take the speed off the balloon, I bounce up, slam down on the ice again and ricochet back up to a hundred feet. I still have the candy-striped rope tugged taut beneath my foot, but otherwise I am clinging on for dear life as *Britannic*

Challenger takes me on a roller-coaster ride every bit as terrifying as the *Eagle*'s bumpy journey across the pack ice in 1897.

Before the balloon smacks back into the ice, I pull the solid red cord. It is meant to release all the helium in the inner cell of the envelope, but it doesn't work. Thinking that maybe this is where my luck runs out, I am thrown off my feet when the basket crashes into a pressure ridge, bounces over it and drags along the bumpy ice at twelve knots. As the basket judders around me, the last five days flash before my eyes. I see the launch, the decision to keep going when I reached 85° and the fright when I nearly stepped out of the balloon. I remember the relief and joy of crossing 89° and reaching the Pole, and the exhaustion during the journey back. But it doesn't stop there; my life flashes like a movie running in my head. I see Claire and my daughters, my father and mother, and all the friends with whom I have climbed mountains and trekked across ice. It culminates with Rune, hauling me out of the icy water of the Arctic Ocean, the last time I thought I was about to meet my maker.

The scraping of empty propane bottles on the outside of the basket against ice brings me to my senses, and I manage to grab hold of the candy-striped rope just before the basket plunges into the black water. A frigid torrent rushes through the wickerwork, rising within seconds up to my knees and slowing *Britannic Challenger*'s headlong lurch. Before I have time to pull myself upright, a gust of wind hooks the balloon back onto the ice and *Britannic Challenger* speeds up again.

And so it goes on for fifteen terrifying minutes and several miles, the bitter wind tossing me from ice floe to water and back again. It is, without doubt, the most dangerous thing I've ever done. The fighter pilot training course hardly prepared me for this; it was a sedate dip in the sea by comparison. As the water rises up to my thighs, I realize I might drown as *Britannic Challenger* sinks into a lead about a hundred yards wide. I take to praying.

This, I am convinced, is the end. Everyone's luck is finite, and mine has just run out.

The water slows *Britannic Challenger* almost to a standstill; if it stops now, then I will sink into the water with it. There is no provision for detaching the envelope, just the chimney to let all the gas out, but that isn't working. I realize I am in real danger of being dragged down by the balloon, so I decide to cut my harness so that I can jump clear and be plucked from the water by the helicopter. But before I can free myself, the balloon starts moving again and I am lifted with it, out of the water and onto the ice.

The floor of the basket has become an ice rink. It is impossible to stand upright or cling on. Wishing that I had a huge hook on a trailing rope as an anchor and fearing that the propane bottles dangling from the side of the basket might explode under the battering, I contemplate jumping to safety. But a sense of shame at abandoning the home that has carried me more than 1,600 miles keeps me clinging on. It would be disgraceful for the captain to abandon his ship; if I jumped out, *Britannic Challenger* would shoot up a few thousand feet and I would lose it for ever.

Eventually, the basket thuds against a pressure ridge, tumbles over and stops dead. Enough helium has escaped from the envelope to prevent it taking off again, but I am trapped in the basket. Pinned to the side of the basket by its contents, I can see the helicopter swooping down towards me from above. The crew jumps out and hacks with knives at the envelope to vent the remaining gas and hot air. Gradually, the balloon sinks to the frosty surface and the ordeal is over.

Having clambered free, I run over to the winchman and hug him, my first human contact after 132 hours' solitary confinement above the ice.

'No time for that,' he shouts over the deafening whirr of the helicopter's blades. 'You've got ten minutes until the helicopter has to leave!'

Rushing to collect all my kit, I pull out the electronics and the gas valve – the most expensive items of equipment – while two photographers and a television cameraman who were on board the helicopter try to pack up the envelope. I beckon the winchman over to my pile of equipment and shout through the cloud of snow and ice that the helicopter's blades have blown up around us.

'This has to come back with me.'

'No,' he shouts back. 'We're taking everything.'

'What?'

'We're taking everything back with us,' he shouts again.

'I heard you the first time. I just couldn't believe that I've wrecked the balloon, causing at least five thousand pounds' worth of damage, and now you tell me everything will fit in the helicopter.'

The winchman just shrugs.

We stuff *Britannic Challenger*'s envelope into the helicopter and lug its equipment through the hatch. Minutes later, we are above the ice, headed for two small huts at the tip of Spitsbergen, where, dressed in immersion suits and with only a tiny pistol as protection against polar bears, Bill Haynes and Stuart Nunn of Britannic have been waiting for six hours. They were dropped off on the way up, as the helicopter did not have the capacity for the two of them and *Britannic Challenger*'s envelope.

Bill and Stuart are shivering with the cold and clearly relieved to see us. Bill throws his arms around me. 'Well done, mate. I always knew you would do it.'

'Thanks, Bill,' I say. 'Thanks for it all, but thanks most of all for having the vision and the faith in me.'

Bill shows me inside the hut. 'The pilots told us if they were not back within two hours then it would be three days before we saw anyone, because it would have meant they had a problem.' Pointing at a stack of mouldy mattresses, he continues: 'I lay on one of those and pulled another one on top of me, but I got so cold I was shaking. I thought we had to get moving, so we went outside and dug a bit, then we went for a walk, but we got sweaty inside our immersion suits. Just when I thought I couldn't take it any longer, you turned up.'

After unloading the basket and balloon on the little island, Bill and Stuart board the helicopter bound for Longyearbyen. At last I am on my way back to safety, proud that the mission has been accomplished safely and overjoyed at succeeding where so many had said I would fail. I'm looking forward to celebrating with my wife, daughters and friends the feat of becoming the first person to balloon to the North Pole. But the celebrations will be tinged with sad memories of Andrée, Frænkel and Stringberg's lonely deaths on an ice bound island more than a century ago.

My dream, hatched on the ice with Rune two years earlier, has come true. Several times, particularly during the landing and when I almost stepped out of the basket, I thought my plans, like Andrée's, would end in disaster, but something or someone has helped keep me alive and safe.

I like to think it was the man to whom I dedicate this adventure, the man who dared to take on nature with a vision ahead of his time: Salomon August Andrée.

AUTHOR'S NOTE

TO TELL THE STORIES OF SALOMON AUGUST ANDRÉE, NILS Strindberg, Knut Frænkel, Nils Ekholm and the flight of the *Eagle* as dramatically and authentically as possible, I called on their diaries and journals, various letters, third-party accounts and newly published research. In doing so, this book overturns several previously held convictions, in particular that the deaths of Andrée, Strindberg and Frænkel on White Island were caused either by trichinosis or through suffocation by the stove's fumes or as a result of simple exhaustion from the cold.

Appendix One explains in more detail why botulism is the most likely cause of death. This theory, I feel, fits the evidence better and makes much more sense than any of the other hypotheses. I am indebted to Håkan Jorikson, curator of the excellent Andrée Museum at Gränna in Sweden, who directed me to Mark Personne, a former intensive care physician, now director of the Swedish Poisons Information Centre. Dr Personne's research, published recently in the Swedish physicians' medical journal *Läkartidningen*, was used as the basis for the death scenes in chapter thirteen. To Dr Personne, many thanks for assistance and for permission to reproduce an English translation of his research.

As well as directing me to Mark Personne, Håkan Jorikson answered many questions concerning the Andrée expedition, and gave me permission to quote from the three men's diaries, journals and meteorological almanacs. Once again, many thanks. All italicized excerpts from diaries or letters are as written, subject to translation from the Swedish and, where necessary, editing for clarity. Most of the direct quotes are derived from the diaries, from letters or third-party accounts of events. Again, they have been translated from the Swedish and edited for clarity. However, in a few cases, quotes have been used to advance the story, to put technical or background information in plain words, to give an insight into the characters of the three men or to explain disparities between events as they were officially documented and what was clearly happening. Whereas this was necessary, it was done in as close a spririt to the original source as possible.

Piecing together and then recounting the history of the Andrée expedition was made difficult by conflicting accounts of what happened and what was said at various times. In part this was because the three men's diaries are incomplete and damaged. Often individual words are missing; frequently, it is entire sentences. In these circumstances, words and phrases have been added to fill the spaces. Occasionally, precise timings of events were confused because Andrée and Strindberg used different conventions for recording the time. At other times, it is obvious that, with an eye on posterity, the men sought to present desperate circumstances in a better light. Consequently, some interpretation of events has been necessary. Andrée, Strindberg and Frænkel also used abbreviations and shorthand in their diaries. These have been written out in full to make them easier to understand.

I am also particularly indebted to Håkan Wasén, a

cousin of Nils Strindberg, who gave me translations of letters between Nils and Anna, Nils and his brother Tore, and answered many questions on the Strindberg family and on Nils's romance with Anna. Once again, many thanks.

Robert Uhlig,
January 2001

THE CAUSE OF DEATH

THE FOLLOWING PAPER BY MARK PERSONNE, DIRECTOR OF THE Swedish Poisons Information Centre, was published in 2000 in the scientific journal *Läkartidningen*, the Swedish physicians' medical journal.

Andrée expedition members probably died of botulism
New hypothesis explains the mysterious deaths

In brief

The causes of the deaths of the three members of the 1897 balloon flight to the North Pole have never been established. Through the years a number of theories have been put forward (vitamin A poisoning, freezing to death, carbon monoxide poisoning, suicide, scurvy, trichinosis, dehydration etc.) but none of these has been entirely without fault.

No proper autopsy was carried out on the bodies when their last campsite was found on White Island, northeast of

Spitsbergen in 1930. The human remains were cremated after arrival in Sweden. Other objects are preserved at the Andrée museum in Gränna.

Here, a further three theories as to the causes of death are presented of which poisoning with *botulinus* toxin appears more probable than the others.

The balloon flight of Salomon August Andrée, Knut Frænkel and Nils Strindberg started on 11 July 1897 and ended with a forced landing on the polar ice three days later. It was followed by a trek across the ice, which ended on 5 October 1897, when they went ashore on White Island.

Andrée kept a detailed journal, the last pages of which, however, are so damaged that the text is partly illegible. Frænkel and Strindberg also took notes. These diary notes and studies of the remains of their last camp reveal a number of circumstances that ought to be covered by any death theory if it is to be considered credible.

Strindberg died before the others. He was buried in a shallow grave thirty metres from the camp but without shroud, cross, flag or other memorials. He was wearing trousers and a waistcoat but his jacket and personal belongings were preserved elsewhere.

Remains of Andrée and Frænkel were found close to one another in the remains of their tent, but not in the group's common sleeping bag. Frænkel was wearing a cap. A pair of sunglasses was found next to his cranium.

The ice trek lasted for almost three months, while the landing on White Island took place a few days before they met their death. The walk over the pack ice had, at times, been exceptionally laborious, but there is nothing to indicate the three were dying when they arrived at White Island.

The diaries mention the following symptoms of illness: recurrent diarrhoea (all three men), a period of constipation (Andrée), stomach pains, running noses (all three men), muscular cramps (Frænkel), snow blindness at the beginning of the ice trek (Frænkel), pronounced muscular tiredness (Frænkel and to some extent Strindberg). Towards the end

311

of the ice trek there are no written descriptions of symptoms.

The diary entries stop around 7 October and, as far as can be judged, the deaths occurred shortly thereafter. On the last fragmentary pages of Andrée's journal there is no mention of illness, death, accident, confusion or other clues to the cause of death. There are observations of nature, reconnaissance, weather, the naming of their landing site and other things. The writing is legible, no misspellings or other signs of seriously affected mental ability are found.

Assuming that all three died from the same cause, the course of death was clearly sufficiently protracted for one member to be buried after a fashion but at the same time so rapid that there was no time or possibility to make notes of the first death in the diaries.

Near Andrée's body a rifle was found, but it was unclear whether it was loaded. There are no reports of bullet-holes or other injuries to the bodies or damage to clothing, except for a small tear in Strindberg's jacket. In the camp there were large quantities of food, mainly raw meat and conserves in tins. Meat and fat from seal, walrus and polar bear that had been shot during the ice trek were carried on the sledges.

The Primus stove, a bottle, a mug and a plate with remains of food were still in the tent. The stove was functional and when found contained three quarters of a litre of paraffin. The valve was shut. No remains of a fireplace were seen anywhere in the camp.

Trichinae larvae were later found in remains of polar bear meat collected from the place where the three men were found.

The expedition carried: cooking spirit, opium and morphine.

Theories on the causes of death – old and new
Trichinosis The Danish physician E.A. Tryde, who wrote an entire book on the subject, presented this theory during the 1950s. His main argument was that *trichinae* were discovered in remains of polar bear flesh taken from the place where the three men were found. Certain non-specific symptoms of disease mentioned in the diaries agree with trichinosis (diarrhoea, constipation, muscle pain – but these were transient). Expected

symptoms are lacking (periods of raised temperature, eyelid oedema [excessive swelling due to fluid retention], conjunctival bleeding, persistent muscle pain, pneumonitis [inflammation of the lungs]). If lethal myocarditis [inflammation of the heart muscle] occurs, it commonly happens between four and eight weeks after ingestion of *trichinae* larvae. Even untreated trichinosis is normally not fatal. It is very improbable that three persons should die more or less simultaneously of this infection. Nansen and other polar travellers survived well in this region despite repeated ingestion of polar bear meat.

Appraisal: Possible cause of certain symptoms of disease but very unlikely cause of death.

Scurvy A well-known cause of death among seafarers of old living on a diet low in vitamin C, but three months is too short a time to develop life-threatening symptoms. There was continual access to food containing vitamin C, such as fresh meat and algae. No typical symptoms are described in the diaries. No loosened teeth were observed.

Appraisal: Excluded as cause of death.

Vitamin A poisoning It emerges from the diaries that polar bear liver, which is rich in vitamin A, was not eaten. No typical symptoms such as severe headache, scaling skin, loss of hair, oedema and tendency to bleed are described. It is also improbable that vitamin A poisoning could kill all three within such a short period of time.

Appraisal: Excluded as cause of death.

Carbon monoxide poisoning According to this theory, the Primus stove was the source of carbon monoxide release. It is, however, improbable that the Primus stove was used at night for heating in view of the need to conserve their fuel. The deaths of the two people in the tent probably occurred during the day as the bodies were found outside the sleeping bag. A person who is awake notices symptoms of carbon monoxide poisoning and ends the exposure. The worn tent would probably have been draughty and well ventilated. Two people who initially survive, but later die of carbon monoxide poisoning, cannot manage to carry out a burial. There was some paraffin left in the Primus stove and the valve was shut, which indicates that it was not in use when the deaths occurred.

Appraisal: Very improbable cause of death.

Lead poisoning It has long been known that members of Arctic expeditions frequently had very high levels of lead in body tissue. Corpses belonging to two members of the 1846 Franklin expedition were found well preserved on Beechey Island in the Canadian High Arctic. During the 1980s, samples were taken from these bodies and the lead contents in pieces of tissue were analysed from skeleton, soft tissues and hair. Levels of 110 to 228 parts per million were found in the skeleton. In a contemporary study, normal values for lead in fingernails were found to be approximately 5 parts per million.[1] Poisoning has been suggested as a contributory cause of the Franklin expedition,[2] but opinions differ.[3]

Andrée, like Franklin, took provisions packed in metal cans sealed with lead seams. It is known that this type of tin may leak dangerous quantities of lead into the contents.

In the collections at the Andrée museum in Gränna, three pieces of fingernail were found in a mitten in 1979. The lead content of the nails has now been analysed with two different techniques. In December 1997 an X-ray fluorescence analysis was carried out on a $0.25cm^2$ area in the centre of one of the nails. A content of 60 parts per million was measured there, ten to twenty times more than normal current reference values.

To confirm this finding, in June 1998 a fresh analysis with proton-induced X-ray emission was undertaken at Lund College of Technology. The lead content was measured at twelve points along the longitudinal axis of another fingernail. In this case, the samples were taken on the underside of the nail to eliminate as far as possible the risk that the nail could have been contaminated by exogenous [outside] lead. The analysis showed raised lead values in the area of 27 to 486 parts per million (with an average value 65 parts per million).

In a contemporary Swedish study of people exposed to lead over a long period, a content in the finger of a skeleton of 55 parts per million was found (a control group had 3 parts per million).[4] In another study, thirteen occupationally exposed patients had skeleton values ranging from 26 to 410 parts per million (control persons 4 to 18 parts per million).[5]

Symptoms of chronic lead poisoning are initially stealthy: tiredness, moodiness and loss of initiative may occur. On increased exposure, symptoms are frequently added from the gastrointestinal tract, with loss of appetite, diffuse stomach pains, constipation or diarrhoea. Muscle pains, aching joints and numbness in the legs are common with further exposure to lead. Then lead colic occurs with serious attacks of stomach pain. Problems of co-ordination, paralysis, confusion and memory disturbances occur. In the final stage, spasms and unconsciousness occur.

The fingernails grow at 0.5 to 1.2 millimetres per week. The expedition lasted approximately eighty-eight days, which gives an expected nail growth of six to fifteen millimetres during this period. Assuming that the growth rate is in between these limits, only the first seven measurement points reckoned from the root of the twenty-millimetre-long nail would have been formed during the expedition. The highest value of 486 parts per million was at measurement point 10, hence definitely outside the relevant timeframe and, if the values are correct, it occurred before the expedition started.

Among the symptoms of disease mentioned in the diaries are various non-specific symptoms compatible with lead poisoning but which may also have several other causes. Since lead poisoning disturbs the higher brain functions one can speculate as to whether the judgement and ability of the expedition members to make rational decisions had been affected. However, the journal contains no obvious signs of mental or functional impairment, which would be expected during the last few days of fatal lead poisoning.

Lead poisoning alone cannot explain the deaths of the three men within the course of one or a few days.

Appraisal: Possible cause of certain symptoms of disease, very improbable as cause of death.

Methanol poisoning The expedition members took cooking spirit and two empty cans of spirit were found at the camp on White Island. It has so far been impossible to establish whether the spirit contained methanol. One possibility is that they unknowingly drank the cooking spirit. Since driftwood had been found, the need to save cooking spirit was reduced, and wine and ordinary spirits had run out by the time they arrived at White Island.

A shot of four to six centilitres of pure methanol can be lethal. The course of the poisoning takes place within one to two days with large individual variation.

The impaired vision that methanol poisoning can cause makes it difficult to write a journal. At Strindberg's burial his companions appear to have been in poor shape. This theory presupposes that the cooking spirit had a high methanol content and that all three drank a quantity corresponding at least to a large schnapps shot, more or less at the same time.

Appraisal: Possible cause of death with low probability.

Suicide No farewell letters were found. No indications of suicide thoughts appear anywhere in the diaries. Extended or collective suicide is extremely uncommon. The personalities and the spirit of the times are against this. The survival instinct was probably strong under the prevailing circumstances. It can be expected that the burial of Strindberg would have been more careful if the two survivors had been fully capacitated, as they would have been if their deaths were the result of suicide.

Appraisal: Possible but unlikely cause of death.

Dehydration, pure hypothermia, exhaustion etc. These conditions have a more protracted course than the circumstances around the deaths indicate. Andrée and Frænkel were found in the tent but not in the sleeping bag, where one would have expected to find persons killed by exhaustion and hypothermia. The possibility that they both crawled out of the sleeping bag because of a terminal fever only to die, appears unlikely. Frænkel, moreover, was wearing a cap when his body was found. Fuel in the form of driftwood and paraffin was available in copious quantities. The bodily exertion required on the island was probably less than during the ice trek. Nothing is mentioned in the last diary entries regarding exhaustion.

Appraisal: Unlikely cause of death.

Attack by polar bears Meetings with polar bears were regular events. A large number of bears were shot. Ammunition had not run out at the time of the deaths.

Appraisal: Can at most explain Strindberg's death, not those of the others.

Botulism *Botulinus* toxin is the most potent poison known to man. It is formed by anaerobic bacteria (*Clostridium botulinum*) in foodstuffs that have been stored for some time. Meat from sea animals is particularly exposed since *clostridi* live in the seabed slime. Botulism is heavily over-represented in the polar countries among the native inhabitants since these traditionally eat food (commonly seal, walrus and whale meat) which has been kept for a long time and not sufficiently heated during preparation.[6,7,8] *Botulinus* toxin type E, which dominates in these regions, does not commonly cause signs of rotting or decay in food.

The toxin blocks neuromuscular impulse transmissions causing general muscle paralysis. Symptoms commonly appear twelve to thirty-six hours after ingestion. Shorter latency times indicate large doses and serious poisoning. The first symptoms are often diffuse: general feeling of illness, nausea, weakness, slurred speech, vertigo, dim vision, light sensitivity, mydriasis [dilation of eye pupils], dry mouth and difficulties in swallowing. Double vision and ptosis [drooping of the upper eye lid] are more specific symptoms. The symptom picture is then dominated by descending muscular paralysis, until the respiratory system is paralysed six to eight hours after the first symptoms appear.

Botulism is compatible with the following data:

- The three men died within the course of one to two days, but not at the same time.
- There was time to bury Strindberg but the burial was shallow since Andrée and Frænkel were weakened by their symptoms of poisoning.
- There are no journal notes of Strindberg's death since

317

disturbed vision and muscular weakness render writing impossible.

- Sunglasses were found next to Frænkel's skull (light sensitivity is an early symptom). It is less likely that sunglasses would normally be needed at these latitudes on 7 October.
- The likelihood that *botulinus* bacteria could grow in the flesh of seals or walruses brought by the expedition on its sledges on arrival at White Island may be considered fairly great. The seal shot on 19 September was mentioned again in the journal ten days later when a polar bear attempted to steal it. Remains of this seal were found in the camp. An intermittently faulty boiler also meant that the meals could not always be heated adequately.
- This cause of death requires no improbable events for its occurrence and accords well with known facts.

Appraisal: Probable cause of death.

Of the above mentioned theories regarding cause of death, *botulinus* toxin poisoning appears the most probable. As far as is known there are no organic remains left in the collection in which this toxin could be demonstrated with modern laboratory techniques. A new archaeological expedition to the site on White Island is planned for summer 2000, when more evidence may emerge.

Acknowledgements

Great thanks are due to museum director Håkan Jorikson at the Andrée museum in Gränna, Sweden, for his collaboration in the investigation, and to Jan Pallon at Lund College of Technology, where the lead analysis was conducted.

References

1. Bu-Olayan AH, Al-Yakoob SN, Alhazeem S. Lead in drinking water from water coolers and in fingernails from subjects in Kuwait City, Kuwait. Sci Total Environ 1996; 181:209-14.
2. Kowal W, Krahn P, Beattie O. Lead levels in human tissues from the Franklin Forensic Project. International Journal of Environmental Analytical Chemistry 1989; 35:119-26.

3. Farrer KTH. Lead and the last Franklin Expedition. Journal of Archaeological Science 1993; 20:399-409.

4. Börjesson J, Gerhardsson L, Schutz A, Mattsson S, Skerfving S, Österberg K. In vivo measurements of lead in fingerbone in active and retired lead smelters. Int Arch Occup Environ Health 1997; 69:97-105.

5. Kiewski K, Lowitz HD. Determination of lead in hydride form in bone biopsies of patients with long past lead poisoning. Arch Toxicol 1982; 50:301-11.

6. Dolman CE. Human botulism in Canada (1919-1973). Can Med Assoc J 1974; 110:191-7.

7. Wainwright RB, Heynard WL. Food-borne botulism in Alaska 1947-1985: epidemiology and clinical findings. J Infect Dis 1988; 157:1158-62.

8. Hauschild AH, Gauvreau L. Food-borne botulism in Canada, 1971-84. Can Med Assoc J 1985; 133:1141-6.

THE EQUIPMENT

David Hempleman-Adams' equipment

Burner/Heater

Heater unit; electric valve; autopilot; sparkers/strikers; chemical warmers; propane tanks; quick shut-off valves; cold seals; fuel usage chart

Flight instruments

Analogue altimeter; altimeter alarm; flytech; two alarm clocks; two variometers; ball variometer; two barographs

Oxygen kit

Liquid oxygen tank; liquid oxygen; three masks; two cannulas; hoses and bag; complete bottled oxygen back-up kit and back-up tanks

Basket equipment

Suntan cream; ship's compass; drinking water; ballast and ballast bags; silicon oil; antifreeze; location beacon; waterproof torch; plotting chart; cut-out partition; insulation and mats; cover; fuel tank ties; fuel tank bleed screws; heater; toilet bucket; steps; chair; cooker stand; cooker; cooker fuel; map board; chinagraph pencils; checklists; three fire extinguishers; fire blanket; first-aid kit; tool kit and spares; waste sacks; loo roll; pee bottle; matches; striker; ice axe; coolbox; helmet; harness; rope; boat hook; dustpan and brush; knife; sleeping bags; boots; clothes; goggles; binoculars; food; food bags; flasks; light sticks

Communication equipment

Two ICOM VHF radios with aerials; lithium AA batteries; mobile phone; satellite phone and batteries; HF radio; frequency and schedule charts; batteries; Argos; two thermometers; Spillsbury radio with two sets of batteries and two antennae; two emergency beacons; three GPS navigation satellite receivers with lithium and AA batteries plus pouches; Iridium satellite phone with batteries

Launch equipment

Flight plan; take-off permit; radio frequency charts; ground sheet; helium; helium hoses; propane; propane hoses; nitrogen; nitrogen hoses; ethane; ethane hoses; liquid oxygen; liquid oxygen hoses; gloves; connectors; adapters; tools; scales; spring balance

Cold-weather survival kit

Boots (Alfa polar boots Mørdre Extreme); two pairs Katangaer strengthened duffel boot liners; two pairs thin socks; vapour barrier socks; three pairs thick socks; two pairs long johns; two Karrimor Polartec tops; one fleece; salopettes; Rab overcoat; windjacket; three balaclavas; bear hat; sheepskin nose cover; four pairs liner gloves; four pairs middle gloves; three pairs outer gloves; fleece pockets; carry mat; two thermal vests; two thin sleeping bags; one vapour-barrier sleeping bag; one thick bag; three MSR stoves with base plates; two billies; handle; wooden spoon; jug; cup with top; spoon; fuel funnel; food for twenty-five days; water and munchie bags; sledge; harness;

rope; skis; poles; tent; ice axe; snow shovel; gun; ammunition; gun licence; heliograph; lighter; matches; tape; toilet paper; bucket; toilet bags; brush and pan for tent; sunglasses; pee bottle; first-aid kit; maintenance kit; female attachments for tent poles; tape for poles; knife; plastic bottles for fuel; MSR bottle; two watches; alarm clock; shortwave radio; AA batteries; two immersion suits; life-raft; life-jacket; flares; French chalk

Other equipment
Fire extinguishers; maps; high-level and low-level charts; pens; diary; beads and pictures; passport; money; credit cards; two Olympus cameras; two Canon cameras; film; batteries; Hi8 video camera with videotapes and batteries; flags (Norwegian; Swedish; United Kingdom; Canadian and Russian)

The Andrée expedition's equipment

This list is as complete as possible. It has been compiled from shopping lists, inventories, lists in diaries and journals, discoveries at White Island and other sources.

On the balloon at launch
Two anchors; three grapnels; 7cwt sand ballast; 11cwt food (to last three and a half months); 4cwt of water and cooking spirit; 2.5cwt reserve rations (to last a further two and a half months); specially designed cooker for balloon; Primus stove; twelve buoys; thirty-six carrier pigeons in individual baskets; three sledges; a boat; a flag

Left at Dane's Island after launch
A wooden balloon hangar; apparatus for producing hydrogen

Clothing
Each man was equipped with six pairs of woollen underpants; three vests; nine pairs of socks; three pairs of thin wool socks; one pair of long wool and hair socks; three flannel shirts; one Iceland jersey; one sweater; one wool-lined leather waistcoat;

four pairs of mittens or gloves; one suit; one pair of English wool-lined boots; one pair of snow boots; two pairs of laced boots; a wool coat; hunting trousers; leather leg and knee protectors; a cap; handkerchiefs

Food

Seventy-two large tins of biscuits and compressed bread; one tin of apples; fourteen small tins of biscuits; one tin of sugar; two boxes of Bovril; one box preserved buffalo meat; seventy-three boxes of milk; twelve boxes of milk powder; twenty-four boxes of Rousseau's meat powder; twenty boxes of butter; thirteen and a half tins of Cloetta's meat powder; cocoa; nine containers of butter; four containers of whortleberry jam; coffee; raspberry syrup; chocolate and lime juice; boxes of sardines; Mellin's Food powder [a gruel]; liver paste; Belgian chocolates; soup tablets

Andrée's sledge

Four ice planks; three bamboo poles; one carrying-ring plank; one boat hook; one groundsheet tarpaulin; one sack of private items (including tubes for collecting scientific samples); one basket; one pot of boot grease; one hose; one large press; one shovel with a spare cross-piece; two baskets of food and provisions; grapnel and rope (total weight 463.7lb until 27 July 1897, after which the expedition dumped about half of its equipment, resulting in a total weight on Andrée's sledge of 284.9lb)

Frænkel's sledge

Boat; one sack of private items; ammunition; altazimuth and stand; various meteorological and navigational instruments (including an aneroid-barometer; a psychrometer; sextant; chronometers; a plumb-bob; a levelling mirror; compasses; hygrometer; thermometer; actinometer) and navigation charts; one photographic apparatus; one cooking stove; two pairs of field glasses; matches; sleeping bag; three blankets; cutlery and crockery; a gun and gun case; equipment for cleaning guns; a sack of books (total weight 298.2lb; this was after 27 July 1897, when Frænkel, Andrée and Strindberg jettisoned about half of their equipment)

Strindberg's sledge

Strindberg appeared to drag mainly food and his personal items, although the following items were also carried between the three men, probably by Strindberg initially: medicine chest; ammunition; several rifles; one sextant; photographic equipment; one tent; two tent poles; tools; sewing materials; theodolite and stand; a spade

INDEX